MICHAEL DOUGLAS

MICHAEL DOUGLAS

A BIOGRAPHY

MARC
ELIOT

CROWN ARCHETYPE · NEW YORK

Library of Congress Cataloging-in-Publication Data is available
upon request.

ISBN: 978-0-307-95236-3
eISBN: 978-0-307-95238-7

Printed in the United States of America

Book design by Lauren Dong
Jacket design by Nupoor Gordon
Jacket photography © Greg Gorman/Icon International

10 9 8 7 6 5 4 3 2 1

First Edition

DEDICATED TO DAVID MILLER,

MY RUSSIAN IMMIGRANT GRANDFATHER,

WHO WAS THE BRAVEST, WISEST, AND STRONGEST

MAN I EVER KNEW. HE WAS MY FIRST TEACHER AND

MY EARLIEST INSPIRATION. HE DIED WHEN

I WAS TEN AND REMAINS MY GREATEST HERO.

THANK YOU, GRANDPA.

◈

AND TO ANDREW SARRIS, WHO LED ME OUT OF

THE DARKNESS AND INTO THE CINEMATIC LIGHT.

I AM ETERNALLY GRATEFUL FOR YOUR KNOWLEDGE,

GUIDANCE, ENCOURAGEMENT, AND FRIENDSHIP.

MAY YOU REST IN HEAVENLY PEACE, IN CINEMA'S

ULTIMATE REVIVAL HOUSE.

CONTENTS

[My father] told me, "Michael, I was watching one of my old movies on television last night and, you know, I couldn't remember the movie at all. I couldn't remember making it. And then I realized, hey, it wasn't me. It was you."

—Michael Douglas

Every kid has to kick his father in the balls.

—Kirk Douglas

INTRODUCTION

Christ, I saw my father as a gladiator, nailed to a cross, as an artist who cut his ear off—and he would be shown doing these superhuman things. I'd think, how can I possibly be a man? How can I be the man this man was?

—MICHAEL DOUGLAS

BEING THE SON OR DAUGHTER OF A HOLLYWOOD icon can be the greatest blessing or the deepest curse. For a child of famous parents who lives in that shadow, the struggle to step into the light of one's own identity often carries a heavy price.

Paul Newman's son, Scott, blessed with his father's good looks but void of his unique talent lived in the shadow of the elder Newman's fame and died of an overdose at the age of twenty-eight. Gregory Peck's son also could not overcome his father's fame and eventually shot himself. Charles Boyer's son, too, committed suicide. Marlon Brando's daughter killed herself after her brother, Marlon's son, another failed actor, fatally shot her boyfriend (and went to prison for it).

There are numerous less dramatic instances. Sydney Earle Chaplin, Charlie's son, although a fine actor and an ambitious one, was unable to compete with his father's old-as-film-itself talent and failed to make it as a box office star either on the screen or stage. It was the same story for Sydney's half sister, Geraldine, who had similar performing ambitions but whose career goals, too, were overwhelmed by the reach and heights of her father's enormous worldwide fame. And despite his singular contribution to 1969's *Easy Rider*, Peter Fonda never achieved the star status or the prestige of his legendary father,

Henry. Although both were alive during the making of *Easy Rider*, Henry never expressed any real desire to work with his son (except for a brief appearance in *Wanda Nevada*, an independent film that disappeared almost as soon as it opened, in June 1979, and which may have been the senior Fonda's long-overdue and failed attempt to acknowledge his son's talent and abilities). Peter's sister Jane did fare a little better. Although she shot her own career in the foot with her "Hanoi Jane" real-life episode, she finally did get to share the screen with Henry in Mark Rydell's 1981 *On Golden Pond*, the dying senior Fonda's Academy Award–winning swan song. Jane went on to have a long and successful career, a two-time Oscar winner, but nevertheless had to battle forever the demons of her own politics and Daddy's long legend. Gender, looks, and her canny ability to choose vehicles that were perfectly suited to her talents helped her to escape the worst of Hollywood's dreaded dynastic curse. And the fact that she was a much bigger star than Peter didn't hurt. By 1981, Henry needed their reconciliation on film as much as Jane did.

Canadian-born Donald Sutherland, who came to prominence in Robert Altman's 1970 *M*A*S*H* and went on to make more than 160 movies and win a cartful of awards (but no Oscar), is the father of Kiefer Sutherland, a successful TV and film actor limited by his range and hampered by his quick temper and substance-abuse battles, as well as by a lack of breakthrough big-screen roles. Kiefer made his name on the TV series *24*, which ran in serial spurts for nearly nine years.

Tom Hanks made himself a force in Hollywood as an actor and producer in film and TV, yet his son Colin has yet to make a solid name in the movies. Sean Connery, film's original James Bond, has a son, Jason, who remains relatively unknown as an actor. To the long list add John Wayne and his actor son Patrick; Lana Turner and her daughter, Cheryl; and the Sheens: relatively sane father Martin, relatively crazy son Charlie, and Charlie's brother, Emilio Estevez, best known as a member of the cinematically inconsequential 1980s "Brat Pack." There are yet dozens more examples of children of filmland famously overshadowed by their more famous parents. Naming them becomes a grim parlor game that could easily last all night.

There are notable exceptions, of course. Jeff Bridges and his brother, Beau, are the sons of affable TV and screen star Lloyd Bridges, a family man and by all accounts a good father, best remembered for his performance on the tube as Mike Nelson in the low-budget independent TV series *Sea Hunt* (1958–61) and on the big screen as the smoldering, immature deputy in Fred Zinnemann's stellar 1952 *High Noon* and in his comic roles in the 1980 *Airplane!* (Jim Abrahams, David Zucker, and Jerry Zucker) and the 1982 *Airplane II* (Ken Finkleman). Eventually both brothers were able to surface from Lloyd's shadow—which, admittedly, was not as long as those of bigger Hollywood legends—and Jeff, relatively late in his career, emerged from the cult film star status he acquired after his memorable performance in Joel Coen's 1998 *The Big Lebowski*.[1] Jeff's bravura Oscar-winning Best Actor performance some years later as Bad Blake in Scott Cooper's 2009 *Crazy Heart* finally made him a bankable star.

Ben Stiller became a superstar, eclipsing both the small-screen success of his stand-up comedian parents, Stiller and Meara, and Jerry Stiller's late-in-the-day sitcom and commercial spokesman career. James Brolin was a minor-league actor; his son Josh is one of the hottest Hollywood leading men of the decade. But far more often in Hollywood, the exceptions prove the rule.

Let us now meet the Douglas dynasty, beginning with Kirk, the son of Russian Jewish immigrants, who went on to international fame and glory and by doing so cast a shadow from which all his progeny, with varying degrees of success, tried to emerge. Perhaps without meaning to, he nonetheless laid down a complex set of twists and turns on their particular yellow brick road of movie dreams of fame, fortune, and glory.

Kirk married his first wife, socialite Diana Love Dill, while he was

---

1   Ethan Coen is the uncredited co-director.

still an unknown actor trying to make it on Broadway. He was ruthlessly and singularly ambitious, and what he may have lacked in raw talent, he more than made up for with a fierce determination that perhaps only the child of poor immigrants can truly comprehend.

At the same time, he showed little interest in domesticity. He fathered two boys with Diana—Michael was born in 1944, Joel in 1947—and to both he remained distant, mostly physically unavailable, and emotionally unavailable to his wife, while craving the affection and approval of his Russian-born father. After a middling career on the boards, Kirk took off for Hollywood alone, leaving his wife behind with two-year-old Michael. A self-confessed notorious womanizer, Kirk's arrival in Hollywood was not unlike that of a child with an insatiable sweet tooth given the keys to the best candy store in the world.

After the release of his first film, Lewis Milestone's 1946 *The Strange Love of Martha Ivers*, Kirk found regular work in bigger and better movies. After several heated affairs, he and Diana began talking divorce. Diana "had some inkling that something was going on with him and his various leading ladies, one in particular." Kirk never denied any of it: "Yes, I liked women. I liked Marilyn Maxwell, she was beautiful. . . . I was a bad boy, yes, I had lots of women."

Diana repeatedly pleaded with him to stop his incessant womanizing, and when Kirk wouldn't, or couldn't, in 1950 Diana went ahead and filed for divorce.

Michael, six years old at the time of his parents' split, was profoundly affected by what he could not help perceiving as his father's abandonment. He drew ever closer to and more dependent on his mother. In his first memoir, *The Ragman's Son*, Kirk describes a scene just prior to the divorce while visiting his wife and two children in New York: "When Diana and I were having an intense argument in the kitchen, we saw Michael, who was about six, walking toward us. We stopped immediately, before he entered, but he burst out crying. . . . That's when we realized that staying together for the sake of the children wouldn't work."

Michael recalls, "I think my earliest memory was about three and it was them fighting. Not physically fighting, but arguing. Voices being raised." Those voices would reverberate in Michael's head for years, even as Kirk's absence turned him into something of an invisible god. Michael's most frequent contact with his father was watching his giant image on the screen performing heroics and making love to other women. Kirk was there and not there, real and not real, an object of worship and an object of longing. These feelings would grow inside Michael until, as a young man trying to find his place in the world, he realized he wanted to be just like his father, and at the same time, nothing like him.

The divorce was finalized in January 1951. Diana received sole custody of the children, with liberal visitation rights for Kirk. That February, she moved into an apartment on Central Park West. As Diana recalled not long after, "Michael . . . was showing signs of deep anger since the divorce and from being a compatible, tractable child, had suddenly become very stubborn and rebellious. He challenged me at every turn. I took him to a child psychologist who observed him in play therapy and then lectured me gently. 'This is not a deeply disturbed child at all. He has suffered a great loss and blames you for it.' [He advised me to] ease up on the discipline and give him loads of love."

The "loads of love" was meant to deflect what was a not uncommon reaction of young children whose parents divorce: that it is somehow their fault. As a child, Michael struggled with whom to blame for his parents' breakup, his mother, his father, or himself. At times he blamed his father for abandoning the family. Other times he blamed his mother for somehow driving his father away. And still other times he blamed himself and, later, younger brother Joel for not being good enough children. Michael's guilt and anger expressed itself in outbursts and mini-rebellions. (Joel handled the trauma differently. He put on weight that he carried on his frame his entire life, as if wishing to insulate himself from his own emotional needs.)

Michael would carry his childhood emotional baggage into his first marriage, which in many ways mirrored his father's. Kirk had married a moneyed sophisticate; so did Michael. Kirk was a serial cheater; Michael, too, loved women. Eventually Michael left his first wife and remarried a woman who closely resembled his father's second wife. The duality of Michael's identity struggle is vivid; it is as if, on the one hand, he strove to become a better version of his dad, while on the other, he feared he was destined to exactly follow in his father's heavy footsteps.

Diana got the message from the psychiatrist, and this early counseling helped Michael improve his social skills and lessen the periodic traumatic flashes that would occur whenever his father came back to New York City to visit the two boys. On one visit to the West Side apartment, Kirk recalls in his memoir, he "walked in and kissed Diana on the cheek. Michael started to cry. Thirty-five years later, he told me it bewildered him. He thought Mommy and Daddy were angry at each other. . . . [T]here was a wall between us. Maybe [the boys] felt that I had abandoned them. We never discussed it."

It was a wall that was to remain up for nearly a lifetime. Michael, the more obviously sensitive of the two boys, would avoid expressing anger and arguing in his marriages, the passive Jekyll to the aggressive Hyde of his movie characters. The ghost of his father's philandering (and the shadow of his own) would emerge in such films as *Fatal Attraction*, *Basic Instinct*, and *Disclosure*. All three characters he played in those films were sexually troubled men, and with the exception of *Fatal Attraction*'s Dan Gallagher they had no apparent connection to or desire to care for their children. According to film critic and historian David Thomson, troubled men became Michael's best roles. He was "capable of playing characters who were weak, culpable, morally indolent, compromised, and greedy for illicit sensation without losing that basic probity or potential for ethical character that we require of a hero."

ALTHOUGH IT IS not unusual for sons to follow in the professional footsteps of their father, Michael always maintained he just sort of wandered into the profession: "I went into theater because I didn't have a major. . . . It was my junior year in college [University of California, Santa Barbara] and I really didn't know what the hell I wanted to do. I really had never thought about acting at all. So when I jumped in, I hadn't done any high school plays or anything. Earlier in my career . . . I was basically someone who was struggling for confidence. . . . I was withdrawn."

Perhaps Michael's greatest satisfaction was being able to accomplish what his father could not: at the age of thirty-one, after a middling film and TV career, Michael managed to get a movie made out of Ken Kesey's semi-autobiographical Beat-influenced novel *One Flew Over the Cuckoo's Nest.* Kirk had originally purchased rights to the book in 1962, before its publication, for $47,000, and he brought it to the Broadway stage in 1963. Kirk played the lead role, Randle McMurphy, a symbolically sane man trapped in a metaphorical insane asylum, surrounded by other inmates he eventually realizes are all the sane victims of a crazy world, whose authority figures are sadistically insane. The Broadway production was intended as a showcase for what Kirk hoped would be his greatest film achievement and win him an Academy Award, an accolade that had eluded him despite his enormously successful film career.

Cuckoo's Nest opened on November 13, nine days before John F. Kennedy was assassinated. In the immediate aftermath of those dark days, the last thing anyone wanted to see was a downcast play about injustice, manipulation, and the misuse of power and murder. Kirk reluctantly closed it on January 25, 1964, confidently believing that the next step, bringing it to the screen, was a cinch.

It wasn't. By the mid-sixties, Kirk's film career had peaked and was on a downslope. Ten frustrating years later, in a last-ditch effort, he handed the rights over to Michael and gave him his blessing to run with it. Michael ran, all right, and, with his producing partner, Saul Zaentz, won the Academy Award for Best Picture of 1975. Over Michael's initial objections, his friend Jack Nicholson, rather than his father Kirk Douglas, played McMurphy. Nicholson also took an Oscar home, the Oscar that Kirk never won.[2]

Cuckoo's Nest marked the moment when Michael changed places with his father and became the more powerful figure in Hollywood. It signaled the beginning of Michael's great run as a producer, actor, and sometimes both in a series of top-grossing, award-winning films that would culminate in his winning a second Oscar, this one for Best Actor for his memorable portrayal of Gordon Gekko in Oliver Stone's 1987 *Wall Street*.

What follows, then, is the story of how Michael fought to step out of his father's shadow even as he struggled against falling deeper into it and become his father. It is the story of a search for self-identity, inner peace, lasting happiness, and enduring love. It is the story of how the firstborn son of Kirk Douglas finally succeeded in becoming his own man.

---

2 *Cuckoo's Nest* wound up winning the "Big Four": Best Picture; Best Actor, Jack Nicholson; Best Director, Miloš Forman; Best Actress, Louise Fletcher. It was the first time one film had won all four major awards since Frank Capra's 1934 *It Happened One Night*. It also won Best Adapted Screenplay, Lawrence Hauben and Bo Goldman.

PART ONE

PARENTS

Kirk Douglas greeted by his sons, Joel, six (left), and Michael, nine (right), at a New York airport after arriving from Europe to spend Christmas together. Kirk was by then divorced from his first wife and the boys' mother, Diana Dill. AP Photo

CHAPTER 1

*As an actor, it was really intimidating watching my father
because his personality, his presence was so strong and so dynamic
that, forget acting, you just didn't even know how to be a man.*

—MICHAEL DOUGLAS

MICHAEL K. DOUGLAS INHERITED MORE THAN HIS
famous father's dirty blond hair and familiar face. He inherited
his freedom. Kirk, the son of Russian Jewish immigrants, was born
in Amsterdam, New York. Herschel Danielovitch, a tailor, had fled
Moscow in 1908 for Belarus, like so many Jews did under the threat
of endless Cossack-led pogroms and conscription that forced them to
fight for the tsar in the Russo-Japanese War. Two years later, taking his girlfriend, Bryna Sanglel, a baker, with him, he left Belarus in
1910 bound for America's promise of safety and rebirth. They passed
through Ellis Island, the gateway to the New World, and settled in
upstate New York, where that same year they married and started a
family.

By 1924 they had seven children, six girls and one boy: Pesha (born
1910), Kaleh (1912), Tamara (1914), Issur (1916), twins Hashka and
Siffra (1918), and Rachel (1924). Issur would later change his name
from Issur Danielovitch to the more American (and less Jewish) Kirk
Douglas.

Herschel was not a warm man. He liked to eat by himself in restau-
rants, or alone late at night at the kitchen table when everyone else was
already in bed. When not plying his rag trade on the streets of Amsterdam, he would spend hours in town, drinking at the local saloon.

Occasionally he would take Issur with him on the rag route, to show him how much hard work it took to put food on the family table. Issur was a quick learner but not especially ambitious. To help feed the family he preferred to break into neighbors' houses and steal food from their kitchens.

Sometimes, to supplement what he earned from the rag business, Herschel sold fruits and vegetables off a cart. Issur used to steal from him, too, and then bring the food home to the family. Sometimes he would keep a potato or two for himself and roast them in the basement, until one time he "accidentally" burned the house down. As Kirk recalls in his memoirs, "I have always suspected that this was . . . subconscious arson. I really wanted to destroy the whole house. There was an awful lot of rage churning around inside me . . . my mother was always saying, 'Don't be like your father. . . .' That made me angry. Who should I be like? My mother? My sisters?"

Herschel was a bad drinker, and since the only other person in the house who wasn't female was Issur, he received the brunt of his father's frustrations via regular beatings. If he angered Issur to the point where he wanted to burn down the house, he also managed to toughen him up, and it was that intense combination of anger and toughness, along with his blond Russian good looks, that would one day help make the boy an international movie star.

DESPITE THE New World dreams of Herschel the refugee, being a Jew was not so easy in America. Anywhere outside the protective environs of New York City's Lower East Side was considered dangerous turf. For Issur, living in Amsterdam surrounded by Christians necessarily kept him a loner, and as a result, he turned increasingly inward and let his mind take him where his body couldn't.

As soon as he graduated from high school, Issur tried to save some money to make a planned getaway. He got a job in the local M. Lurie department store, where he quickly devised a scheme to steal cash by altering the receipts.

While becoming an increasingly clever sneak thief, Issur accidentally discovered another way to act out his inner frustrations when he tried out for the role of Tony Cavendish in a small community theater production of *The Royal Family*, a popular and successful Broadway play that parodied the Barrymore family. He was curious about what all those people in that little building were up to, so he walked in one night and was handed a script. After he read, he was offered a part and said yes. It turned out to be a fun experience for him, but a limited one with very little in the way of monetary rewards. He then went back to working and stealing until, after another year had passed, his sisters convinced him to take his life savings, about $200, travel north to the town of Canton, and try to enroll in St. Lawrence University, a college education being his best chance to make a better life for himself.

The night before he left, he said good-bye to his father, who handed him some bread rubbed with garlic and slices of herring, wished the boy good luck, and went to bed.

ONCE AT ST. LAWRENCE, Issur felt deep pangs of homesickness, loneliness, and hunger. And there was never enough food to sate him. As a result, he was constantly grubbing food from his friends at the dorm and scrounging off their trays in the cafeteria, until one angry matron loudly dressed him down and humiliated him in front of all the other boys.

Issur hung in there, trying to find new ways to get some more food and maybe even learn something—until girls came into his life. One in particular, Isabella, a WASP beauty attending the university, caught his eye. Too shy to talk to her, he sent her a poem instead, and soon enough they were going together. But Issur knew there was no possibility of any kind of permanent relationship with Isabella. It wasn't just the religious thing. Isabella was simply not that interested in him.

There weren't many other extracurricular activities that attracted him besides theater and girls, and there wasn't much of either of those. He decided to join the wrestling team, where he was easily able to take down all the boys bigger than he was. Wrestling became an effective outlet for his frustrations and anger, and soon he was the best wrestler in the school. Self-pride was something new to him, and he wore it like a badge of honor.

During his first summer vacation, Issur wrestled for cash in carnivals, but his second year he managed to land a job with a summer stock acting company at the Tamarack Playhouse on Lake Pleasant in the Adirondack Mountains. He wasn't hired as an actor; he did not have anything like the training or experience of the other cast members, most of whom had come to Tamarack together from the Goodman School of Acting in Chicago. Instead, he was a paid stagehand, with the promise of maybe a line or two here and there if needed.

Issur didn't get a chance to do much acting that summer, but he did manage to steal one of the Chicago actresses from her boyfriend and sneak away and have sex with her. The only other friend he made was one of the regular cast members, Mladen George Sekulovich, who had just changed his name to the easier-on-the-tongue Karl Malden. Taking his cue from Malden, Issur proudly began calling himself Kirk Douglas.[1]

Back at St. Lawrence for the start of his junior year, he quickly resumed his role as the star of the wrestling team. He was so good he was encouraged to try out for the Olympic team, but Kirk turned all of it down. He knew now what he wanted to do with his life, and it had nothing to do with athletics. He couldn't get the smell of that girl out of his head, or the thrill of stealing her away and having to pretend they hardly knew each other when her boyfriend was around. He was going to be an actor!

In 1939, after graduating from St. Lawrence, Kirk traveled down to New York City, where he was promptly turned down by the

---

1   It is unclear when Issur legally changed his name to Kirk Douglas.

Academy of Dramatic Arts (located at that time in Carnegie Hall), not because he wasn't a good enough actor but because he couldn't afford the annual $500 tuition and he didn't qualify for a scholarship. Instead, he found work downtown in the Village at Greenwich House, putting on plays and skits with immigrant children.

That fall, after spending another fun-filled summer at Tamarack, Kirk returned to New York City, and this time the Academy of Dramatic Arts admitted him, even waiving the tuition. Soon enough he caught the attention of another student, Margaret Mary "Peggy" Diggins, a raven-haired, wide-eyed beauty who also happened to work as a model and was, as Kirk recalled in his memoirs, the current Miss New York.[2]

They fell in love, and Kirk asked her to marry him. She said yes, and in a heated rush, they took a train to Newark, New Jersey, since an acting friend of Kirk's had told him it was the quickest place to get married.

It wasn't. Kirk and Peggy had problems providing the necessary papers, and no wedding was performed that day. They returned to New York disappointed but determined to get back to Newark and get married as soon as possible.

However, before that could happen, Peggy was offered a Hollywood contract to join a group of girls who called themselves the Navy Blue Sextet, *the six most beautiful girls in the world!* And just like that, she was gone.

Peggy never wrote or called Kirk.

He was crushed and tried to forget her. To keep himself busy he took a job at Schrafft's on Broadway and Eighty-Sixth Street, one of a citywide chain of ice cream and sandwich palaces where a lot of unemployed actors found work. With salary and tips he made enough money to rent a small room on the West Side for $3 a week. And whatever food remained on patrons' plates when they left he considered fair game.

---

2   No other source has been found stating that Peggy Diggins was ever Miss New York.

He continued to work at Schrafft's even after he left the Academy in the spring of 1941. He was one of only 80 out of 168 students to make it through the senior year of the program. The rest either couldn't afford to continue, were drafted into the army, or simply were deemed not good enough to graduate.

Going to school was one thing, but making a living as an actor was another, and despite his job at Schrafft's he was always just one step ahead of eviction. Then, after the December 7, 1941, attack on Pearl Harbor, twenty-five-year-old Kirk decided to enlist in the air force, but he was rejected for being too old.

So it was back to working Schrafft's at night and making the rounds during the day, finding no prospects, until one day he arrived at the Katharine Cornell–Guthrie McClintic production offices, one of hundreds of doors he had knocked on. Only this time the people in the office didn't just ask him for a photo and résumé and show him the way out. This time he actually got to meet one of McClintic's assistants, who liked what he saw and arranged to have Kirk audition for a new Broadway play they were producing, *Spring Again*. Much to his surprise and delight, Kirk landed the four-line role of a singing telegram boy. The pay wasn't much, and he'd have to give up Schrafft's in order to make every performance. To make ends meet, he took the job of stage manager and understudied four other roles.

As Kirk tells the story in his memoirs, one night McClintic invited him to dinner and made a sexual pass that shook Kirk up—about McClintic, about acting, about the theater, maybe even about his own manhood. Not long after, he joined the navy.

Times had changed: it was 1942 and the war was raging; now the military was willing to take anyone who could breathe. Kirk was sent to South Bend, Indiana, where he spent four months in training as a naval officer at Notre Dame Midshipman School. One day Kirk was surprised to see one of his fellow students from the Academy on the cover of *Life* magazine. Diana Love Dill was as much a beauty as he could imagine.

Her father was descended from one of two brothers who had been born in Northern Ireland and set sail for Virginia in the early seventeenth century; but when they stopped in Bermuda they decided to settle there instead, eventually amassing a great fortune in shipping. Diana's mother, Ruth Rapalje Neilson, could trace her roots back to Northern Ireland as well. Ruth had married Thomas Melville Dill, four years her senior, a former commander of the Bermuda Militia Artillery, and future attorney general of the island.

Their seventh and final child, Diana, born in Bermuda in 1923 to a mother who was forty-three and a father who was forty-six. At the age of six, Diana was sent off to London to attend the Doreck School at the far end of Kensington Garden Square and receive a proper British upper-class education. Diana lived in London until 1930, when she relocated with her sister Frances, or "Fan," and the rest of the family to the Isle of Wight. There the girls attended the Ryde School with Upper Chine for Girls.

Diana and Fan stayed on the Isle of Wight until 1933, when they returned to Bermuda. Eventually, as war loomed ever closer and it was feared that the British island might come under attack, Diana and her family moved to the relative safety of the American mainland and New York City. When Diana was old enough, she tried out for and was accepted by the Academy of Dramatic Arts, which was where she first met Kirk.

They became friends. Diana liked to call him "Doug"—short not for "Douglas" but like "dog," as her accent made it sound, when she became aware of his relentless pursuit of women. In her memoirs she remembers him as not an especially good actor but a terrific ladies' man, "always with one pretty girl or another."

It didn't bother her all that much. She found him charming in his own way; she had grown up with aggressive military men. Soon enough their friendship turned romantic, and at the start of her senior year, Diana asked her parents for permission to stay in New York permanently. With the war continuing, they agreed, as long as she lived in housing for women only.

Then an offer came to her from an agent for the movies. Kirk couldn't believe this was happening—déjà vu all over again—and begged her not to give in "to the tinsel of Hollywood." They fought furiously about it, but Diana's mind was made up. She left Kirk and New York for the West Coast, where she hoped for a career in movies.

Now, after seeing her picture on the cover of *Life*, Kirk decided to write to her in care of the magazine. He was pleasantly surprised to receive a warm letter back. As it happened, she told him, Hollywood had not welcomed her with the open arms she had hoped for. She had since returned to New York, where she worked as a nurse at night, first at Bellevue before transferring to St. Anne's Maternity Hospital, and occasionally worked as a model for the John Robert Powers Agency.

Kirk, still stationed in South Bend, began traveling to New York City to visit her every chance he got, but when he received word that he would soon be shipping out overseas, he asked Diana to fly to South Bend to marry him. She said yes.

On November 2, 1943, they were hitched in Indiana by the navy chaplain and then again, at Kirk's insistence, by a rabbi, who agreed to perform the ceremony on the condition that their children would be brought up Jewish. They agreed, but Kirk assured Diana he would not hold her to that promise.

They spent the next month and a half together in South Bend until the day Kirk was sent to the South Pacific. Fearing she might never see her husband again, Diana moved to New Jersey to live with her oldest sister, Ruth. Diana thought it unseemly to be modeling while her husband was at war, so she took a full-time day job in Manhattan with E. R. Squibb.

Not long after, she discovered she was pregnant.

ABOARD SHIP, Kirk was caught in a non-combat-related explosives accident that nearly killed him. He was sent to San Diego to recover. Diana immediately quit her job and flew to the West Coast to be by his side for the duration of what looked to be a long recuperation. In June 1944, Kirk was given a medical discharge from the navy. They decided to move back east and settled temporarily at Ruth's house in New Jersey to await the arrival of the baby.

When he was well enough, Kirk started making the audition rounds and soon found work on Broadway, due partly to his talent and partly to the severe wartime shortage of leading men. While he acted, Diana searched for a place for them to live and found a walk-up on West Eleventh Street in Greenwich Village, complete with a bedroom balcony. However, on September 24, 1944, before they could move in, Diana went into labor. It proved a difficult delivery, but at ten thirty the next morning, the twenty-fifth, their baby boy was born. Upon her release from the hospital, the Douglases moved into their New York City apartment.

Choosing a name for the baby had been something Kirk and Diana disagreed about. If it was a boy, Diana wanted to call him Kirk junior. Kirk vehemently refused, because in the Jewish religion, children are named not after the living but after the dead. Kirk finally agreed to Michael K. (for Kirk) Douglas.

And so it was that the son of this handsome, struggling actor and his beautiful Bermudan socialite came kicking and screaming into the war-torn world.

CHAPTER 2

I didn't grow up in Beverly Hills, thank God. I could think of nothing worse than growing up in the richest city in the richest state in the richest country in the world. How could you possibly preserve any sense of reality?

—MICHAEL DOUGLAS

ALL THROUGH HIS BABY YEARS MICHAEL ALMOST never smiled or laughed, and the more anybody tried to get him to do so, the less of it he did. "As a child, he was very shy," Kirk recalled. Not that Kirk was around all that much to notice. He was appearing on Broadway steadily now, and it was during this period, Diana later remembered, that the seeds of their marital problems were planted. "His deep, dark Russian depressions and sudden rages," as she described them, confused and frightened her and highlighted the differences in their backgrounds. She was WASP, upper-class, and always wearing a happy face; he was Jewish, working-class, prone to emotional outbursts, and almost never smiled. He was an unhappy person with fits and starts of happiness; Diana was a happy person with occasional small bumps in the road.

Still, to the outside world, they appeared to have a solid marriage. Their Village apartment was the frequent locale for parties filled with actors and artists and writers, and their love life was as strong as ever, no matter how many additional sexual adventures Kirk was having.

The appearance, however, was not enough to mask their increasingly difficult relationship. For one thing, Diana felt she needed more in her life than motherhood. If Kirk could work, she wanted to as well, and leave the gilded cage of her marriage. In what was considered an unusual move at the time for a newlywed mother, and something of a compromise to her, she decided to go back to school part-time, to take a short-story writing course at New York University.

This led to a whole new level of tension between her and Kirk. One night they had a down-and-out about, of all things, the Sacco and Vanzetti case, their opposite positions underscored by their ethnic differences. Although Sacco and Vanzetti were heroes to the working class, Kirk was against them, while to Diana they were innocent and should not be made to pay the price for any so-called crimes.[1]

The Sacco and Vanzetti case was the first time in their marriage Diana stood up to Kirk and dared to openly disagree with him, despite his insistence that he was (always) right, and it put another layer of tension on what should have been simply a family discussion. The fact was, Kirk wanted her to be a stay-at-home mother. It was an era when married women who worked were viewed as either economically deprived or unhappy at home. Kirk did not want people to think his wife *had* to work, that he couldn't support his family on his own.

Late in 1944, against Kirk's wishes, Diana resumed her acting career while he successfully auditioned for a role in Betty Comden and Adolph Green's upcoming musical *On the Town*, with a score by Leonard Bernstein. Kirk was given one of the leads until he suddenly lost his voice. The show was postponed twice while he went to see a series of specialists, but finally it went on without him. His part was given to actor John Battles, and the show opened on December 29, 1944, without Kirk.

◇

---

1   Ferdinando Sacco and Bartolomeo Vanzetti were accused of armed robbery and murder in Braintree, Mass., in 1920. They were tried twice and were executed in 1927. The trial became a showcase for everything from class division in America and anti-immigration sentiment to anarchy. The evidence was flimsy, and the case remains controversial to this day. Kirk and Diana were arguing about it in 1945, and they were not alone. Several movies and plays have been made about the two men, their trials, and their execution.

EARLY IN 1945, after finishing a brief run in *Measure for Measure*, Diana took off for an extended stay in Bermuda at the family compound, a jovial retreat where, after serving dinner, the staff would gather around a piano and entertain the guests by singing old familiar tunes.

She took Michael with her. Because of the Dill family wealth, rumors had surfaced that the boy might be the target of an impending kidnapping. Not wanting to leave Michael with Kirk, who worked six evenings and two matinees a week, Diana felt safer having her son by her side.

Meanwhile, on Broadway and alone in New York, Kirk became reacquainted with a young actress by the name of Lauren Bacall, whom he had dated when both were students at the Academy of Dramatic Arts, and who would play a pivotal role in his becoming a movie star. As a favor to Kirk, she recommended him to her friend, film producer Hal Wallis, who had been complaining about the shortage of young male actors in Hollywood and was looking for one to star in his new picture, *The Strange Love of Martha Ivers*. Wallis tested Kirk, liked him for the part, and offered it to him.

Kirk had never thought much of Hollywood as a place where he could seriously practice his craft—an attitude not unusual among New York–trained actors, who preferred the continuous nature of stage performance to the chopped-up mechanics of film acting. But with Diana away and nothing new showing up on the boards for him, he took Bacall's advice and that of his good friend David Merrick, a Broadway producer and future impresario, both of whom urged him to accept Wallis's offer. Merrick also set him up with big-time talent agent Charles Feldman to close the deal.

Early in 1945, Kirk boarded the fabled Twentieth Century Limited to Chicago and from there traveled on to Hollywood by himself, while his wife and son remained in Bermuda.

Diana eventually decided she wanted to be with Kirk while he made his movie, and so she surprised him by showing up that winter without advance warning, with Michael and her mother in tow. Diana, no stranger to Hollywood, knew all too well what a playground it was for good-looking young men like her husband, whose philandering had been one of the reasons she had unofficially separated from him.

He was caught off guard by Diana's arrival, especially since, in her absence, he had decided not to return to New York—Wallis, pleased with Kirk's work on *Martha Ivers*, had offered him a five-picture deal. Now, he would have to put a damper on his living it up and revert, at least for the time being, to playing the dutiful husband and father, until he broke the news of his new deal to Diana. She had a surprise for him as well. She was pregnant with their second child.

UPON HER ARRIVAL, Diana set about finding a place in L.A. for them and settled on a small Swiss-chalet-style cottage on Vado Place in Laurel Canyon, in the Hollywood Hills.

On January 23, 1947, one day after her twenty-fourth birthday, she gave birth to Joel Andrew Douglas. As soon as she could, she moved both boys into the guesthouse and hired a full-time nanny.

Almost from the start, Diana saw a troubling sibling rivalry develop between the two boys. Michael was proving to be increasingly insecure with a need for constant attention, and he was not much of a sharer, especially when it came to the affections of his mother. One of the first times Diana held baby Joel in her arms in front of Michael, he started crying and screaming, "No, Mommy! No, Mommy!" Diana quickly handed Joel to the nanny and tried to comfort Michael. "It's okay, Mikey, it's okay . . . that's your little brother and you can help me take care of him."

AS KIRK BECAME more successful on his way to major stardom, his marriage continued to deteriorate. At one point, after a series of arguments that had been going on for weeks (and were really one long argument about who-knows-what), Diana angrily suggested he needed to see a psychiatrist, which Kirk took as an insult. And if he didn't, she added, they would have to separate again, this time for good.

It set off one of the worst fights they had ever had. So involved were they in this argument they didn't notice young Michael standing right in front of them, crying, while he stared at his parents screaming at each other.

DIANA KEPT a busy social calendar while Kirk ground out one movie after another, often staying at a studio bungalow, sometimes alone and sometimes in the company of an eager young starlet. One evening Diana went alone to a party at the home of Charlie Chaplin and Oona O'Neill. Oona, the daughter of Eugene O'Neill, was a long-time friend of Diana's, from before Oona's marriage to the much older film great. At the time, Chaplin was considering Diana for the role of the dancer in *Limelight* but ultimately gave it to Claire Bloom. After this latest disappointment, Diana had had enough of both Hollywood and her husband and decided to return alone to New York City. Early in 1949, Katharine Hepburn, another good friend, recommended her for Philip Barry's new play, *Second Threshold*. Diana was happy to have this excuse to leave L.A., fed up with Kirk's increasing self-absorption, constant philandering, and, perhaps worst of all, his almost lackadaisical attitude about cheating. He had even gone so far as to introduce to Diana at dinner one night a woman he had been seeing in New York and whom he had newly relocated to L.A. This was Kirk's version of one big happy family.

Diana flew to Manhattan, leaving the boys with Kirk and the nanny until she was settled. A few weeks later, while living in a Midtown hotel, she decided early one evening to call and let Kirk know she was okay. A woman answered the phone. Diana asked to speak to Michael. When he came to the phone she asked him who that was. "Oh," he said, "that was Auntie Irene. She's living here now."

Auntie Irene was Irene Wrightsman, a twenty-year-old beauty who was the daughter of the president of Standard Oil of Kansas. Kirk had been seeing her secretly before Diana left; once Diana was gone, Kirk moved Irene into the house. Diana hung up, called her lawyer, and told him she wanted a divorce.

Kirk refused to accept the fact that Diana was serious. In one last, desperate attempt to save his marriage, at Diana's insistence he agreed to see a psychiatrist, but only for a week. (He would stay in analysis for five years.) However, to Diana, it was a showy, empty gesture that came too late. In 1951, she went forward with the divorce. Diana would keep the boys with her on the East Coast, which meant among other things that Michael would have to be uprooted once again, this time with little brother tagging along.

The divorce came just as Kirk was hitting the stratosphere. The year before (1950), he had been nominated for a Best Actor Oscar for his performance in Mark Robson's 1949 surprise hit boxing saga, *Champion*, based on a short story by Ring Lardner, in which he gave a performance of conflicted ferocity as a man whose moral strength erodes as his professional career rises.[2] At one point, he begins an affair with a hot blonde and throws over everyone who has helped him get to where he is. It is a stinging fight film with a convenient Hollywood ending dictated as much by the censors as by the story. In this, his eighth film, Kirk was able to show more of his real inner self than he ever had before, playing a mean, self-centered, enraged, and hard-ass character he felt completely at home in. As the 1950s arrived, Kirk had become a star, and the last thing on his mind was domestic family life.

◈

---

2   The other nominees that year were Broderick Crawford, who won for his performance in Robert Rossen's *All the King's Men*; Gregory Peck in Henry King's *12 o'Clock High*; Richard Todd in Vincent Sherman's *The Hasty Heart*; and John Wayne in Allan Dwan's *Sands of Iwo Jima*. It was Kirk's first nomination. He would receive two more, one in 1953 for Vincente Minnelli's *The Bad and the Beautiful* (1952) and one in 1957 for Minnelli's *Lust for Life* (1956). He lost both times.

DIANA, NOW twenty-seven years old, managed to find an apartment in the postwar housing crunch that had hit Manhattan. When a family friend died, she was able to grab his place before it was listed on the open market. The two-bedroom apartment with maid's room was located on Central Park West and Eighty-Fifth Street, not very far from her old apartment. Diana especially liked that now each of the boys could have his own room.

Once settled in, she decided to take the increasingly withdrawn six-year-old Michael to see a child psychiatrist. He was constantly crying and begging his mother to get back together with his father. He felt the emotional pain of the divorce intensely and broke out in tears over the smallest of things. When these outbursts eventually stopped, they were replaced by shyness and a resistance to showing any type of affection. The surface passivity and the inner turmoil were traits that would stay with Michael for the rest of his life.

After several visits, the doctor concluded that Michael was not deeply disturbed or especially antisocial. He was simply acting out the anger he felt at the loss of his father's presence. He told Diana that Michael had developed a "core of sensitivity that he guarded jealously."

Joel, whose natural temperament was somewhat milder than Michael's, appeared less bothered by the divorce, or by anything. He was apparently a happy, if increasingly overweight, little boy. Diana put him into a morning nursery program while Michael attended an ultra-exclusive all-boys private school on the Upper East Side, Allen-Stevenson, where every student was required to wear a blazer and flannel pants. She also hired a full-time governess so she could continue to pursue her career as an actress. However, the more she left the boys with their governess, the more mischievous they got, and they soon took to physically fighting with each other all over the house. After seeing the psychiatrist, Diana was no longer worried that this was abnormal. This behavior, she now believed, was what all boys did.

IN JUNE 1951, Kirk called and asked if he could have the boys with him in Hollywood for the summer. Diana agreed. As it happened, she had been offered the leading role in *Light Up the Sky* with a summer stock company in Ohio, and Kirk's offer made it possible for her to take it. An actor in the company, Bill Darrid, would eventually become Diana's second husband.

Kirk often brought Michael and Joel to the set so they could watch their father work. He was putting the finishing touches on what would be one of the more important films of his career, Vincente Minnelli's *The Bad and the Beautiful.* While there, Michael liked to roam around the studio exploring, enjoying getting lost in the small spaces between walls and flats. One time he happened to return to the sound stage just as Kirk was filming a love scene with Lana Turner, with whom he was allegedly having an offscreen affair (he has always denied this).

Kirk saw him, called "Cut," and waved Michael to go away until the scene was finished, but Michael snuck back and watched. "I was very shocked. I remember looking at my father doing this love scene, and his catching my eye (as if to say, embarrassed, 'Move out of my sight')." Afterward Michael asked his father why he was kissing another woman.

For Kirk, the question, as well as the answer, was both complicated and simple. He didn't know what to say, nor did he feel comfortable talking to Michael about such things. About anything, really.

KIRK NOW DECIDED he wanted to buy a bigger apartment in Manhattan for Diana and the kids, and put it in the boys' names so that if they ever needed cash they could sell it. Diana rejected the notion out of hand, not wanting any of Kirk's guilt money. She really wanted nothing more to do with him at all, other than sharing custody of the children. She had moved on. After her summer stint in Ohio, she continued seeing Darrid, and their relationship deepened. A relatively unknown actor with a normal-size ego, Darrid wanted to marry Diana and was willing to take her two children as part of the package.

For Diana, it was a difficult proposition, and not something she wanted to rush into. Being Mrs. Kirk Douglas had been a nightmare, as she saw her once-unknown husband grow famous, distant, increasingly insecure, and, by his own admission, serially attracted (if not addicted) to sex with other women. The only lasting bright spot from their union was her two boys. Diana was sure she loved Darrid, but she was also aware of the disruption that marrying a new man might cause for Michael and Joel.

CHAPTER 3

I was able to watch my father live in the limelight with all the publicity. . . . [B]eing the second generation takes the joy away from any success you may achieve . . . What do you do about kids born with silver spoons in their mouths? . . . Most kids of successful parents . . . are usually late bloomers.

—MICHAEL DOUGLAS

DURING THE 1953 EASTER HOLIDAYS, KIRK WAS filming Anatole Litvak's *Act of Love* on location in Paris and invited his two boys and Diana to visit. Besides seeing his sons, he had another reason for asking them all to join him. He said he had someone he wanted them all to meet. Kirk had recently fallen in love with Anne Buydens, a public relations woman working on the film. He was enthralled by her Germanic beauty and deeply moved by her life story. She had somehow survived despite having suffered mightily during the war at the hands of the Nazis. Kirk had asked her to marry him, even though she was married at the time to someone else and Kirk was engaged to actress Pier Angeli. He asked Anne shortly after Angeli dumped him.

Before they arrived in Paris, Michael and Joel came down with chicken pox, and then Diana succumbed while they were in the City of Light. By the time they finally recovered, they had just enough time left to attend the opera and, on their last day, finally meet up with Kirk, who explained his situation to them. After Diana congratulated him, they all walked together along the Bois de Boulogne; Michael took his father's hand and put it in his mother's. "Now the family is together," he announced happily.

Kirk and the newly divorced Anne Buydens were married on May 29, 1954.

AFTER THE WEDDING, Anne quickly became good friends with Diana, a development that was key in helping to reduce Michael's anxiety about his new stepmother—a word that frightened him at first because it reminded him of the evil characters in *Cinderella*.

Both boys were overjoyed when Diana decided to move the family back to the West Coast for the summer of 1955 so that they could see their father and she could once again try to revive her acting career. She had done well enough on the stage in New York City, but now she wanted to make another stab at the big screen.

Kirk, meanwhile, had started his own production company, Bryna Productions (named after his mother), in the hopes of making more money with his acting and gaining greater creative control over his projects. With a reputation for being difficult—quick on the trigger with his directors and line producers, according to one who knew and worked with him—he had developed a reputation as being "a talented but stubborn prick. Nobody liked him in Hollywood. He treated everyone like they were servants, and no one looked forward to working with him. He always had to be right about everything." Perhaps because he simply couldn't work for anyone else, he decided to work for himself, and continue his quest to find the one role that would deliver him an Oscar and confirm to himself his place in Hollywood's acting pantheon.

In 1955 *The Indian Fighter* was Bryna's first production, an action Western shot in Cinemascope on location in Oregon and written by Frank Davis and Ben Hecht, veteran writers with solid credentials. The script was based on a story by Robert L. Richards, writing as Ben Kadish, due to the blacklist, and directed by Andre de Toth. Production began when Diana and the boys returned to L.A. Now that he was the boss, Kirk wanted to help Diana out, and after talking it over with Anne and getting her okay, he offered her a part in the film. Anne, who was pregnant at the time, volunteered to keep the boys with her while Diana filmed on location with Kirk up in Oregon. During the final weeks of shooting, Diana brought the boys up north to be with her, and Kirk wrote in a few lines for each of them ("*The Indians are coming! The Indians are coming*"), so the film would be a true Douglas family affair (minus Anne).[1]

When the picture was finished, Diana enrolled the boys in public school in Westwood. Michael was placed in Emerson Junior High School, a far cry from the privileged halls of Allen-Stevenson. Joel went to Bellagio Road Elementary in Westwood. Because of the differences between New York private schools and California public schools, ten-year-old Michael was jumped into the seventh grade, placing him alongside thirteen- and fourteen-year-old boys and girls. It was the first time he had gone to school with girls. He felt awkward and shy among the older L.A. kids until one girl gave him his initial taste of the joys of coeducation. Michael remembered it this way: "The first girl I ever kissed had her mouth wide open!"

That part was great, less so the proliferation of Hollywood gangs that had begun to infiltrate Emerson and set up factions that ruled the hallways, something that Michael, a pampered product of East Coast private schools, had no prior experience with. When he complained to his mother that the gangs scared him, she immediately pulled him from Emerson and enrolled him in what was considered at the time the best private school in California, the Los Angeles Black-Foxe Military Institute. Michael felt relieved, even if it was an all-boys school.

IN 1955, AFTER the commercial success of *The Indian Fighter*, Kirk was able to produce his second feature. But that's not all he produced that year. On November 23, 1955, Anne gave birth to a baby boy, Peter Vincent. The child was given his middle name after the talented and tortured painter Vincent Van Gogh, whom Kirk had brilliantly

---

1   The boys' footage did not make it into the film's final cut.

portrayed in Vincente Minnelli's *Lust for Life*, Kirk's newest smash-hit Bryna production.

Both Anne and Diana worked hard to make sure the boys understood that Peter was their new brother. Surprisingly, Michael seemed easier with it than Joel. The younger boy was having problems at Bellagio and continually ran out of his classrooms and all the way back to his mother's small rented house nearby. Diana decided that it was Joel's turn to see a psychiatrist.

After several visits, Joel was diagnosed as mildly dyslexic, which manifested in uncontrollable behavior such as running away. This was intensified by the sibling rivalry reinvigorated by the arrival of Peter Vincent.

AT THE SAME TIME, Diana and Bill, who had been communicating by phone, agreed to put an end to their separation by marrying. They set the date for December 1956 so that Diana could take the full year's tax benefits from her alimony and child support. The alimony would end, of course, on her wedding day, but the $540 a month Kirk paid for child support would continue.

It was a happy time for her but signaled yet another major disruption for the boys. Diana agreed to give up her movie career and move back east with them to a new place Bill had decided to buy, a nineteenth-century farmhouse in Westport, Connecticut. Joel, especially, had difficulty adjusting to the new surroundings. Not long after they moved in, he kept calling for glasses of water at night during what proved to be the most inopportune times for the newlyweds. Diana decided to hire a tutor rather than have Joel try to adapt to another new school. Bill had another, simpler solution: he believed that anything that was wrong with the boy could be fixed by getting him a dog.

Bill also resisted dealing with Michael in any but the most basic, nonthreatening ways. Michael had entered puberty around the time of that first kiss, and his interest in girls had since exploded. Diana pleaded with Bill to explain the birds and the bees to him, as his real father was three thousand miles away making a movie and there was no one else. Bill reluctantly agreed; he asked Diana to fix him a strong scotch, then braced himself for what was to come, and sat down by the fireplace with Michael. What was awkward at first soon turned into an elbow-sticking, roaring hell of a good time, the two of them emerging from the sex education chamber laughing out loud, arms entwined. Mission accomplished.

When it was Joel's turn, a year or two later, he had a much more difficult time with "the talk," and did not emerge from it with so much as a trace of any one-of-the-boys camaraderie. Shortly after, Joel had what amounted to something between a breakdown and an extended anxiety attack that required a brief hospitalization.

MICHAEL, MEANWHILE, having hurdled over the awkward stages of puberty, became a prince among princes at the coed junior high school in Westport. All the girls loved him, and he enthusiastically loved them all back. He lost his virginity with "I think it was somebody older . . . as hard as guys that age are trying to get it and it doesn't seem possible—there are those girls who just make a decision. No romancing, you know; they just make a decision they're gonna go for it. And there are a few surprised guys." Diana fretted about how her "skinny little fourteen-year-old [had become the neighborhood teenage] Lothario."

Michael went on to attend Choate Rosemary Hall, a private high school in Wallingford, Connecticut, where he participated in football, basketball, track, wrestling, weight training, the dance committee (he was chairman), the art club, and the auto club (he was president)—everything and anything except activities related to dramatics.

KIRK, MEANWHILE, was making some of the best, if most controversial, films of his career. In 1957 he hired a still largely unknown Stanley Kubrick to write and direct a new Bryna project, *Paths of Glory*, which would become one of the most blistering and least commercial antiwar movies ever made. For his next project, Kirk wisely picked an entertaining, noncontroversial big-budget action-adventure picture called *The Vikings*, directed by Richard Fleischer.

That same year, following *The Vikings*, Kirk chose to make *Spartacus*, his mighty film adaptation of Howard Fast's controversial story of a pre-Christian slave who led an uprising that nearly brought down the republic. *Spartacus* took three long, hard years to make, and all of Kirk's time, energy and attention. Later he would quip that the film "took more time than the real-life Spartacus spent waging war against the Roman Empire."

Kirk saw very little of his children during those years. He missed all of the emotional difficulties the overweight Joel was having, and how Michael was slowly turning into a new, younger version of himself. If Joel's problems stemmed from his inability to adjust to the absence of his real father and the presence of a new one, Michael went around telling anyone who would listen that his father *was* Spartacus.

SEVENTEEN MONTHS after Kirk had finished filming Richard Fleischer's *20,000 Leagues Under the Sea* for Walt Disney Studios, he brought the boys out to Hollywood and accepted Walt Disney's invitation to bring them to his house, where Disney took some home movies of Kirk and the boys riding the backyard train. It was considered a privilege to be invited to Disney's home and even more special to get to ride his train. However, when Disney ran the footage as part of his weekly TV show, *Walt Disney's Wonderful World of Color*, Kirk wrote Disney an angry letter demanding that he never again exploit his family in that way. It was Kirk's understanding that the films had been made for Disney's home use and not for any personal gain, he wrote, and he had not given Disney the right to use footage of his children and himself as part of that week's episode. Walt was apologetic and promised Kirk it would never happen again.

Two months later the show was rebroadcast, with the train-riding footage intact. Kirk, now furious, decided to sue Walt Disney, but just as the case was about to go to trial, he withdrew the suit. In a famous moment, Kirk shrugged and told the press, "You can't sue God."

Those two TV broadcasts mark the first television appearance of eleven-year-old Michael Douglas.

IN 1958, ANNE gave birth to another child, Eric Anthony, completing a second set of sons for Kirk. Peter and Eric would grow up under the same roof as their famous father but ultimately would not be able to get any closer to him emotionally than either Michael or Joel. Nor would they bond especially well with their half brothers. Each set tended to orbit within the universe of their respective mothers.

BY THE TIME Michael graduated from high school, his mother and stepfather had long been on a campaign to convince him to attend Yale, where he somehow was accepted despite considerably less than Ivy League–level grades.

But he had a different plan. He wanted to head back to the West Coast, to attend the University of California, Santa Barbara, in a lovely coastal town about a hundred miles north of Hollywood. He had discovered through the promotional brochures he had received from the university that the ratio of female students to male students there was four to one.

PART TWO

CONNECTICUT
TO SANTA BARBARA
TO NEW YORK

A publicity still from Michael's TV series The Streets of San Francisco.

CHAPTER 4

I think having a famous father was a pain in the ass for him. . . .
Michael, of all my four sons, had the least ambition.

—KIRK DOUGLAS

IN THE FALL OF 1963, UCSB WELCOMED NINETEEN-year-old English major Michael with open arms and loving, bikini-clad coeds. Music filled the air alongside the pungent clouds of pot smoke and other assorted social accessories of physical pleasure that filled this campus-by-the-sea, reassuring Michael he had made the right decision.

Not long after classes began, his frequent communiqués home to his mother were filled with descriptions of his great new life, lots about the weather, the ocean, and of course much about the girls, but hardly any news of his academic achievements. A red flag went up for Diana when Michael wrote to say he was moving in with a girl, but not to worry because they were still going to date other people.

It was, indeed, that now-fabled dawning of the age of Aquarius, and everyone under twenty-five wanted entrée to the anything-goes Youth Club of America. And at UCSB Michael stood at the head of the line. He let his hair grow long, wore dirty ripped jeans and tie-dyed shirts, was having far too much fun enjoying himself with the pleasures of excess, and missed most of his classes.

By the end of his first year, Diana and Kirk each received letters from the dean regarding Michael's failing status. His grades had fallen below the minimum acceptable level. The dean strongly suggested Michael take a year off to find himself and to make sure he was ready and willing to take on the responsibilities of full-time college studies.

Michael agreed, dropped out, and returned to Westport. To pass the time, he picked up some day work in a local Mobil gas station. "I was into hot-rods," Michael said later, and in his after-hours he tried to build himself a racing car in the family garage. That July, he was named "Mobil Man of the Month."

When Kirk heard about the honor, he called Michael, asked him if he intended to work in a gas station for the rest of his life, and then hung up. He wasn't pleased.

KIRK WAS, at the time, licking his wounds over the failure of *One Flew Over the Cuckoo's Nest*, his attempt to bring his movie-star magic to Broadway.

One Flew Over the Cuckoo's Nest was based on Ken Kesey's semi-autobiographical novel of the same title about a so-called sane man who gets himself imprisoned in a mental institution to escape criminal prosecution. Kirk had optioned Kesey's 1962 novel after reading it in galleys prior to its official release and had hired Dale Wasserman, the screenwriter for *The Vikings*, to turn it into a stage play. Kirk intended the Broadway run to be a tune-up for what he hoped would make a terrific, Oscar-worthy movie. The show opened on November 13, 1963, despite the poor to mixed reception it had received in its pre-Broadway tryout in Boston.

Unfortunately, the New York reviews for *Cuckoo's Nest* were not very good ("murderous" was how Kirk described them). Everyone had advised him to get out as soon as he could, not to throw good money after bad, but Kirk, always a stubborn man, believed the play would eventually find an audience.

It wouldn't. Nine days into the show's Broadway run, President Kennedy was assassinated. In the months that followed the awful deed, no one was in the mood to be entertained by a play about someone who might be dangerous and crazy and was stuck in a metaphorical mental prison. Kirk managed to keep it going for two more months on sheer star power but finally pulled the plug on January 25, 1964.

AFTER THAT, Kirk returned to the commercial sanctuary of the big screen and made John Frankenheimer's *Seven Days in May*, co-starring his good friend Burt Lancaster. Based on a popular novel of the day by Fletcher Knebel and Charles W. Bailey II, it is a paranoid thriller about an attempted military overthrow of the American government. He followed that immediately with Otto Preminger's *In Harm's Way*, a star-studded ensemble reenactment of the Japanese attack on Pearl Harbor. Besides Kirk, John Wayne was in it, along with Patricia Neal (whom Kirk had dated briefly a few years earlier but could not pry out of the bed of Gary Cooper, the self-proclaimed love of her life), Tom Tryon, Brandon DeWilde, Burgess Meredith, and dozens of other up-and-coming, here-and-now, and over-the-hill Hollywood stars.

Kirk had decided to bring along Anne and their children, Peter and Eric, to Hawaii, where the on-location film was being shot. Neither of the boys from his first marriage was invited. Joel, Kirk decided, was too emotionally frail to make the long trip, and he was still angry at Michael for becoming an award-winning gas station attendant.

Kirk's next picture was Anthony Mann's *The Heroes of Telemark*. By then, he had finally gotten over his anger at Michael and took him along on location in Norway, where he got him a job in the wardrobe department. Kirk figured if the boy wasn't going to complete his education, maybe he could learn something about the film business.[1] Kirk took Mann aside and told him to work the boy as hard as he could. Mann, known for his directorial toughness that at times seemed to border on the sadistic, promised Kirk he would make sure Michael didn't think he was on some kind of a picnic.

To everyone's surprise, no one's more than Kirk's, Michael proved

---

1   Michael is listed in the credits of the 1965 release as assistant director.

he could take whatever Mann dished out. He did anything and every-thing he was told to, including assignments no one else wanted—sloppy, dirty work, physically demanding but dull jobs—and he liked it. He was energized by being around film people, especially his father, and began to think that this was a world he wanted to belong to.

Meanwhile, impressed with his son's work ethic, Kirk invited Mi-chael to join the next production, an American film shot almost en-tirely in Israel. Melville Shavelson's *Cast a Giant Shadow* was the true story (Hollywood style) of American colonel David "Mickey" Marcus, who helped Israel fight for its independence. It was another cameo-fest, with Kirk's cronies John Wayne (whose Batjac Productions financed the film), Frank Sinatra, and Yul Brynner making appearances.

This time Kirk assigned Michael to a specific position, production assistant, and also let him do some stunt driving, all of which Michael loved. Kirk also brought along Joel, who had pushed through his pu-berty and in doing so lost some of his emotional confusion. He was now a strapping, husky six-footer. Kirk made him his bodyguard.

The film was completed early in the summer of 1965, just in time for Michael to enroll in UCSB's summer session. Kirk was elated that Michael had decided to go back to school, but he made it clear he wanted to see some positive results this time.

HE NEEDN'T HAVE WORRIED. Michael couldn't wait to get back to school, and the first thing he did upon his return was to change his major from English to drama. He tried out for UCSB's summer production, Shakespeare's *As You Like It* and landed a small role and threw himself into it.

When it came time for the performance, Michael invited both Kirk and Diana to see him act in it. Both accepted, and each arrived separately. Kirk viewed the production as something of a test. Know-ing of Michael's decision to want to become an actor, Kirk decided that if his son did a good job, he would encourage him to pursue his new dream, maybe even give a helping hand. There were a lot of doors Kirk could open.

But as it turned out, Kirk hated Michael in the play. "You were terrible," he told him backstage afterward, and walked away, leaving his son speechless. Diana was much more positive after seeing him perform in a school production of *Escurial*, but it was Kirk's opnion that meant the most to Michael.

AFTER THAT, Michael quickly fell back into his campus-style hippie living. He once more took up pot smoking, and now became an enthusiastic user of LSD. In the spring of 1966, he moved out of his dorm and into a commune situated in a bunch of abandoned buildings near Mountain Drive, high in the hills of Santa Barbara, with its heady views of the beautiful aqua-blue Pacific.

The members of the commune busied themselves rejecting "straight" society and nourishing their minds by growing their own pot and taking daily doses of acid. Not surprisingly, they had no interest at all in doing anything that smacked of tradition. "There were, I suppose, between 100 and 150 of us at any one time," David Garsite, another member of the commune, later remembered. "We were the 'Smile on your brother' brigade. . . . I have this vision of Michael in torn jeans and velour shirt flashing around on his big motorcycle, with his long hair trailing in the wind, and a blonde with the most fulsome bosoms you ever saw riding behind him."

Michael was content to live in a no-running-water shack on the edge of the commune, his bike parked at the front door, dreaming of putting on agitprop street shows with the commune to protest the war in Vietnam. Only he couldn't get himself off his mattress long enough to organize any of it. Besides always being stoned, a rare venture out on a ski trip had resulted in an accident that left Michael with an injured vertebra, forcing him to wear a back brace (despite doctor's orders, he only wore it occasionally). The injury left him ineligible for the draft, which may be why he wore it at all, although he insisted at the time that if drafted he would not go into the army but would instead flee to Canada for the duration of the war.

He was enjoying a doob one day when a visitor came to call.

It was Kirk, banging on the door. When Michael let him in, Kirk screamed bloody murder about how his son was living his life. Michael reacted by not reacting. He calmly watched as his father finished his rant and bolted down the road, pushing aside anyone and anything that got in his way.

DESPITE BEING a stoner and seriously injured, Michael managed to attend some classes and did fairly well. When he returned to Connecticut that summer he was together enough, with Bill Darrid intervening, to land a position at the prestigious Eugene O'Neill Memorial Theater's National Playwrights Conference in Waterford, Connecticut. Michael did backstage work and served as a gofer, both unpaid positions, all for the promise of a small part in one of that season's plays. In many ways, to Michael the O'Neill was not all that dissimilar to the commune, except here everyone put on plays every night instead of getting stoned.

He wasn't enjoying himself all that much, and was thinking about bailing and returning to the West Coast when he met another backstage member of the company, a balding, pug-size young man to whom he took an instant liking. The fellow's name was Danny DeVito, the unlikeliest of wanna-be actors.

The intense, gnomish five-foot DeVito and the laid-back, five-foot-ten Michael quickly became inseparable. They kept their distance from the coffee-drenched neo-esoterica that filled the smoky nights of most of the other actors in the company; Danny and Michael preferred pushing wheelbarrows filled with dirt, cutting wood, pouring concrete. Alone it was drudge work, together it was fun.

The dynamic of their friendship is not all that difficult to understand. Michael was a silver-spoon baby without any pressing need to make a living. Being a nameless member of a commune fit him perfectly, even if (or perhaps because) it enraged his famous and famously intense father. DeVito, Italian and Catholic, was the child of an immigrant mother and was burning with ambition. He was a working-class Jersey boy who had to survive on his own wits and talent. He was rough-hewn, small in size but large in stature. Their mutual attraction was complementary; if Michael desired to be accepted as one of the workers-of-the-world-united, DeVito longed to get off the mean streets and move among the socially elite. Each envied the other. And there was something else: girls. Both were crazy for them. With his good looks, Michael could always get all the women he wanted, while DeVito wanted anything he could get. To that end, Michael was happy to share, and DeVito was happy to take.

DeVito was born in Neptune City and grew up in Asbury Park, not far from where a young Bruce Springsteen was honing his craft and where, a few generations down the road, a couple of shore kids would chronicle the vapidity of their lives on MTV.

Although he spent much of his childhood at the Jersey shore, DeVito's heart belonged to Brooklyn. Every week he looked forward to traveling with his parents to see his grandmother, who still lived there. As he remembers, "On Sundays we'd take the Staten Island Ferry, get on the Belt Parkway, and drive to Flatbush. I always loved driving through the streets. But I also loved living at the shore. It was a resort, and every summer the city girls would come down. . . . There were six or seven movie theaters that were constantly changing their programs. Until Labor Day, when everything would change and it would become Bergmanesque. . . . Beautiful light, not a lot of people, family. Really a beautiful place to grow up."

DeVito quickly became addicted to movies and wanted to be in them, but he believed it was simply impossible for a guy who looked like he did to get from here to there. After graduating from high school, he lowered his sights and let his sister pay his tuition at the

Wilfred Beauty Academy. Not long after, DeVito took a job in her parlor. After a while, he decided he wanted to expand his realm and get into makeup. He thought it would be a great way to get even closer to the women who had quickly become his regulars. The only problem was, he had no idea where to go to study makeup.

Then he saw an ad in a New York newspaper for the Academy of Dramatic Arts (the same acting school that Kirk had attended), which offered a course in makeup technique. "One night, I was eighteen or nineteen, I went down [to the Academy] and said I want to enroll in makeup. They told me I couldn't enroll just to learn makeup, I had to enroll as an acting student. So my dream was forced upon me! I did a monologue, from *Teahouse of the August Moon*, because that was how you got in. I'd never seen a play before, except *Mr. Roberts* done in a tent out in Neptune, New Jersey. But I got in and I enrolled in night classes."

DeVito proved something of a natural, and despite his height of only five feet (some sources list him at four feet eleven inches), he was able to find work quite easily as a rather distinctive character actor in several summer stock companies, including a 1966 summer residency at the O'Neill, where he met and befriended Michael.

WHEN THE SUMMER ENDED, DeVito went back to Manhattan and resumed looking for acting work, while Michael drove his motorbike cross-country all the way to Santa Barbara, ostensibly to resume classes but really to take up residence once more at Mountain Drive. "I got into the Maharishi, and was doing some meditation. . . . You had your motorcycle or whatever, and your renaissance velour shirts. It was fun. Marijuana and psychedelics had a real influence . . . that had to do with rhythm and perspective. I was not, in that period, career-conscious at all."

Only a few days had passed before Michael next heard from DeVito, who called to say he'd landed a big-break audition in Hollywood for a film role he desperately wanted. Michael wished him luck, and told him he was welcome to stay at the commune as long as he wanted or needed to. DeVito took him up on his offer. Despite the distance between Hollywood and Santa Barbara, the price of a round-trip bus back and forth would be cheaper than finding a place in Hollywood.

DeVito arrived in Santa Barbara wearing a black full-length coat, white sneakers, and a beret. It was Method preparation, DeVito explained to Michael, his way of fitting into the part prior to the audition, which was set for the following week. In the interim, he took a great deal of pleasure from admiring the naked, pot-smoking women who lounged around the commune like it was a poor man's Playboy Mansion.

DeVito thought he had a real shot at playing the dark and merciless killer Perry Edward Smith, one of the two subjects of the movie Richard Brooks was making based on Truman Capote's bestselling self-described "nonfiction novel" *In Cold Blood*, about the murder of the middle-American Clutter family by Smith and his partner, Richard "Dick" Hickock.

He did not get the part; it went instead to Robert Blake. DeVito lingered for a while in Los Angeles before heading back east.

MEANWHILE, PERHAPS feeling some of DeVito's energy and determination, Michael finally began to grow weary of the lifestyle he was living. Plus, more and more strangers were showing up, either to try to get laid or to sell drugs to the group. The idealism of Mountain Drive, like the sixties themselves, was fast devolving into slippery hustling, fake hippies, and a legal mire of narcs and cops. Feeling he'd had enough, in the fall of 1967 Michael decided to return to regular classes at UCSB to try to salvage his academic career.

He once more quickly became a familiar and likeable presence on campus. He was known partly for being the son of a celebrity, partly for his natural good looks (including flowing blond hair and a soft chin made firmer looking by the family's trademark cleft), partly for his acting, and partly for his robust liberal political activism.

In June 1967, the end of his junior year, Michael returned for another go-round at the National Playwrights Conference. He was hired as an actor and was determined this time to concentrate more on performing than on girls.

For this season, the O'Neill focused on newer playwrights. Among them was Michael's assigned roommate, Cincinnati-born Ron Cowen, a self-styled playwright. He had managed to get the theater company to produce an early version of one of his plays, *Summertree*, a vivid antiwar story about an all-American young man determined to avoid the draft. When his number is called, he decides to flee to Canada, only to have a last-minute patriotic change of heart; he allows himself to be conscripted, winds up in Vietnam, and is killed. Michael loved the play, seeing a lot of himself in the main character. Cowen cast him in the leading role.

IN MAY 1968, with his parents in attendance, Michael received his BA from UCSB. The next day he left for New York City, intent on becoming a Broadway actor. Upon his arrival, he immediately called DeVito, who offered to let Michael stay with him at his apartment on West Eighty-Ninth Street, for only half the rent.

DeVito remembered, "Our apartment in New York City was $150 a month. I think I was struggling more than he was. But he did the laundry. He fluffed and folded really well. He left me when he went to do *The Streets of San Francisco*, but he still paid half the rent when he was away. Now we often talk about how stupid we were to let this low-rent apartment go."

No sooner had he unpacked his bags than Michael headed for the Neighborhood Playhouse, one of the more prestigious acting schools in Manhattan. He had scheduled a fall audition for the Playhouse's acting guru, Sanford Meisner. Michael's goal was to secure a place in the next semester's roster.

Evenings Michael and DeVito became regulars of the Greenwich Village bar and Soho nightlife circuits, where the food was lousy, the pot plentiful, and the women easy. They often piled into DeVito's old Chevy, a muscle car "which Danny drove with total authority," Michael recalled. "You know, ticking the side-view mirrors of the double-parked cars, never moving a muscle, never easing off." "Ya can't worry about it," DeVito told a reporter. "Just go through, like Zen." This was the era when bombing around Manhattan in a car and driving downtown was still feasible, especially in Soho, where DeVito could pull up on almost any street, get out, and leave his car there and it would remain safe and unticketed. In those days, the police stayed away from Soho as if it were Siberia, and the oversize illegally converted lofts and lax street security made it the perfect locale for New York's anything-goes art community of the late 1960s.

When taking a break from picking up girls (their favorite pastime), they loved to play practical jokes on the uptown crowd. A typical stunt involved DeVito accompanying Michael to a party in one of Madison Avenue's snootier neighborhoods wearing a pair of grotesque stage teeth and imitating a hunchback. They noted carefully how the room warmed up only when Michael smoothly, and falsely, introduced his friend as the star of the new Richard Brooks movie.

That fall, Italian film director Michelangelo Antonioni was in New York searching for the lead in his next film, *Zabriskie Point*, about the American sixties as seen through the eyes of the outside world, meaning Antonioni. Michael, still waiting for his audition call at the Neighborhood Playhouse, decided to try out for the film. As he remembered, "This talent scout hunt was a big event in New York. Antonioni was looking over people at the Cheetah Club [one of the hottest disco clubs in New York City at the time]. I remember there were crowds stretching all the way around the block. They had us come in three at a time, like a lineup."

In a pre-interview with an assistant, Michael related a Vietnam "war game" exercise he had done in one of his drama classes at UCSB. When he was finally brought before Antonioni, that same assistant asked him to repeat the story to the director. "I'm talking about it," Douglas recalled, "and Antonioni's looking at the guy next to me. He's not interested in me at all, but he lets me go on talking. So I'm telling him about this one gory time, and he's ignoring me, so I said in the same voice, 'And of course, all Italians eat meatballs.' Antonioni didn't even notice. There I was spilling my guts, so I said, 'Fuck this,' and walked out."

Michael was more certain than ever that he was never going to be the next Kirk Douglas.

CHAPTER 5

I don't think Kirk ever learned to enjoy money. He's got a big
house in Beverly Hills and a big fence around it—and himself.
Money doesn't mean that much to me.

—MICHAEL DOUGLAS

AS IT TURNED OUT, THE NEIGHBORHOOD PLAY-
house was not Michael's thing. At least part of the problem was
the regimentation—too academic, too much lecture-and-listen, too
much like regular school.

He soon quit the Playhouse in favor of studying at Wynn Handman's American Place Theatre. In the fifties and sixties, because so
much of live television and radio dramas, and some movies, were produced on location in New York City, Manhattan was thick with training grounds for actors, and the American Place Theatre was one of the
newer and more dynamic ones. It was founded in 1963 by Handman,
Sidney Lanier, and Michael Tolan.

A Manhattan native, Handman was less interested in training actors than in incorporating them into a community of writers, directors,
and performers to discover and produce new American plays. Training
included teaching actors how to perform in full-length scripts in front
of the public rather than doing individual scenes for the classroom.
Among his better-known students in the 1960s were Richard Gere,
Alec Baldwin, James Caan, Christopher Walken, Joanne Woodward,
and . . . M. K. Douglas.

Upon landing his first paying job in New York City, Michael discovered he could not use his real name on stage. In 1969, after almost
two years of looking for acting work, Michael had landed a part in the

CBS Playhouse production of Ellen M. Violett's *The Experiment*, play-ing a scientist who compromises his liberal views to accept a job with a major corporation. It was a theme he was familiar with, youthful rebels against the corporation, and a character he knew he could play. The other two principal players in the cast were John Astin and Barry Brown. All three, including Michael, were relatively unknown, but when he applied for mandatory membership in AFTRA (the Amer-ican Federation of Television and Radio Artists) he discovered that television was considered a closed shop and actors had to be members of AFTRA in order to get work, though the conundrum for most was that they couldn't get a card without a job and they couldn't get a job without a card. AFTRA informed him he couldn't use the name Michael Douglas professionally, even though it was his real name, be-cause it was already registered to a popular Cleveland-based daytime variety host, Mike (Michael) Douglas.[1]

The videotaped broadcast of *The Experiment* aired on February 25, 1969, and the next day Jack Gould, then the *New York Times*'s television critic, wrote that "Mr. Douglas gave a remarkably lucid and attrac-tively relaxed performance." That much was great. He then continued, "[He] could easily go as far as his father; he has a promising knack for intuitive versatility." That part wasn't. This would be the first of many reviews that would compare him to Kirk. Michael knew now that he would need to push to have his work recognized before his heredity.

AFTER THE CRITICAL and ratings success of *The Experiment*, CBS approached Michael about joining the rotating acting roster of the net-

---

1   For television, Michael was allowed to use M. K. Douglas. Later on, in film, the Screen Actors Guild let him use his real name, as the other Michael Douglas was not a member of that union. Hence, on TV and in live performances, he was M. K. Douglas, and in film he was Michael Douglas. When Mike Douglas left TV, he gave his permission for Michael to use his full name on TV. "I hated being billed as M. K. Douglas," Michael said later. "It sounds so pretentious, like some old character actor" (Edwin Miller, "Chip Off the Old Block," undated).

work's new feature-film unit, Cinema Center Films, which would create product for both the little and big screens. Before the ink was dry on the deal, Bob Thomas, the nationally syndicated Associated Press journalist, interviewed Michael for his April column and later wrote that the public should "add Michael Douglas to the ever-growing list of movie stars' children who are making it in films." It was the last thing Michael wanted to read; he had hoped that Thomas wouldn't go there. The rest of the piece wasn't as bad. "He also is an instant star, thanks to the recent CBS Playhouse drama, *The Experiment*. . . . Mike himself wears his brown [*sic*] hair in the fashionable long style, though he appears to have passed through the hippie stage. That happened in his university days. Mike went the whole route: guru, pot, LSD. His experience with narcotics proved worthwhile, he believes, 'because it taught me about rhythm in living. You know how some days you feel dull and listless and other days you feel alive? Everyone has certain rhythms and using narcotics dulls the senses and you need the sharp edges for acting.'"

And just like that, via official anointment by influential Hollywood scribe Bob Thomas, the laid-back, anti-authoritarian former free-love hippie and political and social activist swam from the outer shores of the counterculture into the show business mainstream.

IN THE SPRING OF 1969, Cinema Center Films put Michael up for the role of Carl Dixon in a new big-screen feature to be called *Hail, Hero!* But his star status wasn't quite there yet, and he was forced to stand in line with other company contract players in what amounted to a cattle-call audition. At first the film's director, David Miller, passed on Michael until, without Michael's knowledge, and believing it would help get him the part, his agent called to let Miller know that in case he wasn't aware of it, M. K. Douglas was Kirk Douglas's son.

That resonated with Miller, and not necessarily in a positive way. In 1962 he had directed Kirk Douglas in the Bryna production *Lonely Are the Brave*, which Kirk often cited as the favorite among all his films. (Michael worked on the film for eight days as an assistant cutter.) However, as with most directors who worked with Kirk, things had not gone smoothly. Here is Kirk's rather cold description of his experience being directed by Miller: "I took David Miller as a director, and regretted it. I felt that he did a far from brilliant job. He was unhappy on location. I played pimp and introduced him to a girl. Anything to keep him happy and get him through the picture. I thought he was the only one who didn't come up to the high standards of all the other elements in the picture."

Miller had directed only two big-screen features between *Lonely Are the Brave* and *Hail, Hero!*, neither of which was successful. Perhaps to make amends, perhaps to end what he might have felt was some kind of industry-wide ban against him instigated by Kirk, or maybe because he suddenly realized Michael was the best actor for the film, Miller reversed himself and gave Michael the role.[2]

THE SCREENPLAY FOR *Hail, Hero!* was an adaptation of John Weston's popular, controversial 1968 antiwar novel of the same name. In it, Carl Dixon is a pacifist with conservative parents; it was another in an increasingly long line of Hollywood films depicting America's generational divide during the Vietnam years.

Although the film opened softly in October 1969 and faded quickly, to those who saw it the surface resemblance between Michael and his famous father was difficult to avoid. They are the same height, and Michael had his father's Fosdick jaw, only not quite as fearless, as well

---

2   Kirk later claimed he had no hand in helping to get Michael the part. John L. Scott wrote in the *Los Angeles Times* shortly after Michael got the part that "Kirk knew nothing about [Miller's choosing Michael for the role] and was recuperating from a minor throat operation when he heard the news. Not allowed to use his voice, and not believing his son could actually get the movie on his own, and for Miller, Kirk jokingly scribbled his reaction on a pad—'I'm speechless!'" John L. Scott, "Kirk Douglas' Son Ready to Start Career in Films," *Los Angeles Times*.

as that famous trademark dimple. Michael's eyes, like his father's, were dark, but cooler and gentler than Kirk's burning browns. Perhaps the biggest difference between them was what they projected: Michael was at home playing laid-back sixties-type youth, while Kirk was never young nor laid-back on film (or in real life). There had always been a gritty, adult authority to Kirk's performances, as well as a naturally intense style of talking through clenched teeth and reddened cheeks. He played muscle-bound cowboys on horseback, or quick-fisted characters who had no patience for other men and always a bend-them-back kiss for the women. Kirk's characters, with one or two notable exceptions (Vincent Van Gogh), resembled his real-life personality—steely, instinctive, sexual, invincible. Michael's, by comparison, were less heroic, more vulnerable. Seen together, which they rarely were offscreen and never on it until decades later, they were less similar than when each was seen in a film by himself that made audiences recall the other.

Vincent Canby, reviewing *Hail, Hero!* for the *New York Times*, acknowledged some individualistic talent in Michael: "It's not an especially memorable performance, but it's an energetic one and without Douglas, *Hail, Hero!* would not even be tolerable. . . . It is, I suppose, an anti-Vietnam movie, but it's the sort of neutral anti-Vietnam movie that one might expect to find at Radio City Music Hall, where it opened yesterday."

Cinema Center promoted the film heavily, and almost every time Michael was interviewed he was asked if Kirk had pulled any strings to get him the part. The question visibly annoyed him, and that was reflected in his answers. Talking to the *Hollywood Citizen News*, Michael tried to point out the folly of that logic. He had gotten the part in *Hail, Hero!* because of his work in *The Experiment*, he said, and in some cases coming from a movie family made it more difficult to gain credibility as an actor. "In Hollywood, when you're a star's son, they think, 'Yeah, for him it's easy.'"

Despite the failure of *Hail, Hero!* Cinema Center put Michael up for another feature, Robert Scheerer's 1970 *Adam at Six a.m.* The character of Adam is a linguistics professor in an unnamed Southern California college who decides to drop out for a summer to be a laborer in Missouri (the film was shot on location in Excelsior Springs, Missouri) to see how "the other half" lives—hence the early wake-up time of the title. There he falls in prole love, and at the end of the picture he remains undecided about in which direction he wants to go with his life.

Adam at Six a.m. was released on September 22, 1970, received almost no distribution, and did nothing at the box office.[3] At this point, the question of whether Michael would be able to continue to make films at all if he *wasn't* Kirk Douglas's son became more relevant. When asked by reporter Shaun Considine about it, Michael replied, "Of course it's helped being the son of Kirk Douglas. It's made [making movies] easier, but not in the way people assume. It can get you past the front door but it can't get the job for you. That's up to you." And then he added testily, "My mother, Diana, is a wonderful actress."

THE TRUTH WAS, whether or not any doors had been opened for him, Michael's career was going nowhere. For that matter, neither was Kirk's. He had aged out of the big-budget action-and-romance movies that had become his trademark. From 1946's *The Strange Love of Martha Ivers* to Elia Kazan's 1969 *The Arrangement*, Kirk had appeared in forty-nine feature films and some made-for-TV movies, but as the years went on, his box office boffo proved increasingly elusive. He had had high hopes for reviving his career by working with Kazan, but the film was a critical and box office disappointment. In his younger days Kirk had brought an intense sexuality to the screen. In his fifties he came off more sour than sexy.

---

3 CBS was unimpressed with the finished product and prior to its release sold off the film's distribution rights to National General, which was looking for cheap product to play overseas and to warehouse for future videotape inventory. Although several years away from commercial video reaching the market, the video concept was already percolating through Hollywood.

Indeed, by 1969, Kirk, at fifty-three, had been pushed aside by a younger generation of leading men: Robert Redford, Steve McQueen, Paul Newman, and Clint Eastwood. Kirk was reduced to accepting mediocre work like the starring role in Dick Clement's nondescript *To Catch a Spy*, which never made it to American commercial movie screens. All of it left him angry and frustrated, and whenever he could, he liked to demonstrate that he still had some clout left in show business.

So when a furious Michael told his father that he had been fired from the long-awaited Broadway stage production of his O'Neill Playhouse buddy Ron Cowen's antiwar play *Summertree* (which Michael had appeared in at Waterford in 1967) in favor of up-and-coming actor David Birney, Kirk, who was in New York filming *The Brotherhood*, angrily had Bryna buy the film rights from Cowen and then gave the starring role in the film version to Michael. It was an unusually generous move for Kirk, and on the surface it had all the markings of a father coming to the rescue of his son. But on a deeper level, there may have been some sense of personal vengeance at work, fury at the director rather than salvation for the son. Kirk remembers, "The director was Jules Irving, and he fired my son. So what did I do? I bought the screen rights and developed it into a movie for Michael . . . *who didn't want to do it!*"

Indeed, Michael was reluctant to make the film precisely because he didn't want to lend credence to the ongoing talk throughout the industry and in the press of nepotism. He didn't want anyone (including himself) to believe he couldn't make it on his own. However, after thinking it over, he realized it was a role he had originated and deserved to play on film, and he agreed to be in the movie.

"A lot of people think that *Summertree* was what *Love Story* should have been," Michael told an interviewer shortly after the film's disappointing June 6, 1971, opening, suggesting that the characters of Jerry, a reluctant soldier who suffers an untimely death in Vietnam, and his girlfriend, played by Michael's real-life girlfriend, actress Brenda Vaccaro, did not resonate with audiences the same way Oliver and Jenny did in *Love Story*, Arthur Hiller's weepy Ivy League remake of *Camille*. *Love Story* had made stars out of its romantic leads, Ryan O'Neal and Ali MacGraw (who were involved with each other during the making of the film). Ironically, Michael had turned down a chance to try out for *Love Story* to make *Summertree*.

Besides a curious lack of on-screen chemistry between Michael and Brenda, there were other reasons the film didn't work, beginning with Kirk's choice of director, British music-hall singer-songwriter-actor Anthony Newley. Despite having created a couple of offbeat Broadway musical hits (*Stop the World—I Want to Get Off* and *The Roar of the Greasepaint—the Smell of the Crowd*) and having starred in dozens of mostly British movies, Newley had little film-directing experience.

Roger Greenspun, reviewing for the *New York Times*, said, " 'Summertree' is a bad movie, but its badness proceeds not from its intentions, which seem honorable, or from its stylistic analogies to past modes, which in different hands could have been interesting . . ."

Another reason for the film's failure might have been the casting of Vaccaro as Michael's love interest. Although their lack of heat on-screen was evident, there was plenty of it offscreen, especially since the two decided to share a trailer during the making of the film. "It was a gradual process over two or three months of working with her on the film" was the way Michael described their falling in love. When asked by one reporter on the set about the obvious romance blooming between the two, Michael said, "She is a fantastic actress, a beautiful girl and . . . ah . . . well, you know how it is." When he was asked what he would do if the film didn't make it, he turned humorously philosophical. "I'll keep on trying for a while at least. I want to do more plays. You learn more about acting on the stage. There's talk of a movie to be made in Spain. I may do that. But eventually if I find myself beating my head against the wall continuously, I'll take my father's advice. He only ever told me one thing: 'If all else fails . . . *fuck it.*' "

As soon as Michael and Vaccaro finished their scenes, they took off together for ten days in Vermont.

◈

KIRK, MEANWHILE, was continuing to search for a way to revital-ize his film career. He had been offered TV series fare but had little interest in working on the tube, fearing everyone would believe his film career was over for good. Instead, what he really wanted to do was make one last attempt to film *One Flew Over the Cuckoo's Nest*. "I loved the role of Randle P. McMurphy, and I was determined to see *One Flew Over the Cuckoo's Nest* on the screen. . . . But I didn't know it would take more than ten years."

In 1969, independent film producer Joseph Levine's Avco Embassy, riding a wave of success after Mike Nichols's 1967 box office bonanza *The Graduate*—it grossed over $100 million in its initial domestic release—was looking for new projects. Levine, a smallish, heavyset man who prided himself on bringing in films others thought impossi-ble to make, briefly considered *Cuckoo's Nest* before deciding that even he wasn't enough of a cinematic alchemist to turn this leaden project into box office gold.

In 1970, director Richard Rush, who had made two films with lit-tle-known Jack Nicholson prior to the actor's explosive arrival in Den-nis Hopper's 1969 *Easy Rider*, also wanted to make the movie, but he, too, could find no studio or investors willing to take a chance on it.[4]

By early 1972, nearly ten years had passed since the show had closed on Broadway, and Kirk could still find no interest in Hollywood to turn it into a movie. The response from all the major studios was the same: the material was too downbeat to be turned into a mainstream commercial hit movie. To try to push the deal, Kirk offered the rights to any studio that wanted it for a low-ball package of $150,000, less than his acting fee alone would have been, but found no takers.

---

4   The two films are *Hell's Angels on Wheels* (1967) and *Psych-Out* (1968). Rush later directed *The Stunt Man* in 1980, for which he was nominated for an Oscar for Best Director. In 1981, François Truffaut called Rush his favorite American director.

And then new problems arose. Dale Wasserman, Kirk's long-ago partner in the project, sued Kirk over the film rights to *Cuckoo's Nest*. The lawsuit didn't get very far, as it was without merit—no provisions for Wasserman to participate in any ancillary rights had been included in his original deal—but it proved an expensive legal battle for Kirk.

As Michael said later, Kirk "was getting discouraged and the book was showing up on college reading lists and the play was being revived on both coasts with great success." Michael had read the book several times and loved it. "I said to my father, 'Why don't you let me take it over, and I promise that I'll at least make your original investment back for you.'"

Kirk, with no other options on the table, finally and reluctantly agreed to let Michael take his best shot.

As Michael remembers, that was when "My long saga had begun."

PART THREE

INTO THE
CUCKOO'S NEST

The 1976 Academy Awards night, just after 1975's One Flew Over the Cuckoo's Nest *sweep. Not since 1934's* It Happened One Night *had a single film won all four major awards, including Best Picture of the Year. L to R: Saul Zaentz, co-producer; Jack Nicholson, Best Actor; Louise Fletcher, Best Actress; Michael Douglas, co-producer. It also won for Best Adapted Screenplay.* AP Photo

CHAPTER 6

My producing career evolved out of my inability to get parts as an actor.

— MICHAEL DOUGLAS

KIRK'S DECISION TO WAIT SO LONG BEFORE GIVING *Cuckoo's Nest* to Michael was ill-timed; in the interim between settling the Wasserman lawsuit and handing over the project, Michael's acting career had progressed. He filmed two more movies after *Summertree;* neither was a hit. *When Michael Calls*, made for Fox TV, was first broadcast in February 1972. His co-star was Elizabeth Ashley, with whom he was romantically linked at the time (it may have been nothing more than part of the publicity push for the film, which aired during the winter sweeps, but the rumors persisted even after the film aired). *When Michael Calls* was a straight whodunit on the order of Agatha Christie's *Ten Little Indians*, but not nearly as clever or entertaining. The other was a feature for Disney, *Napoleon and Samantha*, directed by Bernard McEveety and originally intended for TV but released instead as a feature in theaters. It opened in July 1972 and quickly disappeared, then did turn up eventually on the small screen.

Brenda Vaccaro accompanied Michael to the London opening of *Napoleon* and stayed with him for the Paris premiere, where the film again quickly faded.

UPON HIS RETURN to the States, Michael, with Kirk's deal still warm in his fist, was offered one of the leads in the TV series *The Streets of San Francisco*, which he agreed to do. The exposure was great and he believed he could appear in one, possibly two seasons and still actively develop *Cuckoo's Nest*. He formed a company called Bigstick Productions, whose only goal was to get a film made of *One Flew Over the Cuckoo's Nest*. At first Michael was quite enthusiastic about the project and thought he could easily succeed where his father had failed. "It was," he remembers, "a classic story, the story of an individual man fighting the system. Particularly in the sixties, people identified with this individual trying to overpower the establishment and at the same time breathe life into a group of men who had been buried by the system. There were larger-than-life images in it, combined with the sort of hallucinogenic style, which a lot of us related to and had never seen [on screen] before. It was just a great, great story."

However, the job of turning it into a film proved just as difficult for Michael as it had for Kirk. Frustrated but determined, he spent days working on the TV series and nights going over the detailed files his father had kept on the project, looking for anything or anybody who Kirk had overlooked and might possibly want to invest in the film. "I remember trying to raise the money for this. I was talking to people who had never read the book and trying to describe how funny it was and when I finished they'd ask me, 'So how come you want to make another *Snake Pit*?' "[1]

The Streets of San Francisco was a weekly *policier* that followed a basic and familiar formula. When the enormously successful TV Western genre of the 1950s and early 1960s began to fade in popularity, the networks simply updated it, turning cowboys into police officers and horses into motorcycles and patrol cars, and continued to crank out the same well-worn good-guy-bad-guy shoot-it-out, shoot-'em-up stories.

The Streets of San Francisco, originally based on the detective novel *Poor, Poor Ophelia* by Carolyn Weston, was conceived by veteran TV producer Quinn Martin, of QM Productions (*The Fugitive, Twelve*

---

1   *The Snake Pit* was Anatole Litvak's 1948 award-winning drama of life inside an insane asylum, the "snake pit" of the title. Historically, American films that dealt with mental illness did not do especially well.

O'Clock High, The FBI), and followed the classic action-cop TV format. Each week two detectives investigate a murder. One is a veteran and (as always on TV in that era) a widower, the other a tough, young no-nonsense type who happens to be single. The veteran solves the crime; the youngster catches the criminal.

To play the detective Lieutenant Mike Stone, Quinn chose aging pro Karl Malden, who had made his name playing Mitch more than two decades earlier in the 1947 stage version of Tennessee Williams's *A Streetcar Named Desire* and in the 1951 film version, winning the Best Supporting Actor Oscar for it. He was also nominated for Best Supporting Actor for 1954's *On the Waterfront*. Both *Streetcar* and *On the Waterfront* were directed by Elia Kazan and starred Marlon Brando. Because of his training and close association with Brando and Kazan, Malden became one of the leading proponents of the American style of Method acting. His entry into episodic television marked the inevitable downturn of his distinguished stage and screen career.

Michael's films had not succeeded to the point where being in *The Streets of San Francisco* could be taken as a decline for him, but it was not considered a positive career move by any of the film studios.[2] Nor was this the only TV he had done. He had appeared in a 1971 episode of *Medical Center* called "The Albatross." Michael recalls, "The best work that I actually did [to date] was a *Medical Center* in which I got to play a retarded boy. It was my first opportunity to play someone other than a 'sensitive young man.' I was real pleased with it. I did my homework, spent some time in hospitals and homes in L.A. getting the voice, the movement, everything like that." It would also help later on, with Michael's research for *Cuckoo's Nest*.

He also appeared in an episode of Quinn Martin's *The FBI* ("The Hitchhiker"), which is how Michael first came to the attention of the producer. "Michael had stuck in my mind after that *FBI* episode,"

---

2 Many TV stars in the 1960s and 1970s had difficulties making the transition to the big screen. David Janssen, the biggest star on TV after a four-season stint in Quinn Martin's *The Fugitive*, failed in his attempt to become a big-screen star and eventually returned to TV series.

Martin later recalled. "He had a kind of presence that we were looking for in the role of sidekick to the star, Karl Malden. He was [relatively] tall and good-looking. He had to be good but—let's be honest about this—not overpoweringly so."

When it was announced in the trades that Michael was going to co-star with Malden, rumors began to spread that Kirk must have had a hand in getting his son on the show to play opposite his close friend. Once again the nasty shadow of nepotism hung over Michael's career.[3]

Michael was cast as twenty-eight-year-old college graduate and assistant inspector Steve Keller. He was already nervous about having to co-star in a weekly series with an actor as revered as Karl Malden. It didn't make things any easier when Kirk called to congratulate Michael and told him, "Michael, you're going to learn a lot but you're never going to be able to keep up the pace that Karl will set."

If Michael was already insecure about playing Steve Keller, Kirk's words of "encouragement" didn't help. Michael recalls, "When I started out, I hated acting [on television]. I had a bucket off-camera because I got so sick with nerves. When I used to look at the camera, it used to look to me like an X-ray machine because somebody told me that the camera can tell when you're lying. And then one day I realized that was bullshit, that acting was about looking people in the eye and lying your brains out. After that I was fine."

That "one day" was when Karl Malden gave him some advice Michael never forgot: "I said, 'Michael, when you do crap, do it fast. And we're doing crap.'"

The show debuted on September 16, 1972, using the pilot as its opening episode, and clicked immediately with audiences.

---

3 John Parker, in his biography of Michael, suggests, without attribution or source, that despite a number of other actors that were being considered for the role, Karl pushed Martin to choose Michael because he wanted to support the son of his good friend Kirk. Everyone involved with the show, including Quinn Martin, has always denied that Kirk had anything to do with Michael's being cast in *The Streets of San Francisco*. Martin maintained it was Michael's stint on *The FBI* that had got him the part.

Because the show's location was crucial to the series, with many scenes shot literally on the streets of San Francisco, both Malden and Michael decided to move into the city itself to save on commuting time. Michael took an apartment at the top of exclusive Russian Hill that overlooked the Golden Gate Bridge. He could see Alcatraz from his living room window and hear the signature foghorns that sounded regularly from the barges and ships out on San Francisco Bay.

Brenda, with whom he had been living in Los Angeles in a beautiful rented house in Benedict Canyon, decided to stay put. Michael had naturally assumed she was going to come with him, but despite a temporarily flagging career, or because of it, she said she needed to be in L.A., where the work was. They fought over it, but the real argument was the unspoken one: Brenda wanted to get married and Michael didn't. Not long after, during a short break in his schedule, he took Brenda away with him to Bali. When the press found out, they wanted to know if this was an elopement. Michael assured them it wasn't and had little more to say about it, but Brenda wasn't as reticent. Possibly as a way to push Michael closer to the aisle, she sat for a long interview with Dorothy Manners of the *Los Angeles Times*, who then wrote that Michael "has fallen in love with a young actress, Brenda Vaccaro, who is just as immersed in the love of acting as he is. They have a fine relationship in their private life, which he does not talk about. She does. 'Ever since we made *Summertree* together we have been in love, together constantly and we talk about everything—except marriage!'"

Back on the set, Michael saw the show's success reflected in the increased number of guest stars, a signature of Quinn Martin's style. As Michael put it, "*Streets* is good because the stories are good and because Quinn Martin never stints on the budget. . . . He pays top salaries to get good guest stars and except for the mockup of police headquarters, sets are never used. Everything is shot on location, even the interiors of apartments." Among the stars who appeared in the course of the series were Robert Wagner, Andrew Duggan, Tom Bosley, John Rubinstein, Carmen Mathews, Kim Darby, Brad Davis, Mako, Naomi Stevens, Bill Quinn, Leslie Nielsen, James Woods, Nick Nolte, Arnold

Schwarzenegger, Stefanie Powers, and Martin Sheen. Even Michael's mother, Diana, was given a guest shot, as was Brenda Vaccaro, even though their relationship was by now effectively over.

Michael grew to love being in San Francisco without Brenda. There was still a strong feel of the hippie generation, most notably at the intersection of Haight and Ashbury, and no end to the supply of women happy to make his acquaintance. During the shooting of *The Streets of San Francisco*, he lived the life of a wealthy young bachelor and had no intention, as he saw it, of putting a noose around his own neck by putting a ring on Brenda's finger.

The show was drawing a healthy twenty-five million viewers a week, and Michael's star continued to rise. He was happy on it, except he could never forget it was television, where sex and politics—in an era where the two filled the air, and Michael's interest in both was fundamental to him—simply did not exist beyond the narrow range of crook and cop, with no social background to explain why these crimes were committed and no compassion for the criminals. It made him realize he had no interest in staying in the inherent artificiality of series television. He wanted to get back to making movies as soon as possible, and so, no matter how busy he was, he still found time to regularly fly down to Los Angeles and continue to go through his father's *Cuckoo's Nest* files, to search for some overlooked tidbit that would allow him to move the project forward.

One day in December 1972, while the show was on its holiday break and he was in L.A. searching Kirk's *Cuckoo's Nest* files, he came across the name of Saul Zaentz, and everything in Michael's world was about to change.

CHAPTER 7

Vintery, mintery, cutery, corn,
Apple seed and apple thorn,
Wire, briar, limber lock
Three geese in a flock
One flew east
One flew west
And one flew over the cuckoo's nest.

—OLD-TIME CHILDREN'S NURSERY RHYME

MICHAEL BELIEVED HE COULD SUCCEED WHERE his father had failed and get Saul Zaentz to put some money in *Cuckoo's Nest*. Zaentz, although several years older than Michael, was nonetheless a product of the same California sixties hippie scene of sex, drugs, and especially rock and roll. He was also an extremely wealthy and canny businessman.

To Michael, Zaentz represented the best of both worlds: he was one of "them" and one of "us," a hippie honcho who was equally at home listening to Jefferson Airplane and reading the *Wall Street Journal* (often at the same time). Michael contacted Zaentz and discovered that he had already tried many times to secure the rights to *Cuckoo's Nest* from Kirk, which was why his name was in the files, but he had never been able to strike a deal, because Kirk always insisted that he had to play McMurphy and Zaentz thought he wasn't right for the part. As Michael discovered, Zaentz was still interested, even more so after he had seen the long-running San Francisco version of the play, which for six years had attracted a steady stream of sympathetic liberal Berkeley students and others to the theater in Jackson Square.

When Michael first got in touch with Zaentz, he was in the midst of his takeover of the small, independent Berkeley-based Fantasy Records, founded by Sol and Max Weiss, who had operated a record-pressing plant before deciding to get into the talent and retail side of the business. Fantasy hit it big in the late 1940s and 1950s, mostly with recordings by jazz greats Dave Brubeck, Cal Tjader, and Vince Guaraldi, and several live albums by the late, legendary comedian Lenny Bruce, whose recordings made the tiny label not just cool but edgy and ultra-hip.

By the mid-fifties, Fantasy had prestige to burn but not a lot of money. In 1955 the Weisses hired thirty-four-year-old Saul Zaentz to help increase the label's revenues. Zaentz had a solid background in booking tours for such jazz greats as Duke Ellington and Stan Getz, and was in charge of distribution for several small jazz labels. The Weisses' goal was a major expansion of Fantasy, and they believed that Zaentz was the person to get it done.

They were right. By 1967, he had turned Fantasy into the largest independent jazz label in the world, and then, along with a couple of newly acquired partners, with Zaentz maintaining a controlling interest, they bought out the Weisses, and together they took ownership of the company. Almost immediately Zaentz added rock and roll to the label and signed several acts, one of which, San Francisco–based Creedence Clearwater Revival, fronted by John Fogerty, became Fantasy's all-time biggest-selling act. Zaentz, balancing his cultural awareness with his business acumen, also signed Creedence to a management contract and assigned Fantasy the publishing rights to Creedence's songs, thereby effectively partnering himself with every one of the group's income streams. (This would eventually lead to a highly acrimonious split between Fogerty and Zaentz.)

Zaentz continued to diversify his company, buying several small jazz and R&B labels as he built Fantasy into a giant money machine, complete with a new, modern office headquarters in San Francisco. By the early 1970s, Zaentz wanted to expand Fantasy into film; when he saw the local revival of *Cuckoo's Nest*, he tracked down the rights and tried to buy them from Kirk. After Kirk said no, Zaentz went on to make another movie that made no money but turned him into a legitimate player in the film business

Everything Kirk had disliked about Zaentz, Michael loved—his hippie veneer, his pushiness, his know-it-all attitude, and his always needing to be in charge. Michael was content to let Zaentz be the upfront man and offered him a full partnership between Fantasy Films and Bigstick to make *Cuckoo's Nest*. Zaentz agreed and, to seal the deal, put up the film's entire $2 million budget.[1]

What followed was eighteen months of preproduction, all done while Michael was still starring in *The Streets of San Francisco*. One of the first things Zaentz suggested was that they go directly to Kesey and commission him to adapt his own novel into a screenplay. Michael hesitated. While he loved *Cuckoo's Nest*, he sensed that Kesey might be something of a one-trick pony. He hadn't written anything after *Cuckoo's Nest* that was comparable to it, and besides, he had no experience as a screenwriter. Nonetheless, Zaentz insisted they should at least meet with Kesey, and Michael agreed.

Their new production company opened an office in Los Angeles, where the meeting took place. They offered Kesey a percentage of the film's earnings to write the screenplay. Michael remembers, "Ken came in not believing in agents and contracts and all that, so we shook hands. He went ahead and we paid him more than members of the Writers Guild get, plus a percentage."

Four months later, Kesey delivered a script that both Michael and Zaentz hated. "It was too surreal," Michael said. "There was one scene

---

1 A year earlier Zaentz had invested heavily in Daryl Duke's *Payday*, a modern-day Western starring Rip Torn. According to Dennis McDougal, Zaentz's Fantasy Films brought *Payday* in at $746,000—$62,000 under budget. The film made no money, but Zaentz benefited financially from the tax shelter it provided. Part of his reason for wanting to put up the entire budget for *Cuckoo's Nest* was the fact that it allowed him to renew his film-based tax shelter.

that had a nurse, wearing a Vularian helmet, and she reached her arms out between two walls and scraped her hands, and blood ran down the walls."

The original viewpoint of the novel and the play is that of the silent Indian chief Bromden, a kind of sacred totem come to life. In the novel, characters change shapes and forms, time stands still, the walls sprout arms that try to grab inmates as they walk by, and there are other surrealistic touches that seemed, if not impossible, at least not in synch with what Zaentz and Michael wanted, an accessible, commercial mainstream film. They eliminated the chief's unseen narration. And they wanted to alter the war-of-the-sexes theme of the battle between McMurphy and Nurse Ratched and elevate it to what they felt was a much stronger and more dramatic power struggle between the empowered nurse and her prisoner/patient—a war for justice and humanity.

They not only wanted to deemphasize the psychedelia, they wanted McMurphy to be a less cynical symbol of freedom and creative individuality, while portraying Nurse Ratched as one of institutional (corporate) repression. All of these changes Michael discussed by phone with Kesey, whose reaction worried Michael. He told Zaentz Kesey wouldn't go for any of it, but Zaentz told him not to worry. They would fly up to Oregon, where Kesey lived, go over their changes, and get him to agree to them. However, when they arrived at Kesey's home, he refused to even talk to them directly. He had since hired someone to represent him, and the script talks quickly devolved into a four-way shouting match.

Michael and Zaentz flew back to L.A. with the same version of the script they had brought with them, and with Kesey now threatening to sue. They then hired a relatively unknown screenwriter, Bo Goldman, to write an entirely new script. Goldman's only previous screenwriting credits were for a TV remake of Alfred Hitchcock's 1947 courtroom melodrama *The Paradine Case*, a 1956 episode of the TV series *Playhouse 90*, and a 1964 episode of TV's *The Defenders*. Zaentz liked his style, and the price was right. They also brought in Larry Hauben to help with the rewrite.

When Kesey heard about what was being done to his script, he threatened to publicly discredit the movie when it came out and call for a general boycott of it. Zaentz and Michael decided to pay Kesey $10,000 plus expenses and 2½ percent of the net to go away. As Zaentz knew he would, Kesey took the money and faded from the scene.

Next, Zaentz and Michael began to look for a director, another step that proved more difficult than either had anticipated. Michael returned once more to his father's files to see who had previously been up for the job and noticed the name Miloš Forman underlined and with cross-outs and exclamation marks. As it turned out, in 1966 Kirk had taken Anne with him on a trip to the Soviet Union and Prague, Czechoslovakia, as a goodwill ambassador for the U.S. State Department. Kirk loved the still-Soviet-dominated burgeoning film industry in Czechoslovakia. There was one director he especially wanted to meet, a young man by the name of Miloš Forman, who had made a name for himself in 1965 with *Loves of a Blonde* and was considered a leading proponent of the Czech New Wave. A year later Forman's reputation grew international when *Loves* was nominated for a 1967 Golden Globe for Best Foreign Film and an Academy Award for Best Foreign Language film.[2]

Kirk, still actively looking for a director to helm *Cuckoo's Nest*, asked Forman if he would be willing to read Kesey's book and consider making a movie out of it. Forman agreed. When he returned to the States, Kirk promptly sent Forman the book, but he never heard from the director again. Offended by what he thought was the director's rudeness, Kirk angrily crossed him off his list.

In 1967 Forman made *The Firemen's Ball*, a Czech and Italian

---

2   The film lost both nominations to Claude Lelouch's *A Man and a Woman* (France).

co-production, and that film, too, was nominated by the Academy for Best Foreign Language Film.[3]

Forman's first post-Czech-liberation American film was 1971's *Taking Off*, a comedy directed and co-written by Forman, John Guare, Jean-Claude Carrière, and John Klein about a group of parents whose children have run away, setting off a series of self-evaluations by the befuddled parents, who eventually turn into adult versions of their rebellious children. The film was a little late in dealing with the contentious nature of the children and parents of the sixties and did not find an audience at the box office. It wasn't a total disaster, as it helped to further establish Forman as a director with international reach and universal appeal.

By the time Michael approached him about directing *Cuckoo's Nest*, Forman had become a bankable Hollywood director. "I met with three or four directors who held their cards very close to their chest. Miloš Forman came and sat down, opened the script on the first page and told us page by page what his vision was for the movie. You could just close your eyes and picture that movie in your head," Michael remembers. "We wanted Forman because he is a realistic and a funny director. We knew we needed someone to handle the comedy. He has a very delicate eye: a great ability to go from humor to pathos, sometimes in the same frame. He's been living in the States long enough to understand the peculiarly American aspects of the book but he still has that profound Central European sensibility." That he was a foreigner brought him closer to the sensibilities of both Zaentz and Michael, each of whom had immigrant backgrounds. As Michael remembers, he and Zaentz were so happy to have found Forman, "we turned to each other and started crying."

Forman added another layer to the film: that of the outsider. McMurphy is an outsider, an immigrant if you will, in the world of the prison hospital to which he is confined, a world he can never really

---

3   The film lost to Sergei Bondarchuk's *War and Peace* (Russia).

be a part of because he is not truly insane. The notion of the outsider, or the immigrant—the foreigner—played right into Forman's hands. Michael and Zaentz believed he could make McMurphy come alive in a way no other director could. As far as Forman was concerned, the script also evoked the political repression he had lived through: "This was a Czech movie . . . about a society I lived in . . . everything I knew."

All they needed now was the right actor to play McMurphy. And as far as Forman was concerned, like Zaentz, he insisted it wasn't going to be Kirk Douglas. Michael put up a valiant fight for his father, but in the end he was outvoted by Forman and the ever-practical Zaentz. In his heart, Michael knew they were right—at fifty-seven, his father was far too old to play McMurphy.

Michael insisted he be the one to break the bad news, knowing all too well what his father's reaction was going to be. Sure enough, Kirk angrily blamed Michael for betraying him. Others were surprised that Michael didn't step into the role himself. He always insisted he wasn't a big enough star, but it is hard to turn away from the obvious conclusion that Michael didn't want to directly compete with his father or be compared to him (or show him up). He didn't want to read in the reviews that his McMurphy was so much better (or so much worse) than his father's. It was bad enough that Michael had to take the role away from him; he didn't need to be told for the rest of his father's life how awful he was in it. He'd been through that before. He would produce and let someone else play McMurphy.

Kirk eventually came to accept Forman as the director, even believing his (true) story that he had never received the book. But as for not playing McMurphy, it put a fresh distance between him and Michael. It was, according to Kirk, "almost incomprehensible. They wanted someone else for McMurphy. Why? That was *my* part. I'd found him. I could create him, make him breathe. But after ten years of telling everybody what a great role it is . . . now I'm too old. . . . I could *still* play that part."

Forty years later, the pain was still there. "*I* bought the book from

Ken Kesey, *I* paid Dale Wasserman to write the stage play. . . . I thought I would get to play it in the movies . . . it was not to be. It was the low point for me . . . [Michael] was the producer, he should have insisted that I play the part."

Michael always put all the blame on Forman for the decision: "The director makes the casting calls. Whenever there's a good part and you don't get it, it's a disappointment because there are so few out there. That was what was so hard about it."

THE FIRST TWO obvious choices that Michael and Zaentz approached to play McMurphy, Marlon Brando and Gene Hackman, both immediately said no. So did James Caan, an early favorite of the producers. Miloš Forman, for some reason, was "also fascinated with Burt Reynolds," Michael recalls, and wanted him for McMurphy because he thought he had cheap charisma. "Before Miloš Forman got involved, I was talking to Hal Ashby about directing the film and Hal was pushing Jack [Nicholson]. . . . Jack had done passive characters in *Easy Rider* and *Five Easy Pieces*, but when I saw him [at an advance screening] as the flamboyant yet sensitive shore patrolman in *The Last Detail* [1973], I was sure he could play the part."

Michael knew Jack casually through his girlfriend, Anjelica Huston, daughter of famed film director John Huston, yet another director Michael had considered for the film. "Michael Douglas talked to me early on about *One Flew Over the Cuckoo's Nest*," Anjelica Huston recalled. "I don't know if I was the instrumental factor in that, but I mentioned to Jack that Michael wanted to see him about it."

When Michael finally did meet with Nicholson, he said he was interested, especially when he learned that McMurphy was going to be less of a cowboy type (as in the novel) than a more realistic street person. However, Michael and Zaentz had to wait in line, as Nicholson's recent run of hits had made him the hottest star in Hollywood. Ashby wanted to use him again right away (even before the release of *The Last Detail*) to play Woody Guthrie in the biopic *Bound for*

Glory, but Nicholson turned it down.[4] Bernardo Bertolucci also wanted Jack to play Dashiell Hammett's Continental Op in *Red Harvest*. Nicholson turned that down as well. Tony Richardson then offered Jack the lead in *The Bodyguard*, based on a script Richardson had co-written with Sam Shepard. That project initially appealed to Nicholson, who gave it a potential yes—until he'd read Bo Goldman's adaptation of Kesey's novel and said yes to that instead (so powerful was Nicholson at the time that without him attached, neither *Red Harvest* nor *The Bodyguard* were able to keep their original deals alive at their respective studios).[5]

As it happened, Jack, like Kirk, had read Kesey's novel before it came out, and had tried himself to option it for the movies in 1963. However, Nicholson had not been able to match the $47,000 put up at the time—by Kirk Douglas.

While Nicholson was ready to sign on, Zaentz and Michael were nowhere near going into production. Then Polanski's *Chinatown* came Nicholson's way, and he was busy filming that for the rest of 1973. After it opened in June 1974, he maintained he was still interested in *Cuckoo's Nest*, but the film still wasn't ready to go, so Jack went instead into Mike Nichols's production of *The Fortune*, co-starring Nicholson's buddy Warren Beatty, with a script by Carole Eastman, who had also done the screenplay for *Five Easy Pieces*.[6]

Once *The Fortune* was completed, Jack promised Michael that if it was ready, *Cuckoo's Nest* would be his next project, despite the fact that Jack now had some real doubts about his own ability to play McMurphy. He had told a friend, Helen Dudar, just before he officially signed on that "the starting problem with *Cuckoo* was that everybody thought

---

4 Ashby then offered the part to Bob Dylan, who also passed. The role eventually went to David Carradine.

5 *Red Harvest* did not get made. *The Bodyguard* was reconceived for Steve McQueen and Diana Ross. The deal fell apart because McQueen would not accept second-position billing after Diana Ross. The film was finally made in 1992 with Kevin Costner and Whitney Houston.

6 She wrote both *The Fortune* and *Five Easy Pieces* under the pseudonym Adrien Joyce.

I was born to play the part, and in my mind it was going to be difficult for me. I felt, 'They already think I'm supposed to be great in this, and I'm not sure.'" As he explained further, the real reason he took the role was to prove to himself he could pull it off. (To do so he agreed to a small salary and a percentage of the profits to help get it made, a deal that eventually earned him millions.)

THE NEXT IMPORTANT piece of the puzzle was casting the role of Nurse Ratched. All the top actresses of the day—Anne Bancroft, Jane Fonda, Faye Dunaway—said no. The next two on Michael and Zaentz's list were Geraldine Page, best known for her stage work, who turned them down, and Angela Lansbury, not yet the major American star she was to become a decade later thanks to the long-running TV series *Murder, She Wrote*.

It was Forman who suggested a relatively unknown actress by the name of Louise Fletcher, whose first major credited film was Robert Altman's just-released *Thieves Like Us*, which anticipated Ridley Scott's 1991 *Thelma and Louise*. Forman called her in to read, and he, Michael, and Zaentz all agreed she was the actress they were looking for. They signed her on the spot.

Michael then sat beside Forman for every one of the nine hundred auditions held to cast the all-important ensemble. They discovered their Bromden on a tip that took them to Mount Rainier National Park, where Will Sampson was working as an assistant warden. They offered him the part. He quit his job at the park, packed his bag, and left for location.

At Michael's insistence. Danny DeVito was quickly added to the group as Martini. Early on, while both were still total unknowns, De-Vito and Michael had made a pact that whoever "made it" first would bring the other along for the ride.[7]

---

7   DeVito had previously played the role of Martini in an Off-Broadway revival of the play.

Most of the other actors chosen for the ensemble were relatively unknown, although some would go on to a certain measure of stardom after the film: William Redfield as Dale Harding, Brad Dourif as Bill Bibbit, Sydney Lassick as Charlie Cheswick, Christopher Lloyd as Max Taber, Dean R. Brooks as Dr. John Spivey, William Duell as Jim Sefelt, Vincent Schiavelli as Frederickson, Delos V. Smith Jr. as Scanlon, Michael Berryman as Ellis, Nathan George as Attendant Washington, Mews Small as Candy, Scatman Crothers as Orderly Turkle, and Louisa Moritz as Rose.

By the spring of 1973, Michael and Zaentz were ready to begin production on the film. They made their official announcement in the May 12, 1973, edition of the *Hollywood Reporter*: "Michael Douglas will spend his summer hiatus from *Streets of San Francisco* producing [the] *One Flew Over the Cuckoo's Nest* movie with Saul Zaentz, head of Berkeley-based Fantasy Records. Michael's father, Kirk, starred in the play on Broadway in 1964 but neither Kirk or Michael will appear in the movie."

They were on the record now, there was no turning back. At this point, Michael wanted to drop out of *The Streets of San Francisco* to devote all of his time to making the film. But not only would Quinn Martin not release Michael from his contractual obligation to play Steve Keller, a character very popular with audiences, he "promoted" Keller to full inspector. With an aging Malden unable to keep up the show's snap-snap pace, Martin shifted most of the action to Michael, in effect switching their roles so that Michael's was the main character and Malden's the supporting one. Not that Michael couldn't have gotten out of his contract if he had pushed hard enough, but it wasn't his nature. He was too passive to break his contract with Quinn and too attached to Malden to hurt him by leaving the series and endangering its continuing run. This was, Michael knew, likely Malden's swan song as an actor.

Nor was he able to leave Brenda despite the fact that their relationship was over. By now, with Michael's schedule loaded with the series and the movie, he couldn't have spent very much time with her even if he had wanted to. As Brenda recalls, there was a passivity on both their parts that had kept them together: "I think the warning signs had been around for some time. We should have split long before we did, but there was a reluctance by both of us to call an end to it. We had been through a lot together, at a particular time in our lives when the support and encouragement of a partner really mattered." True enough, except that now Michael had a new partner of sorts, Saul Zaentz, and a child he was raising with him called *One Flew Over the Cuckoo's Nest*.

Brenda recalls, "We were a beautiful couple. People loved us. Mike was charming, brilliant: women fell over him, men admired him. And I am, naturally, a good complement to such a man. But when you're done with a man, you are done. I just began to find it boring with Mike. I realized he wasn't the man I was going to marry, and my relationship changed at that point . . . and I don't think he really wanted to marry me. Everybody but us seemed to think that marriage was a good idea."

Michael completed the second season of episodes for *The Streets of San Francisco*—twenty-three mini-movies, two less than the first season (not counting the pilot)—just as United Artists agreed to distribute *Cuckoo's Nest* for Bigstick, the final crucial piece of the puzzle. Michael would go on to do another two seasons of the show, plus the first two episodes of the series's fifth (and final) season. During the making of *Cuckoo's Nest*, Michael was allowed to film his scenes in batches. But when it became clear that Michael's future was in movies, Quinn did let him out of his contract, replacing the character of Steve Keller with a new one played by Richard Hatch.[8] After the series ended, Malden was reduced to hawking American Express cards in a series of commercials in which he closely approximated the character of Mike Stone and admonished audiences not to leave their homes without it.

By then, Michael had become the most successful feature film producer in Hollywood, perhaps of all time.

---

8   Michael appeared in 98 of the series's 120 episodes.

Chapter 8

It was magical. It was pure. Because we did it outside of the system, and we didn't know what we were doing, there was an innocence on the part of all of us.

—Michael Douglas

Filming on *Cuckoo's Nest* began in January 1975, on location at Oregon State Hospital in Salem, where the events that had formed the nucleus of Kesey's novel actually took place. To obtain the location, Michael had personally prevailed upon the hospital's current superintendent, Dean R. Brooks, who happened to have loved the book, felt the system that had produced it was so much more enlightened now, and thought that the film would be a historical look back at how far they'd come. (It didn't hurt that as part of the deal Brooks was given a small part as the superintendent.) Brooks even allowed Forman to spend six weeks working on the final script while living in the institution and let two cast members sit in on actual therapy sessions.[1]

Because of that exposure, Forman discovered something that would help his ensemble cast avoid the easy clichés of "playing crazy": "We think of drooling and people going booga-booga and climbing the wall. These are exceptional cases. It's like playing alcoholics. Only naive actors play drunkenness with—blah—big sloppy gestures. Real alcoholics are desperately trying to act sober. It is the same with mentally disturbed people. They are basically normal except for one thing which may not show up for weeks or may be so subtle you can hardly

---

1   DeVito and Lloyd. Later on, Nicholson would be given similar "privileges."

notice it. . . . In Czechoslovakia, we consider Kafka a very funny man. A humorist. I first realized that Americans think differently when I saw Orson Well[e]s' *The Trial* [1962]. I think one of the reasons it didn't come across is because he made it a deadly serious film. And if you read the book, it is very very funny." Apparently Forman thought he was making a comedy—admittedly, a dark one, but in classic European fashion a comedy nonetheless.

To film *Cuckoo's Nest*, Zaentz and Michael hired cinematographer Haskell Wexler, whose previous credits included such blue-chip productions as Mike Nichols's 1966 *Who's Afraid of Virginia Woolf?*, for which Wexler won an Oscar for his cinematography; Norman Jewison's 1967 *In the Heat of the Night* (which garnered Wexler another Best Picture Oscar); Jewison's 1968 *Thomas Crown Affair* with Steve McQueen and Faye Dunaway; and two edgier films that probably got him *Cuckoo's Nest*—1969's controversial, counterculture *Medium Cool*, which Wexler filmed, wrote, and directed, and George Lucas's 1974 smash hit *American Graffiti*, which, like *Cuckoo's Nest*, was essentially an ensemble production.

However, early in, stylistic differences developed between Forman and Wexler. Whereas Wexler was familiar with how to shoot group setups and shoots—he had learned a lot from George Lucas's precision lining up of shots—Forman was more freewheeling with his directorial eye and heavily improvisational in his mise-en-scène. Looking for spontaneity, Forman had relatively little worked out before he ordered the camera to roll, and he was always seeking out the comic bits that developed among the inmates themselves and between them and McMurphy.

Wexler thought the film required a moodier and more precise look, but Forman continually rejected his suggestions. Push eventually came to shove, and Forman insisted it was either him or Wexler—they could not continue working together. Reluctantly, Zaentz and Michael let Haskell go. Zaentz rather easily assumed the role of "bad cop" and fired the cinematographer; Michael was the "good cop" who expressed deep sadness and genuine regret. Wexler was replaced by Bill Butler (who, as it happened, had replaced Wexler once before, when he was fired from Frances Ford Coppola's 1974 *The Conversation*).[2]

Cuckoo's Nest was proving extremely difficult to make. There were problems with lighting, problems with sound—it's always more difficult to shoot on location than it is on a sound stage, and there were problems with Jack Nicholson's growing empathy with the real inmates. It was said that Jack was so moved by what he saw that he personally used the finished film to try to convince then-Governor Ronald Reagan to institute reforms to California's housing and treatment for the mentally disturbed. Jack was not alone in his sympathetic feelings for the inmates; many were given minor technical jobs by Forman during production and paid for their work.

The acting-school tenet of staying in character that the film lent itself to led to a peculiar camaraderie among the actors playing inmates. They never broke character, even at meals. To make it easier for them (but more difficult on the technicians), except for one boating scene, the film was shot in sequence.

Nicholson, ever the basketball junkie, rented an apartment near the hospital so he could spend evenings and weekends watching college basketball at Corvallis or Eugene or even an occasional Blazers game in Portland. But as he told *Newsday*, during much of the shooting he felt more like a prisoner than an actor. "For more than four months, I spent the days there and would come out only at night, walking down this little path in which my footprints were indelibly marked by the almost constant rain, to the place where I was living. I'd have dinner in bed and go to sleep and then get up the next morning—still in the dark—and go back to the maximum security ward. It was basically being an inmate, with dinner privileges out."

He had showed up at Oregon State Hospital two weeks early, managed to convince Brooks to let him mingle with the most disturbed

---

2   Little of Haskell's footage remains in *The Conversation*, mostly a few long outdoor shots that were too complicated and too difficult to reshoot within the budget limitations of the film.

patients, ate with them in the mess hall, and was even allowed to watch the administration of shock treatments to some of them. During production, as he continued to get close to several of the real patients, he began to wonder, just as Kesey had, who the real inmates were: who was crazy and who was sane. "Usually, I don't have much trouble slipping out of a film role," Jack said. "But here, I don't go home from a movie studio. I go home from a mental institution. And it becomes harder to create a separation between reality and make-believe." It was even harder for Anjelica Huston, who had come to Oregon to stay with him during filming but couldn't take Jack's total immersion in his character and soon packed her bags and returned to L.A.

By the middle of the eleven-week shoot, Zaentz and Michael, struggling mightily to keep the film on schedule, began to feel the pressure and started to take it out on each other. They disagreed on what seemed like every detail, often out loud in front of the cast and crew, and more than once nearly came to blows. Zaentz was forever guarding the budget and complaining Michael was spending too much money, while Michael was looking for perfection from his actors, director, and cinematographer and was willing to give them all the time they needed to find it. And there were real-life tragedies that nobody could have foreseen: actor Billy Redfield was diagnosed with leukemia during filming. He died ten months after the release of the film.

The bottom line was that Zaentz and Michael were learning on the job how to be producers. They were in over their heads and over budget, and they knew it. This film had so much riding on it that the two of them were continually anxious, unsteady, and insecure.

For Michael, the production was a formative lesson in how to be a head honcho, and it allowed the positive, creative aspects of his personality to overcome the negative, passive ones. Reflecting on his experience co-producing on *Cuckoo's Nest*, Michael said, "Well, I've learned that [film] work is a totally collaborative effort. Half the battle is getting along. If you start pissing people off or alienating them you get nowhere. It's better to bend than get into a conflict. We have conflicts but it makes them more important when they come if you try to d[e]fuse them first. Of course it's your sanity too."

BY THE TIME production wrapped that March, everyone connected to the project was aware that something special had taken place. Michael remembers, "It was a really magical experience for all of us—for everybody except, unfortunately, Ken Kesey, and that has always hurt me, and it has probably hurt him a lot. It is the only thing about the film that I regret."

Cuckoo's Nest opened on November 19, 1975, to mixed-to-positive reviews and overwhelming box office support. Roger Ebert, writing for the *Chicago Sun-Times*, called it "a film so good in so many of its parts that there's a temptation to forgive it when it goes wrong. But it does go wrong, insisting on making larger points than its story really should carry, so that at the end, the human qualities of the characters get lost in the significance of it all. And yet there are those moments of brilliance." Ebert would later upgrade his opinion and include the film on his list of greatest movies.

Vincent Canby wrote in the *New York Times* that the film was "a comedy that can't quite support its tragic conclusion, which is too schematic to be honestly moving, but it is acted with such a sense of life that one responds to its demonstration of humanity if not to its programmed metaphors. . . . Even granting the artist his license, America is much too big and various to be satisfactorily reduced to the dimensions of one mental ward in a movie like this."

Richard Schickel, in *Time* magazine, said. "The trouble [with the film] is that it betrays no awareness that the events are subject to multiple interpretations. . . . [T]he fault lies in a script that would rather ingratiate than abrade, in direction that is content to realize, in documentary fashion, the ugly surfaces of asylum life."

Newsweek's Jack Kroll complained that the movie had "simplified" the book. "What's missing," he said, was the "powerful feeling at the center, the terror and the terrifying laughter. . . . By opting for a style of comic realism, Forman loses much of the nightmare quality that made the book a capsized allegory of an increasingly mad reality."

However, Pauline Kael, the doyenne of esoteric film critics in the 1970s, heaped praise on the film in her highly influential weekly column in the *New Yorker*, calling it "a powerful, smashing, effective movie—one that will probably stir audiences' emotions and join the ranks of such pop-mythology films as *The Wild One*, *Rebel Without a Cause*, and *Easy Rider*, the three most iconic, culture-shifting films of the '50s and '60s."

Reviews really didn't matter because from day one, audiences packed theaters to see it. *Cuckoo's Nest* would go on to gross $108,981,275, most of that in 1975 dollars (before additional video, cable, and Netflix streams of revenue became available, adjusted for inflation, in today's dollars $400 million.)[3] It ranks eighty-two on the list of highest-grossing movies of all time (Victor Fleming's 1939 *Gone with the Wind* is number one; number eighty-one is Ken Annakin's 1960 *Swiss Family Robinson*; and number eighty-three is Robert Altman's *M*A*S*H*). It played to packed houses all over the world; in Sweden it reportedly played in one theater for eleven years. It is ranked number twenty in the American Film Institute's documentary *One Hundred Years . . . One Hundred Movies*.

WEEKS BEFORE the highly anticipated awarding of that year's Academy Awards, Ken Kesey flew down to L.A. and, despite their previous agreement, sued Zaentz and Michael for damages for not using his script to make the movie version of his novel. "They took out the morality, they took out the conspiracy that is America" was the main thrust of his complaint. This time he had hired a team of lawyers who demanded 5 percent of the film's gross for Kesey, along with $800,000

---

3   All box office numbers, unless otherwise noted, are from Box Office Mojo.

in punitive damages. Eventually the case was settled, with Kesey receiving 2½ percent of the film's gross—no small amount, but it did nothing to assuage his anger over what he saw as the bastardization of his work.

THE ACADEMY AWARDS for 1975's best pictures were held on March 29, 1976, at the Dorothy Chandler Pavilion in Los Angeles. The ceremonies were hosted by television and film star Goldie Hawn, representing "young" Hollywood, and veteran song-and-dance man Gene Kelly, holding up the rear. In an unusual twist, additional hosting segments were given over to Walter Matthau, a serious character man who had found real fame late in the day as a comic actor, leading man George Segal of *Who's Afraid of Virginia Woolf?* fame, and the venerable Robert Shaw, who that year had given a remarkable performance in Steven Spielberg's insanely popular *Jaws*.

Michael showed up in a superbly tailored tux with a gowned Brenda Vaccaro as his official date—even though by now the two had officially broken up. "It was a bittersweet thing," Michael later recalled. "I had been with Brenda for years—and we had just separated. She had been nominated that year in a film, coincidentally, that my father was in. So we went together, though we were not together." She was nominated for Best Supporting Actress in Guy Green's *Once Is Not Enough*, and it just seemed to Michael like the right thing to do to appear together, as friends. (Vaccaro lost to Lee Grant for her performance in Hal Ashby's *Shampoo*.)

What made the night truly memorable for everybody was the incredible sweep that *Cuckoo's Nest* pulled off. Not since 1934, when the film industry and the Academy of Motion Picture Arts and Sciences were quite different from what they were in the 1970s, had one film won all four of the major categories—Best Actor (Clark Gable), Best Actress (Claudette Colbert), Best Director (Frank Capra), Best Picture (*It Happened One Night*). This night, against some formidable competition, including Spielberg's heavily favored *Jaws*, *One Flew Over the Cuckoo's Nest*, the film that nobody had wanted to make, was about to make history.

The evening began on a less than auspicious note. Nominated for a total of nine Oscars, *Cuckoo's Nest* lost the first four out of five it was up for, prompting Jack Nicholson to raise his eyebrows, grin, and whisper over to Michael, "I told you," whatever that meant. "You try not to put importance on it," Michael said later, "but it gets you crazy."[4]

Then the broom came out. Louise Fletcher, the sixth choice for the role of Nurse Ratched, won Best Actress. When her name was announced and she went to the stage, she surprised everybody (and confused some) by accepting her award in American Sign Language so that her deaf mother could "hear" her. Translated, her words were, "I want to thank you for teaching me to have a dream. You are seeing my dream come true."[5]

Perhaps the biggest no-brainer of the night was choosing Best Actor. Jack Nicholson was the current prince of Hollywood, and his performance in *Cuckoo's Nest* was right up there with the best of his best. The charismatic personality that Nicholson had exhibited most notably in *Easy Rider*, *The Last Detail*, and Roman Polanski's 1974 *Chinatown*—a combination of leading man and character actor, with charm, sarcasm, a winning smile, and a blast of intelligence—made him irresistible. He had Brando's wounded-animal strength and Dean's pained vulnerability, fortified with a sixties-style skepticism toward authority, all of which perfectly fit into his astonishing immersion-therapy per-

---

4   The four nominations the film lost were for Cinematography, Film Editing, Scoring—Original Music, and Best Supporting Actor (Brad Dourif). It won an Oscar for its fifth nomination, Writing—Adapted from Other Material, which went to *Cuckoo's Nest*'s Lawrence Hauben and Bo Goldman. Kesey had not been listed as one of the screenwriters and did not receive an Oscar.

5   The other nominees were not much competition in the Academy's eyes: Isabelle Adjani in François Truffaut's *The Story of Adele H.*, Ann-Margret in Ken Russell's *Tommy*, Glenda Jackson for Trevor Nunn's *Hedda*, and Carol Kane for Joan Micklin Silver's *Hester Street*. Sign language was not yet a common practice at Awards ceremonies.

formance in *Cuckoo's Nest*. Audiences loved it, and the Academy did too. When his name was called as the winner, the crowd stood and cheered as he ran up to the stage and flashed his zillion-dollar smile for all the world to see. "Well," he said, "I guess this proves there are as many nuts in the Academy as anywhere else!" The audience roared with laughter.[6]

Between the meaningless song-and-dance numbers meant to entertain the home TV viewers and tickle the ratings numbers, the night actually managed to build to a dramatic climax when it became clear that *Cuckoo's Nest* actually had a chance of sweeping the big four. Next on that list was Best Director. The nominees' names were read, and when Miloš Forman's name was called and he got up, the onetime Czech film savant had reached the pinnacle of Hollywood glamour and power.[7]

The audience then hushed, waiting to witness history the way a crowd at a baseball game anticipates a no-hitter, as Gene Kelly introduced Audrey Hepburn to present the night's final award, Best Picture (in Hollywood parlance, Best Producer). In her familiar clipped and elegant fashion, Hepburn read the nominees one last time, said, "The winner is . . . ," opened the envelope, then threw her arms in the air and shouted, "*One Flew Over the Cuckoo's Nest!*" The audience erupted in cheers, and Michael slowly stood up and waved. Then he turned to Forman and said, laughing, "It's all downhill from here." Michael found the white-haired, bearded Zaentz, and together they linked arms and made their victory walk to the podium.[8]

Zaentz spoke first. "The dream started at the Rialto Theater in

---

6   The other nominees were Walter Matthau in Herb Ross's adaptation of Neil Simon's *The Sunshine Boys*, Al Pacino in Sidney Lumet's *Dog Day Afternoon*, Maximilian Schell in Arthur Hiller's *The Man in the Glass Booth*, and James Whitmore in Steve Binder's *Give 'Em Hell, Harry!*

7   The other nominees were Robert Altman for *Nashville*, Federico Fellini for *Amarcord*, Stanley Kubrick for *Barry Lyndon*, and Sidney Lumet for *Dog Day Afternoon*.

8   The other nominees were Stanley Kubrick's *Barry Lyndon*, Martin Bregman and Martin Elfand's *Dog Day Afternoon*, Richard D. Zanuck and David Brown's *Jaws*, and Robert Altman's *Nashville*.

Passaic, New Jersey, a long time ago. But now gratification comes from all over the world . . . dreams do come true."

Then it was Michael's turn. Looking tan, his head tilted slightly to one side, his Oscar held low like a six-gun, he leaned into the long, slim microphone. "I think *It Happened One Night*, 1937, was the last time a film won Picture, Director, Actor, Actress" (it was 1934). "I'd just like to really thank the Academy for all your support, and to our really incredible cast and crew, from whom I think we all learned something about working ensemble . . . and as Louise said, anybody who's got a dream and it's a possibility it's not going to be a reality, just hang on." The music came up, and once more the audience stood and applauded.

After some early scary moments, Michael's big night had burst open like a balloon filled with glitter. As he recalls, "It was a wonderful moment. I remember it well. First of all, Jack Nicholson had lost two years in a row. He lost for *Chinatown* and *The Last Detail* and he was not even going to go [to the Awards]. We had nine nominations but it was still a fight to get him to go . . . And then came the last five [*sic*] awards . . . Then Miloš won . . . then Louise won . . . and then Jack won, and then we did. I think the picture was popular because everybody knew the dark horse history of the project."

That night Michael attended all the parties, including the most important and prestigious, the Governor's Ball, and went on and on about town until dawn.

Without Brenda.

NOT MENTIONED IN Michael's acceptance speech nor in attendance for the Awards ceremonies was Kirk Douglas. He had decided to stay home and watch it all on television.

CHAPTER 9

Everybody was happy to see me. When you have a hit, you are the most popular man in the world. I went around the world and just savored it. Jack and I went on a promotional tour for the movie. We had a blast.

—MICHAEL DOUGLAS

JACK AND MICHAEL SHARED THE SAME TASTES IN A lot of things besides movies, including food, drink, drugs, and women. They toured the world promoting the film like a couple of rock stars with a new hit album, loving the excesses of success and always looking for more. They teetered through England, Sweden, Denmark, France, Germany, Italy, Japan, and Australia, greeted by big crowds, hordes of pot-smoking hot young girls willing to audition for anything the boys wanted, and huge box office receipts wherever they went. Three months into it, Jack finally had to return to the reality of work and begin promoting his newest film, Arthur Penn's *The Missouri Breaks*, in which he co-starred opposite Marlon Brando.

Jack's departure signaled the end of the party. As Jack later said, "We had a blast—I couldn't keep up with Michael. Oh, and by the way, he has a penchant for the bizarre." He may have been referring to their alleged shared liking of kinky sex games, as stories kept leaking about the actors' wild romps, to the point where an angry Anjelica Huston booked a vengeance trip to London with Ryan O'Neal, intending to have some fun of her own.

As far as Michael was concerned, "I was single at the time and I was determined to savor the experience in the most decadent of ways. True, it did get a bit excessive, and people close to us were worried what I was doing to myself, but it was fun and it was meant to be. I knew it could not last forever and never intended that it should."

After Jack left, Michael continued on alone to South America, making stops in Brazil, Venezuela, and Mexico. He did not return to Los Angeles until the autumn of 1976, fully six months after he had won his Oscar. And when he did, his reception by the industry was surprisingly mixed.

Hollywood is nothing if not a petty and jealous place. It's the turf that comes with the chronic insecurity that is the hallmark of an industry where nobody really knows anything about anything, except occasionally how to make a decent movie. Already the word filtering through Hollywood was that Michael had shot to the top too quickly, he had not paid his proper dues, and he was the son of a famous movie star without whom he would not have gotten the necessary breaks. There could be nowhere for him to go now but down. For the most part, he tried to ignore it, more concerned with what he could possibly do to top *Cuckoo's Nest*—if he could top it at all.

That fall, Jimmy Carter was elected president in what was one of the greatest upsets in American politics; he was an unknown peanut farmer from the South who had become governor of Georgia and then ran against Vice President Gerald Ford for the presidency. Carter was so little known that when he was governor he appeared on the television program *What's My Line?* as the celebrity guest, and no one on the regular panel had a clue as to who he was. Ford, politically fatally wounded by his pardon of his predecessor, the disgraced Richard Nixon, was never able to shake the notion that it had all been prearranged to keep the former president out of jail, and lost in the general election to Carter. Many thought that Mickey Mouse could have run against Ford and beaten him. (Still others thought Jimmy Carter *was* Mickey Mouse.)

To thank all those in Hollywood who had supported his campaign, Carter invited many of them to his inaugural gala, Michael among them. He had somehow found time to attend a few fund-raisers during

Cuckoo's Nest to help ensure that the Republicans would not hold on to the White House. Jack Nicholson was invited, and he and Michael arrived together, Jack in shades and Michael reverting to his shoulder-length hair and bushy beard look from his college days. Early on, they were joined by Bob Dylan on the roof of the White House, where they all celebrated the occasion by smoking some pot.

Midway through the festivities, in one of those storybook moments that Rodgers and Hammerstein turned into a love song for the ages, Michael looked across the crowded ballroom and saw for the first time the princesslike Diandra Luker, smiling, shining, utterly resplendent in a flowing white gown.

Michael made his way toward her, and, completely ignoring his official escort for the night, started a conversation with this tall, slim daughter of an Austrian diplomat, who was a student at Georgetown University's School of Foreign Service.

She was polite, but in truth she had never heard of him. She had only been in America three years, never watched television, had never seen *The Streets of San Francisco*, and knew nothing about *Cuckoo's Nest*. According to Diandra, "He had this enormous, burly beard. He looked like a painter or a sculptor. I just thought he was interesting. He was different. He had different perspectives about things. He was sixties, rock and roll, and drugs. . . . We were people from opposite worlds."

After a very short time, he asked what she was doing later, and she said she was going to a private club. Michael confidently said he would see her there, but she smiled and told him he wouldn't be able to get in. Michael showed up at the club with Jack anyway, but despite their confidence and their fame, rules were rules, and they were not allowed past the front door.

Michael got in touch with Diandra the next day and arranged to take her to dinner. Soon after, she accepted an invitation from Michael to spend a weekend in Southern California. When she left for L.A., a cautious Diandra told her roommate, "If my mother calls, tell her I'm in the library."

Eight weeks later, on March 20, 1977, thirty-two-year-old Michael Douglas married nineteen-year-old Diandra Luker.

When Michael told Jack he was getting married, Jack couldn't believe it: why would anyone do that to himself?[1] Evidently many others couldn't believe it either: according to Michael, "A lot of people showed up for the wedding just to believe it was happening."

MARRYING DIANDRA had turned Michael into some bizarre reincarnated version of his father. Diandra was reminiscent of Kirk's first wife, socialite Diana (even their names were similar). Diandra had a lot of British friends and associates because of her father's diplomatic career, and like Diana, she had lived all over the world. That contributed to Michael's attraction to her. And, as it turned out, Michael was more like his father than he had realized. He needed to be married.

The wedding was held at Kirk and Anne's relatively modest house in the heart of Beverly Hills, just north of Sunset. It was a smallish affair with about twenty invited guests, including Nicholson, Beatty, and Karl Malden and his wife. Kirk also invited his good friend Gregory Peck and his wife.

Not long after, Diandra enrolled at UCLA to continue her studies and Michael began to realize how great the age difference between them was: he had married a girl so young she was still going to school. Every day, like a dutiful husband (or dutiful father), he would drive her to campus and pick her up after classes.

Marriage was a new experience for both of them. Having spent most of her time in America in Georgetown, Diandra was not at all used to seeing a grinning Jack Nicholson hanging out around the house, usually half naked and dripping wet from the pool while she

---

1   Nicholson had an early unsuccessful marriage and was now committed to a philosophy that said no matter how great a relationship was, it had to be able to end quickly by simply walking out the door. His pal Warren Beatty had shared this philosophy, as did Michael until he met Diandra.

was studying, or Warren Beatty playfully coming on to her with his beautiful horsey smile and jaded come-hither eyes.

What she was used to was being sheltered and pampered and having her privacy. And Michael quickly discovered that Diandra could be brittle and inflexible when it came to the ways of celebrity life. She was not at all earthy like Brenda. There was not a whiff of the sixties about Diandra.

He also had a career to deal with. He felt the marriage would find its proper level, but his career needed most of his attention now. The one shortcoming for him about *Cuckoo's Nest*, if it may be called that, was that because Michael had not starred in it, a lot of people were left with the impression that he had given up acting in favor of producing. The truth was, he was itching to get back in front of the camera, but he had learned enough to know that in order to enjoy that part of it, he also had to remain behind it, to make sure things were done the way he wanted. In that sense he was no longer an actor, but rather a producer who also wanted to act.

And although he had hit the jackpot with *Cuckoo's Nest*, there was already a new crop of young, eager, and competitive producer-directors mostly out of film's new training ground, Southern California's film schools. They included Steven Spielberg (Cal State at Long Beach), George Lucas (USC), and Francis Ford Coppola (UCLA). To the industry—meaning the people in Hollywood with the money—they were the best bets. Spielberg's *Jaws*, released the same year as *Cuckoo's Nest*, proved far more popular with audiences, and Lucas's 1973 *American Graffiti* was a huge coming-of-age success that preceded *Star Wars*, which would turn him into a one-man billion-dollar industry. Coppola's 1972 film *The Godfather* and 1974's *The Godfather Part Two* had become part of the American cinematic vernacular, among the best American movies ever made, and both would still be remembered when *One Flew Over the Cuckoo's Nest*, which wasn't seen all that much in theaters after its Oscar sweep, was forgotten.

These three filmmakers, along with the European Roman Polanski and to a lesser extent East Coasters Martin Scorsese and Brian De Palma, were the names Hollywood turned to first. Michael, on the other hand, despite his enormous succès d'estime, was still considered something of an anomaly, a one-shot wonder. It was an impression he meant to change. The first thing he did to make that happen was to actively search for a script he could both produce and star in.

ONLY IN HOLLYWOOD does a business open its door and be considered a success when product comes in rather than goes out, even if most of what comes in is worthless. A big part of a producer's job is to wade through the tons of rhinestones to find the one diamond, and that's just what Michael did. Wading might mean reading two pages, one page, a synopsis, or just a title and immediately knowing the script that accompanied it wasn't what he was looking for. He wanted something so great that it could outdo *Cuckoo*. He knew enough about the business to know that every film can't be a blockbuster—his father's career was strewn with failures, interrupted by occasional not-bad movies and one-in-a-million moments of greatness, but he kept searching for that elusive gem.

One such script came across Michael's desk in April 1977 via the U.S. mail—in other words, directly, with no interceding agent or manager. It had been written by a young screenwriter named Mike Gray and was about a disaster at a Connecticut nuclear power plant. Despite some flaws in the plot and technical theoretics, the subject matter connected Michael to the San Francisco protest era that he had so much been a part of. He was then and continued to be against the testing and production of nuclear weapons and the building of nuclear power plants in America. The script was about a nuclear accident capable of producing a meltdown that if unchecked might send radioactive material through the earth all the way through to China—just like what mothers warned children would happen if they dug too deeply in the sand at the beach.

The script was called *The China Syndrome*. Michael saw it as "a great horror movie, a movie about man against machine, a movie about an individual fighting the system. It had an interesting social message with all the aspects of a great thriller." The only real problem Michael could see was that Gray also wanted to direct, and that wasn't going to happen.

For the *New York Times* he elaborated further on the task confronting him: "The Jack Godell part was the heart of the story. There was no woman. The near-accident was observed by three documentary filmmakers. I thought it was a wonderful character study of a man against a machine. I like pictures about average guy heroes who aren't smarter or stronger than anyone else but who make moral decisions and risk their lives, like McMurphy in *Cuckoo's Nest*." Godell was the technician who single-handedly tries to permanently shut down the power plant following a near-apocalyptic accident.

Michael wanted to cast Richard Dreyfuss in the role of the TV news cameraman, but Dreyfuss, whose breakthrough in *Jaws* had led him to *Close Encounters of the Third Kind* in 1977, both directed by Steven Spielberg, and who was set to star in Herbert Ross's *The Goodbye Girl* (for which he would win a Best Actor Oscar), couldn't fit *The China Syndrome* into his schedule and reluctantly passed. The fact that he asked for $500,000 didn't make Michael all that eager to try to change his mind.

Dreyfuss's rejection of the project made Michael start to wonder how much he really had to offer an A-list actor, and not just in terms of money. He didn't have the reputation of a Spielberg or a Lucas, and despite *Cuckoo's Nest* he didn't have studios and distributors throwing money at him. Sure enough, when he made the rounds, he couldn't find any financial backing for *The China Syndrome*. "I had thought after 'Cuckoo's Nest' that all the financial doors would be open to me. I had a bit of a shock when I was turned down by twelve money sources, including two major studios. They thought the nature of the material was uncommercial—awfully talky and awfully technical."

Even Zaentz wanted nothing to do with it. He had since dissolved their partnership and moved on with several new projects, including

1984's *Amadeus*, directed by Miloš Forman, which would win second Oscars for both Zaentz and Forman.

AT THE SAME TIME that Michael was struggling to get his next film produced, Diandra announced that she was pregnant. Now she insisted they had to move out of smoggy L.A. and up to Santa Barbara, where the environment would be much better for their baby. Having to leave Hollywood, where he needed to be every day to hustle his new project, was about the worst news possible for Michael. But he did it for Diandra.

They bought the first house they looked at, a Spanish Colonial Revival villa a mile from where Michael used to live on Banana Road. Diandra loved it (though she would go on to spend $10 million rebuilding it top to bottom) and quickly transferred from UCLA to UCSB to continue her studies. Michael believed that her classes and the redirection project would keep her sufficiently occupied so he could return to L.A. and try to get *The China Syndrome* off the ground. In the meantime, Michael appeared in a quickie movie at MGM called *Coma*.

Coma, a hospital-based horror film from the novel by Michael Crichton, co-starred Geneviève Bujold and Rip Torn. Unfortunately, it was also directed by Crichton. It is never a good idea when a powerful novelist believes he can direct his own movie better than anyone else, especially professional directors. The characters in *Coma* are undefined and the plot muddled, having something to do with missing bodies that are being warehoused (with references to Don Siegel's classic 1956 *Invasion of the Body Snatchers*). The film did well, although exact box office figures remain unavailable.

HE STARTED contacting actors, believing *The China Syndrome* would be a faster sell with a "name" attached. Robert Redford said no in a one-sentence letter. Nicholson actually thought about doing it, but before a deal could be set he signed on with Stanley Kubrick to make the film version of Stephen King's *The Shining*.

Michael then approached Jack Lemmon, another liberal-minded actor who happened to be active in the anti-nuclear movement. He had recently narrated an PBS television documentary called *Plutonium: An Element of Risk* that had upset a lot of network people as well as viewers, marking the end for a while of anything that smelled like a political broadcast by the network during prime time. None of that, Michael knew, helped *The China Syndrome*, but he thought he might try to get Lemmon to be in the film anyway, since he wouldn't be immediately put off by the material.

Sure enough, Jack was eager to play Jack Godell. After only a two-minute conference phone call with Jack and his agent at William Morris, Lenny Hirshan, Jack was aboard.

The way the original script was written, Jack was far too old to play Godell, who was originally supposed to be a thirty-two-year-old fiery idealist. No problem, Michael said, and hired a relatively unknown writer (for a relatively small fee) to revise Godell's character to fit the fifty-something Lemmon.

This project was still going nowhere fast when another major player came in out of left field. Despite her pedigree and having been one of Hollywood's biggest stars, Jane Fonda, at the time, was anathema to the studios, for her outspoken opposition to the war in Vietnam— her 1972 trip to North Vietnam had gained her the dubious moniker "Hanoi Jane," that she would never be able to completely shed.

Columbia Pictures was one of the few studios that didn't turn away from Fonda. Sherry Lansing, high up on Columbia's executive scale and a personal friend of Fonda's, was politically sympathetic and suggested to Michael that she just might be able to get his nukes-gone-wild film moving.

At the time, Fonda was in London with producer Bruce Gilbert trying, without much luck, to develop a film based on the Karen Silkwood story. Speaking to Michael over the phone, she suggested they somehow combine the two similarly themed projects into one film.

Just not right away. Fonda had committed to Hal Ashby's *Coming Home* (for which she and her co-star, Jon Voight, would win Best Actress and Best Actor, respectively, Voight for his portrayal of a paraplegic Vietnam veteran and she for her role as the married woman who falls in love and has a physical relationship with him).

One day during the filming of *Coming Home*, Michael visited the set, and over lunch he, Gilbert, and Jane agreed she would make *The China Syndrome* in partnership, provided she could play the female reporter who works with Godell to help uncover and then publicize his story. (In the final script there is a scene where the car Jane's reporter character is driving is almost run off the road by another car; the scene was added at her request so at least something reminiscent of the Silkwood story would appear in *The China Syndrome*.)[2]

With this team of actors in place, including himself in the role of Richard Adams, a maverick cameraman who plays an integral part in the unfolding plot and its ultimate resolution, Michael, partnered with Jane's IPC Films, went to Columbia, and struck an unusual deal with Sherry Lansing. The studio would not produce the film but instead agreed to finance a $5 million note for Michael to allow his company to produce what would be a small, independent film, which Columbia would then distribute, with the first monies earned going to the studio to pay off the loan.

Hiring Jane Fonda meant that the picture had taken a step up in both budget and (to some) prestige, and that Mike Gray was officially out as director (he had never been a real consideration, but Michael had no reason to eliminate him before a deal was set). Gray vehemently protested that his "little" film was being taken away from him, but Michael calmly explained the facts of Hollywood life. There was no way Columbia would let a first-time screenwriter direct his own script.

---

2 *Silkwood* was made in 1983, directed by Mike Nichols, starring Meryl Streep. Both were nominated for Oscars but neither won.

Michael offered the job to James Bridges, whose credits included 1973's hit film *The Paper Chase*, for which he had been nominated for Best Adapted Screenplay. Bridges initially turned down the project, unsure of where the nexus of the drama lay, and also a little bit afraid the story might be too political and wind up hurting his own career. Fonda, however, kept at him, and nineteen days later she convinced him to make the movie. "Jim's reasons for refusing weren't valid," she said later. "He was just scared of working with stars."

Bridges wanted to shape the story more as a thriller than a straight polemic. To do so, he followed the plot as it unfolded in real time, with very little backstory of the film's characters.

Michael then had to find a suitable location to make the film. As he had with *Cuckoo's Nest*, he wanted to shoot on location. He knew that finding a cooperative nuclear power plant would not be easy. Much to his surprise and delight, the Trojan Nuclear Plant in Oregon—without the cooperation of the Department of Energy—agreed to let the production crew take photographs inside the plant that were later used to create a duplicate of the interior in Hollywood. At the same time, Jane was busy working with Bridges on the script, carefully deleting anything that made her sound preachy or overly technical. She correctly continued to insist that in order to work, *The China Syndrome* had to be an entertaining film with a message, rather than a message film that might or might not be entertaining.

There was relatively little trouble during the shoot, even as Columbia was preparing a seventy-two-page PR document that mentioned the title of the film but not once the word "nuclear," despite the fact that a nuclear accident is central to the film's drama and the fate of Godell, and that mentioned Fonda as little as possible. In fact, in order to sell the film to distributors and theaters, they positioned it as a suspenseful drama without mentioning any political issues at all: it was "a contemporary thriller about a television news reporting team" and "an astonishing look at the uses of power—redemptive as well as corruptive," a "monster movie with technology the monster."

Upon completion of filming, Columbia planned a selective advance screening program, providing cards so that preview audiences could give their opinions. Three weeks prior to its official release, Columbia began a $1.5 million TV ad campaign, something then still relatively new to the film business, and set up dozens of media interviews for its stars. Columbia had managed to book the film into seven hundred venues, a relatively large number for what they still considered a small picture.

Talking with *Look* magazine, Michael downplayed the film's more controversial story line of the nuclear power plant mishap. "In telling *The China Syndrome* story, everyone gets sucked right into this nuclear issue. It's very volatile and we don't want to categorize it as a Jane Fonda anti-nuke film." Michael later told one reporter asking how good it was to work with his co-stars. "Jack Lemmon was such a gentleman—a treat. Jane Fonda was just extraordinary. And she had a great butt. She still does."

THE CHINA SYNDROME opened on March 16, 1979, to respectable box office. The next day Michael, Jane Fonda, Jack Lemmon, and James Bridges went to Central Park's Tavern on the Green for a luncheon that the *New York Times* described, perhaps unintentionally, as a "blinding flash of promotion." Michael, looking pale and slender, told a reporter from the paper that he had spent "time riding around Los Angeles with a television news team to add verisimilitude to his portrayal of the cameraman whose persistence and courage uncovers callous corruption imperiling an entire city in the operation of the nuclear power plant."

In its first two weeks *The China Syndrome* grossed $15 million in its initial domestic release, bringing it close to a profit position (after production and promotional costs), despite an expected corporate-energy-based organized protest against the film. The filmmakers were labeled as irresponsible fear-mongers, with the events of the film dismissed as a never-could-happen scenario designed to turn people against the business of nuclear power. Jane Fonda's name was frequently dragged mance. The film's script also won the 1980 Writers Guild of America award. As Michael, later reflecting on the success of the film, said, "The first thought [for me] about the movie was the end result. . . . I have no formal religious training, but that picture . . . was close to a religious experience for me. It affected me in terms of working with the United Nations [for nuclear disarmament]. That's where all that came from."

AND YET, DESPITE having two of the biggest films of the 1970s, Michael Douglas was still not considered automatically bankable by the studios either as a producer or an actor. The primary reason was that neither of his films had anything remotely resembling what Hollywood likes to call a "love story." They were offbeat and hard to categorize. His two out-of-the-chute successes were considered flukes by the industry. One fluke was bad enough; having two in a row was worse. Three would be too much for any studio to risk.

Which is why, after making the two biggest Hollywood movies of the past five years, going into 1979 Michael couldn't get a job.

Chapter 10

*My producing career evolved out of my inability to get parts as
an actor.*

—Michael Douglas

On December 13, 1978, four months before
the opening of *The China Syndrome*, Diandra gave birth to a
baby boy they named Cameron.

The birth had been a difficult one. She had delivered by cesarean,
and it had considerably weakened her. At their Santa Barbara home,
having returned from Los Angeles and his film commitments, Michael turned domestic and became the dutiful husband and father.
He would often wake up early and brew strong coffee for himself and
Diandra to drink together on their balcony. Around her, Michael
knew, he had to be careful to keep his lingering bachelor ways outside
the front door, to not "be a bad influence. She was so young [when we
married], but she didn't get sucked up into the Hollywood scene. She
held back, picking and choosing her way.

"I guess what I found out before Diandra, was that I was basically
very lonely. I've really only been happy with one person. And I learned
that although I like to get it on—have a good time on a Friday or Saturday night—I can't go out and get crazy all the time like I used to
and recover as quickly. . . . I joke with some of my rock and roll friends
who knew me in my wild, single days, like Joe Walsh [of the Eagles].
A lot of them are still out on the road after fifteen or eighteen years. I
mean, if you've got kids who get up real early in the morning, your life
is going to be different from the way it was. . . . I guess [Diandra] and
I were soul mates—like we knew each other in a different life."

But it was in this life that both of them were having a difficult time. Diandra was trying to work at drafting international charters to protect the environment while caring for Cameron. She regularly complained to Michael that since the baby was born she did not have enough time for herself or quality time together with him. Michael had no answer for that. No matter how much coffee he made or how early he woke up, he was by profession a producer and actor; it was a life that would never allow him to be home precisely at six, kiss the baby, read the paper, and sit down with his wife for dinner. Their different lifestyles had created a physical and emotional divide between them that would only get worse.

IN THE WINTER of 1979, with much fanfare, Michael, under the Bigstick banner, returned to filmmaking, signing a nonexclusive three-picture producing deal with Columbia Pictures, thanks in part to Sherry Lansing. Michael could not deny that he preferred making movies rather than changing diapers.

It was, at the time, a great deal for Michael, because it meant he would no longer have to hustle studios for distribution for every picture he wanted to make or spend all his time trying to raise funds. Columbia was willing to put up all the money. But not long after he made the deal Lansing left Columbia and landed up at Twentieth Century-Fox, the first female head of a major Hollywood studio. After Lansing's departure, Michael felt orphaned, left without an enthusiastic supporter, and his producing career at Columbia stalled.

With nothing else on his plate and eager to work, he accepted a quickie acting role in a small film for Universal called *Running*. He made it simply because there was nothing else to do and he was not quite ready to return to full-time domesticity.

Hollywood always loves health fads, and none was more pervasive in the '70s than running. It was inexpensive, and no equipment was needed beyond a pair of sneakers; it soon became a craze on the order of the 1950s Hula Hoop, something both fun and healthy. When it on Monday they gave Michael the green light to make a preemptive bid prior to auction of $250,000 for the script, an astronomical amount for a first screenplay by a woman at a time when there weren't that many established female screenwriters in Hollywood. Being on-screen was no problem for women; behind the scenes, though, with notable exceptions like Lansing, it was nearly impossible for them to break through the industry's glass ceiling.

Michael, however, with his liberal sixties background, had no problem with Diane Thomas's gender or her lack of experience. "It was a bidding situation and I was always accused of paying too much money for a first-time writer. My take was, if it's a first-time writer or a tenth screenwriter, it's priceless."

Interestingly, no actors came knocking on Michael's door looking to play Jack T. Colton, the Harrison Ford–type male lead. Part of the problem was that the role appeared to be actually modeled after Ford himself, and the film resembled a bit too closely a Spielberg-Lucas project called *Raiders of the Lost Ark* that had just gone into production as a joint venture between Lucasfilm Ltd. and Paramount. One of the reasons Thomas's obviously commercial script had received no previous takers was that no other actor in Hollywood was willing to ruffle those golden Spielberg/Lucas/Paramount feathers.

Except Michael. He had decided to play the role himself.

The reasons that Michael had not made this kind of movie or played this type of role before had more to do with his personal feelings than the rigid dictates of Hollywood. "The role of Jack Colton is closer to my father. I guess I've shied away from the kind of roles he played, shied away from the comparison. Passion and anger. It limits you a little. . . . The Colton role is also closer to me than what I've played before. He's a rascal. . . . [A]s Joan Wilder's publisher says in the script, 'Jack's favorite author is the guy who wrote Pull tab to open.'"

So the dynamics of the emotional and professional competition of son versus father were still there for the both of them. Kirk's reaction to this shift in Michael's career direction and choice of roles? Cautious enthusiasm (heavy on the caution, light on the enthusiasm) with a critical assessment of Michael's having not yet found himself as an actor. "Michael's just scratched the surface as an actor. There are lots of things inside him that haven't emerged on-screen yet, an inner strength, an inner anger. There's a mystery inside him. A seething cauldron behind that face. It's a wonderful quality. A good part for Michael would be a nice, sweet, lovable guy and then—bang—you're suddenly looking into the eyes of a killer. . . . [B]efore *Champion,* I played weaklings, made pictures like *A Letter to Three Wives.* Then, suddenly, everyone thought of me as a tough guy." Including Michael. In effect, Kirk was saying that Michael had not played up to his talents or his abilities, and until he did, he would never be as good an actor as his father.

PRODUCTION ON *Romancing the Stone* had originally been scheduled to begin in February 1980, but because it still had no director, the studio was insisting on a major rewrite, and the location was not set, its start was pushed back indefinitely. It was still a go, but as far as the studio was concerned, it was now only a partial green light.

In the meantime, Michael started looking for another film just to act in, a quick shoot, something to keep him busy that he might be able to squeeze in while he waited for *Romancing the Stone* to go into production.

He talked things over with Nicholson. Michael said he was worried about the long delay getting *Romancing the Stone* going, something he attributed at least in part to Columbia's dragging its feet. Nicholson was less concerned about Michael's producing problems and told him so in no uncertain terms. The reason he had not become a big movie star, Jack told him, was that he had been rendered sexless by the studios. He needed a script with some heat in it.

Michael chose something called *It's My Turn,* in which he played a former baseball player, Ben Lewin, whose mother (Dianne Wiest) is marrying a female mathematician's widowed father. Kate Gunzinger, the mathematician (Jill Clayburgh), is a professor at a Chicago university and lives with her boyfriend, Homer (Charles Grodin). When Kate travels to New York to attend the wedding she meets Ben. Although he is married, he and Kate have a brief but passionate affair. After the wedding, Kate returns to Chicago, unsure what the future holds.

When Clayburgh agreed to do *It's My Turn*, the script had already been knocking around for six years. Back then, Claudia Weill, a television producer (and distant cousin to Kurt Weill), liked the novel it was based on and contacted screenwriter Eleanor Bergstein to ask if she would be interested in writing a screenplay-to-order called *Girlfriends*, similar to the novel in some ways but with some differences.

Bergstein said no, she was too busy working on her next novel.

Several years later, Weill was given significant public TV grant money to make a movie, and once again contacted Bergstein. This time she agreed, as long as she was guaranteed to have input every stage of the way. That screenplay eventually became *It's My Turn*.

When she felt it was ready, Weill gave the script to Alan Ladd Jr. "Laddie," at the time the head of Twentieth Century-Fox, loved it and wanted to make a hefty preemptive offer. However, when Weill told Bergstein, she rejected it, telling Weill she had changed her mind and wanted nothing to do with Hollywood, that she was only interested in writing for public TV.

It took some convincing, but when Jill Clayburgh expressed interest in playing Kate, Bergstein agreed and the deal looked set. Then suddenly Laddie and his entire team were gone, the victims of a studio coup. Either way, the new regime at Fox had no interest in *It's My Turn*.

But not for long. Veteran producer Ray Stark, a longtime Columbia producer whose pictures carried the prestigious credit "A Ray Stark Film," wanted to take over the entire production, and he reconceived it top to bottom, cutting out a key sex scene between Michael and Clayburgh. That scene was one of the reasons Michael had wanted to make the film.

By the time *It's My Turn* started shooting, it was already supposed

to have been in postproduction. This affected preproduction sched-
uling on *Romancing the Stone*. To save time, Michael and Clayburgh
volunteered to rehearse evenings and weekends. It was also his first
experience being directed by a woman, and Claudia Weill made it her
business to get on Michael's good side by appealing to his male vanity and his narcissism. As he recounted, "I have not had many directors come up to me and say, 'You are such a dish.' I was immediately
spoiled, and comforted in an offhand sort of way. There is a moment
in every actor's life when he sees the director, normally male, go over
to the leading lady, put his arm around her shoulder and whisper,
'What's wrong, darling? Let's talk.' Well, I'm sorry, but guys like to
be complimented too. I just loved having the director come to me, put
her arm around my shoulder and ask me if I'm okay."

FILMING WAS COMPLETED on *It's My Turn* in seven weeks at
Columbia's studios in Burbank and one week of location pickups in
New York City. It was scheduled for release in the fall of 1980, but
prior to its opening, a firestorm developed at Columbia. After several
disappointing previews, Michael, who was still upset about that scene
between him and Clayburgh that had been cut, announced he would do
no publicity appearances for the film. At the same time, Marilyn Beck,
who wrote a Hollywood gossip column, claimed that she knew that
Michael hated the film: it had taken far too long to make, he wished
he'd never gotten involved, and he was going to refuse to promote it.[2]

When Ray Stark found out, he blew a gasket. He believed that he
and Columbia had done Michael a huge favor by giving him a lot of
money for a role that he could do in a sleepwalk, and the least he could
do was help sell the film. But Michael had a different view. Besides los-

---

2   The scene, written by Bergstein, was cut by Weill at the urging of Stark, who
didn't like anything approaching explicit sex in his strictly PG films. The most erotic
scene in the script, it had Michael and Clayburgh dancing together. Bergstein later
used it as the basis for another screenplay that became a huge hit, Emile Ardolino's
Dirty Dancing (1987).

ing the one scene he felt he needed to give him some heat as an actor, the film had also cost him his start date on *Romancing the Stone*. To him, it was like giving up an executive position at the office to take on the more pressing task of becoming the head of the typing pool.

Michael was summarily called into Ray Stark's office for a tongue-lashing, during which Stark implied that Michael's entire future at Columbia might be at stake. Michael tried to calm Stark down by telling him that the whole thing had been blown out of proportion, a story planted in the press by someone who didn't like him. Whether or not Stark believed the story, Michael got off with a mild rebuke—mostly, insiders believed, because privately, Stark, like Michael, was not overly fond of either the film or Claudia Weill and knew that Columbia was much more heavily invested in the more important *Romancing the Stone*.

IT'S MY TURN opened on October 24, 1980, and proved a $7 million dud. Weill was especially hurt by the fact that just before the film's premiere Stark wanted to do yet another cut. At that point, though, the studio heads, perhaps fearing an avalanche of lawsuits, gave her cut the final green light.

Weill chose never to work for a major Hollywood studio again.[3]

Michael resumed preproduction activities on *Romancing the Stone*. However, three years would pass before a single footage of film would be shot, largely because of a serious skiing accident that sidelined Michael. To keep busy, he kept looking for new projects he could produce from his wheelchair.

The first was something called *Virgin Kisses*, a novel by Gloria Nagy about a woman who has a one-night affair with a married man and can't let him go when he wants to return to his wife. Columbia

---

3   *It's My Turn* was Weill's second feature film. Her first, *Girlfriends*, was independently made and sold to Warner. It was on the basis of that film that *It's My Turn* was green-lighted. Afterward she returned to independent features, documentaries, and teaching.

hated it, and it was shelved, but Michael kept renewing the rights to *Virgin Kisses*, believing that one day he would get it made.

Another project he liked was something called *Starman*, a sci-fi flick about a space traveler from another world who accidentally lands on earth and then can't leave. It was vaguely reminiscent of an old DC Comics character that appeared in the 1950s, John Jones (J'onn J'onnzz), Manhunter from Mars. (The character eventually became a member of the Justice League of America.) Michael's choice was a prescient one. Within two decades comic books would rule the world of animated and special-effects cinema. But in 1982, Columbia was leery about such a project; finally the studio gave it the green light, if for no other reason than to keep Michael at Columbia.

At the same time, the hottest director in Hollywood, Steven Spielberg, was making his own space adventure film, *E.T.: The Extra-Terrestrial*. He had already made *Jaws* (1975) and the blockbuster *Close Encounters of the Third Kind* (1977) and was about to release the most sure-fire film of the year, *Raiders of the Lost Ark* (1981). Every studio, including Columbia, wanted *E.T.*, but Columbia had to pass because it already had *Starman*. Frank Price, the head of production, believed that between the two projects the studio had chosen the right one. A memo he sent around said that in his opinion, *E.T.: The Extra-Terrestrial* was a children's film, while *Starman* was an adult love story that happened to take place in space.

Despite Price's memo, Columbia was gun-shy about taking on Spielberg one-on-one and put the brakes on *Starman*—not enough to kill it, but just enough to slow it down until *E.T.* was in theaters. But even as *E.T.* was released in 1982, a host of directors, including Adrian Lyne, John Badham, Michael Mann, and Tony Scott, came in and out of *Starman*, while Columbia never came up with a firm start date. "We had *Tootsie* in development for four years," said Frank Price, in defense of the *Starman* delays. "If you're trying to make exceptional pictures, which is what Michael and all of us are trying to do, it takes time."

"What has happened to the movie business," Michael told *Esquire* magazine, "is market research. You would think, and I *did* think, that here I am, I've produced two big movies, and I go to the studio with a new thing I want to do. I've got a track record, but it turns out that doesn't matter."

Instead, the studio turned its attention to Richard Attenborough's *Gandhi*, an epic, widescreen biography of the Indian pacifist leader meant to be the next *Lawrence of Arabia* (1962), except that Attenborough, a British actor turned director, was no David Lean, and Ben Kingsley, as good an actor as he is, was no Peter O'Toole.

But if Michael thought that *Starman* was going to be kick-started by Columbia after *E.T.*'s success at the Academy Awards, he was wrong.[4] The studio continued to drag its feet on *Starman*, demanding rewrite after rewrite, to make sure there was no way it could be considered a "copy" of *ET*. It wasn't until the summer of 1983 that Columbia announced production would begin that fall.

Now Michael set about finding a director. He chose John Badham, whose biggest film to date was 1977's *Saturday Night Fever*. However, even before production began *Starman* was delayed yet again by the studio, and Badham left to make *Blue Thunder* followed by the sci-fi youth adventure *WarGames*.

At that point, Michael gave up on *Starman*, and Columbia. *Starman* was made a year later at Columbia, directed by John Carpenter, and released in 1984, starring Jeff Bridges and Karen Allen, and while not a big moneymaker ($28 million domestic on a $24 million budget) it is considered today one of the better '80s sci-fi films. Michael received a producer credit, but except for hiring Carpenter, he had little to do with the film and severed his ties with the studio before it was released. "My father taught me that a good business deal is one which is beneficial to both parties. In that sense, the Columbia deal was not a good business deal. I discovered that I work best in a funky little office somewhere, with just a reader and a secretary."

---

4   That year *Gandhi* won eight Oscars; *ET* won four. *Tootsie*, another Columbia Pictures film, was nominated for ten Oscars but only won one, for Best Supporting Actress (Jessica Lange).

Whatever story he wanted to tell about what had happened to *Star-man* and his relationship with Columbia, five years had passed without *Romancing the Stone* or, for that matter, any new Michael Douglas film being made. He managed to retrieve the name Bigstick from the studio (it was of no value to them), left his spacious Columbia offices in Burbank, and went back to his small office in Hollywood to try to turn his career around. The one sure project he had was *Romancing the Stone*, the still-undeveloped script he had always liked but that had somehow gotten away from him. Instead he had taken dumb acting parts and followed the lead of the post-Lansing corporate heads at Columbia, the same geniuses who had turned down *E.T.* for *Starman* and then screwed *that* up.

He held the script up and took a deep breath. It had to be his ticket back.

HOWEVER, BEFORE he could resurrect *Romancing the Stone*, another acting assignment came his way, via Fox, something called *The Star Chamber*. He liked the script and decided to do it. He was cast as an idealistic judge who gets drawn into a secret vigilante law group—a plot with echoes of Clint Eastwood's popular 1973 Dirty Harry film, *Magnum Force*.

The Star Chamber takes its title from the feared seventeenth-century English court. It was written by Roderick Taylor and directed by journeyman Peter Hyams. Also in the film was Hal Holbrook (who, coincidentally, had played a major role in *Magnum Force*). Despite an extensive television promotion campaign, the film, released on August 5, 1983, after the season's big summer openings, flopped badly, pulling in just under $2 million on opening weekend and grossing a total of $5.5 million before it quickly disappeared.

If there was any rationale for his doing the film besides wanting to be at Fox where, not coincidentally, Sherry Lansing was now calling the shots, it was to make himself bankable as an actor again, a plan that decidedly hadn't worked. The studio was hesitant about making

Romancing the Stone with Michael playing the lead and preferred either Burt Reynolds or Clint Eastwood, both actors red-hot at the time, but getting Clint was impossible. He had solidly landed at Warner with his Malpaso production company, a total-control setup that Michael could only envy. Whatever Clint wanted to do, he did; unfortunately, he passed on *Romancing the Stone*. And Burt Reynolds said no too. At one point Columbia had gone after Sylvester Stallone to play the lead, but he didn't work out either.

Sherry Lansing believed in Michael's abilities and potential star-power and wanted to keep him at Fox. To do so, before he could make a deal anywhere else, she gave him the green light to both produce and star in *Romancing the Stone* at the studio.

PART FOUR

ACTION STAR

Michael with Kathleen Turner in Romancing the Stone. Rebel Road Archives

CHAPTER 11

Romancing's script included mudslides, problem alligators, multiple stitches for cast and crew. But it had a wonderful virginal quality. After China Syndrome *I'd O.D.'d on grimness. The only way I find a project is if I fall in love. And like when you fall in love with a woman, you wake up at night thinking about it.*

—MICHAEL DOUGLAS

IT WAS LATE 1982. MICHAEL WAS FAST APPROACHING thirty-nine and, despite the Oscar and acclaim he had won in the seventies, he was feeling very much a failure. Nearly a decade had slipped by following the success of *One Flew Over the Cuckoo's Nest* and *The China Syndrome*, the latter's box office was helped immensely by a freakish real-life nuclear disaster. For the longest time Michael found himself without a project to produce, and now having been given a green light at Fox he put himself on a fast track to get *Romancing the Stone* made, and, in behavior reminiscent of his father's when Michael himself was a young child, he had very little time left for playing daddy.

Diandra was not pleased with Michael's decision to move back to L.A. full-time and resume his film career, leaving her holding the baby. It wasn't just Michael's obsession with the film that bothered her. She found the entire film industry personally distasteful. She would never feel at ease in the role of the good Hollywood wife. After six years of marriage, during which time Michael had not spent any significant amount of time at home, she asked him for a legal separation.

She did it almost as a formality, which was even more unsettling to Michael. She spent virtually all of her time in Santa Barbara, she pointed out, while Michael remained at his office in Hollywood. Their marriage had come to a crossroads, and she had taken the first step to end it.

Diandra made her decision after *Romancing the Stone* was picked up by Fox. She knew it meant Michael would be away from her for long stretches of time, on location and in pre- and postproduction. She no longer could keep pretending they had any kind of real, i.e., traditional, marriage, which was the only kind she had bargained for.

There was nothing Michael could do about Diandra's decision to legally separate, even if he had wanted to, which he wasn't sure he did. By now, whatever heat was in their relationship had long cooled. In truth, Michael was not that upset. Although he would miss five-year-old Cameron, Diandra had assured him he could visit the boy whenever he wanted to. She had no desire to deprive her son of a father, nor her husband of his son. Nor did she want to get divorced. She was as reluctant to take that final step as Michael was. For Diandra, remaining married, even if separated, had to do at least in part with her awareness of her social standing. For Michael, it was more a question of passivity.

SHERRY LANSING'S DEAL with Michael and his new partner at Bigstick, Jack Brodsky, came with a proviso that they make *Romancing the Stone* for under $10 million, modest for an action film shot on location. Michael had no problem with the budget; he knew he could both produce and act in this film with relative ease, because Joan Wilder was the leading role, the bigger part, the true heroine of the story.

To direct, as he had with *Cuckoo's Nest* and *China Syndrome*, Michael wanted someone relatively unknown who would take a relatively small salary to help keep the film within its budget. Thomas's script was fresh and original, and Michael wanted a director who also was fresh and original.

After considering several candidates, he settled on thirty-three-year-old Robert Zemeckis. If Zemeckis's résumé was notable, it was also notably thin, but there were things about him that Michael liked. For one thing, he had been among the early students at USC's burgeoning film school. What was different about USC from other film schools, particularly those back east, was that these students' heroes weren't Truffaut, Godard, Rohmer, or Chabrol, the heart of the French New Wave that had led 1970s film students to Andrew Sarris's theory of auteurism. To most West Coast film schoolers, auteurism was already passé, as were the current crop of directors who fancied themselves auteurs, including Martin Scorsese, Francis Coppola, and Brian De Palma. Instead, these film schoolers' heroes were Walt Disney, Clint Eastwood, and Sean Connery (as James Bond), and they sought to emulate their films. They had no artistic rage or fear or guilt about making popular commercial films. The studios weren't their enemies, they were their banks. They longed to swim in the waters of the mainstream, and that was exactly the type of director Michael was looking for. *Romancing* had no message; it was simply meant to be a good time at the movies and make a lot of money.

Early in his career, Zemeckis become friendly with Steven Spielberg, who soon became his mentor and executive-produced Zemeckis's first two features.[1] The financial failure of those films made it more difficult for Zemeckis to find work away from Spielberg because they had become so closely linked. And Spielberg had just laid a colossal bomb of his own, *1941* (1979), also written by Zemeckis with a friend from film school, Bob Gale, and John Milius. The disastrous *1941* made any further collaborations between Zemeckis and Spielberg, at least for the moment, out of the question.

Although Zemeckis continued to write scripts, including one about a boy who manages to travel across in time in a DeLorean car, he could not generate any interest from the studios. He directed no more films until 1983, when Michael decided to take a chance on him for *Romancing the Stone*. After screening his earlier work, Michael was convinced

---

1   *I Wanna Hold Your Hand* (1978) and *Used Cars* (1980). They were both well received by the critics but underperformed at the box office.

Zemeckis could handle it. As Michael later recalled of the director, "At twenty-eight his career was over. At twenty-three [*sic*] his career was back, thanks to *Romancing the Stone*." (When he began the film in 1983, Zemeckis, born in 1951, was thirty-two years old.)

Everything was now in place except one last and crucial element— the casting of Joan Wilder. Word was that Michael had settled on Debra Winger, who had become hot after her turn in Taylor Hackford's 1982 smash *An Officer and a Gentleman*, which had earned her a nomination for an Academy Award for Best Actress (she lost to Meryl Streep for her performance in Alan J. Pakula's *Sophie's Choice*) and even hotter after James L. Brooks's 1983 *Terms of Endearment*, a tour de force for Shirley MacLaine and Jack Nicholson that was all but stolen by Winger, who was again nominated for an Academy Award, this time for Best Actress (and who lost again, this time to Julie Andrews in Blake Edwards's *Victor Victoria*). Michael reportedly wanted Winger badly, but Fox didn't think she was glamorous enough or physically fit for the part. Fox productions president Joe Wizan suggested instead, but really insisted upon, Kathleen Turner. After spending a few years in TV soap opera limbo, Turner's film debut as a femme fatale came in 1981's *Body Heat*, Lawrence Kasdan's loose remake of and homage to Billy Wilder's 1944 dark and exciting *Double Indemnity*, in which she gave a performance the *New York Times* called "jaw-dropping."

Turner got the part.

ROMANCING THE STONE finally went into production on July 5, 1983. The plot centers around Joan Wilder, a writer of romantic novels, whose life turns into one of her own stories when she receives a map from her dead brother-in-law and a phone call from her sister pleading for her to come to Cartagena, Colombia, where she has been kidnapped by a couple of antiquities dealers, played by sleek-headed stand-up comic and actor Zack Norman and Michael's buddy Danny DeVito. There Joan meets American bird exporter Jack T. Colton

(Michael), who reluctantly agrees to help her find her sister for the grand sum of $375.

All of it is silly and goofy, and rightly played that way by Michael and Turner. Their on-screen chemistry elevated the spirited inter-play between the physically awkward Joan and the physically superior Colton. The film's turning point comes when Joan suggests to Colton that they find the treasure themselves, a gigantic emerald, and rescue her sister as well. The picture then shifts into overdrive, and the action becomes nonstop.

Colton fancies himself as something of a ladies' man, one of the reasons Michael wanted to play him. Here, finally, was a chance to show some of his sex appeal on-screen, cartoonishly set as it may have been.

Zemeckis and Michael's first choice of location was Colombia, South America, but it was about to start its rainy season, and so they settled instead on Mexico—where it rained for nearly half the ninety days allotted for production. As Michael later recalled, "I remember arriving on location in Mexico and saying to Bob, 'I don't remember a river being here. Do you remember a river being here?' It was a night-mare." Fox had given Michael his $10 million budget, and there was little room for error. To save money, much of *Romancing* wound up being shot in Veracruz and Mazatlán.

One of the scenes in the film is a major mudslide. The crew spent almost two weeks filming it. As Michael recalls, "Poor Kathleen's double was beat to hell and she'd come back crying, 'I can't do it again.' We had about 200 gallons of water that we would dump behind the stunt people into a trough. It would hit them in the back, all 200 gallons, and they would just take off. We had to have cargo nets in place every once in a while so they could grab onto something because they couldn't do the whole fall—it would kill them, they'd be flying down."

Kathleen Turner later said of the film's production, "I remember terrible arguments [with Robert Zemeckis] doing *Romancing*. He's a film-school grad, fascinated by cameras and effects. I never felt that he knew what I was having to do to adjust my acting to some of his damn cameras—sometimes he puts you in ridiculous postures. I'd say, 'This is not helping me! This is not the way I like to work, thank you!'"[2]

Word spread quickly among the crew and cast that Michael and Kathleen were going at it hot and heavy whenever they weren't on set together. When the rumors hit the press, Michael, who had reverted to his penchant for extramarital escapades but was always careful not to let any of it leak, blew a gasket and took it out on everybody on the set. He shed his nice-guy actor guise and turned into something he had never been before, a tough-guy producer, and because of it everyone gave him a wide berth.

Michael denied the affair and insisted that everything during the making of the film was professional and aboveboard. He told one reporter there to do a story about the making of the film: "Kathleen's a real trouper. It's not always easy working with an actor who's also the producer. Even Bob Zemeckis would sometimes say, 'I don't know whether to talk to you as an actor or a producer.' But Kathleen was great. . . . [A]s for my part [as Colton], I must say it requires some expertise to dive between a lady's legs.'"

Years later, but before his divorce became final, both Michael and Kathleen confessed to having had the affair. MICHAEL: "Mind you, during the making of the film we were carrying on."

"When we were doing *Romancing the Stone* I was unmarried and unattached," Kathleen said later, "and he told me he was separated. We worked so closely together, and he was just so gorgeous and smart and funny and capable. And I fell for him."

MICHAEL: "We carried on like bandits, onscreen and off."

◈

───────────

2   Despite their difficulties on the film, Zemeckis would go on to work with Turner again, casting her as the voice of Jessica Rabbit in 1988's *Who Framed Roger Rabbit?*

ROMANCING THE STONE opened on March 30, 1984, among the first in an unusually crowded slate of spring and summer films that year that included Neal Israel's *Bachelor Party*, with Tom Hanks in his pre-superstar days; Stan Latham's *Beat Street*; Willard Huyck's *Best Defense*, which starred at the time super-hot Eddie Murphy and Dudley Moore; Hal Needham's *Cannonball Run II*; Bruce Bilson's *Chattanooga Choo Choo*, with Barbara Eden and George Kennedy; Thomas Chong's *Cheech and Chong's the Corsican Brothers*; Richard Franklin's *Cloak and Dagger*, with Henry Thomas and Dabney Coleman; Richard Fleischer's *Conan the Destroyer*, starring Arnold Schwarzenegger; Joseph Ruben's *Dreamscape*, starring Dennis Quaid; Ivan Reitman's *Ghostbusters*; Joe Dante's *Gremlins*; John G. Avildsen's *The Karate Kid*; Nick Castle's *The Last Starfighter*; Barry Levinson's *The Natural*, with Robert Redford; Sergio Leone's *Once upon a Time in America*; Stuart Rosenberg's *The Pope of Greenwich Village*, from the hugely popular novel; Albert Magnoli's *Purple Rain*, starring Prince; John Milius's *Red Dawn*; Bob Clark's *Rhinestone*, starring Sylvester Stallone and Dolly Parton; Leonard Nimoy's *Star Trek III: The Search for Spock*; Gene Wilder's *The Woman in Red*; and Steven Spielberg's *Indiana Jones and the Temple of Doom*, the much-anticipated sequel to *Raiders of the Lost Ark*.

Romancing the Stone benefited from an early opening, as some of the monster releases, including the sequel to *Raiders* and Prince's surprise hit *Purple Rain*, wiped out all competitors in the respective weeks they were released. Coming out prior to the Easter holiday, *Romancing* had relatively little competition and grossed an astonishing $77 million in its initial domestic release, $10 million overseas, and another $37 million in the new venues of video rentals and sales, and went on to become the eighth-highest grosser of the year.[3] Michael happily agreed

---

3   According to *Variety*, the top ten films of 1984, according to initial domestic release, were Martin Brest's *Beverly Hills Cop* ($235 million), Ivan Reitman's *Ghostbusters* ($229 million), *Indiana Jones and the Temple of Doom* ($180 million), *Gremlins* ($148 million), *The Karate Kid* ($91 million), Hugh Wilson's *Police Academy* ($81 mil-

to do an extensive PR tour, showing up everywhere and even doing a stint as guest host on *Saturday Night Live* despite the fact that the show had two resident stars in the competing summer film *Ghostbusters.*

Until now, Michael had consciously avoided making the type of films that had turned his father into a superstar, hard-action adventures with healthy doses of romance thrown in for good measure. Even *Spartacus* had managed to include a love story in between crucifixions. Michael had made his name based primarily on two nongenre (nonaction, nonadventure) films, one that dealt with the subject of legal insanity, the other with the dangers of nuclear power plants. Now *Romancing the Stone* had not only brought him back to prominence but also put him up there as an actor with the big boys. When reporter Roderick Mann pointed out how much Michael in *Romancing* resembled his father's familiar film character—same determined jaw, same piercing eyes, same way of talking—Michael shrugged it off: "I've been told that. . . . [A]nd if it reminds anyone of my dad, that's fine with me."

In private, Michael knew *Romancing the Stone* was no *Spartacus,* but it didn't have to be. If audiences loved *Romancing,* it was good enough for him. Still, everything he did, it seemed, reminded someone of Kirk Douglas—even himself, when eight years into his own marriage, Diandra read about Michael's reported affair with Kathleen and informed him she was considering filing for divorce.

---

lion), Herbert Ross's *Footloose* ($80 million), *Romancing the Stone* ($77 million), *Star Trek III: The Search for Spock* ($76 million), and Ron Howard's *Splash* ($69 million).

CHAPTER 12

My first responsibility is to producing, but I love acting. It's fun. It's make-believe. It's a license to steal. Whether you're playing dramatic parts which allow you a certain amount of self-analysis, or doing a comedic part. It's all fun. My seven-year-old son Cameron sees me acting and says, "Gee dad, that's what I do in the park every day."

—MICHAEL DOUGLAS

UPON COMPLETING *ROMANCING THE STONE*, Michael sheepishly returned home to an increasingly unhappy Diandra, who, even as he was preparing for his promotional tour for the film, had decided to give him one last chance in the form of an ultimatum: either they move east, away from Hollywood and all that came with it, or she would make good on her promise and file for divorce.

Her newest demand came as a shock to Michael. He knew that Diandra was not ecstatic about living mostly by herself in Santa Barbara. Even though it is one of the most beautiful places in the country, it was just too laid-back and casual for her tastes and lacking in the culture and high society she felt far more comfortable among. She did not like anything about Hollywood. She thought it was sleazy and that it took Michael away from her for long periods of time, when he surrounded himself with beautiful and available women. She did not like living in the shadow of her husband the superstar while their marriage (and his fidelity) took a backseat.

At first Michael tried to reason with her, patiently explaining that his career was based in Hollywood and therefore he had to be based there, but Diandra didn't care. He pointed out all the privileges his career had given them, but Diandra wasn't impressed. She came from money and already had all the privileges she needed.

By the end of the summer of 1984, as *Romancing the Stone*'s first theatrical run was winding down, Michael told interviewer Jane Ardmore, "To balance my family life and work is really tough. I promised my wife, Diandra, that the minute [the film's run] is over, I'll give her and our son, Cameron, all my time. Focus totally. That's how I do it. I go from one extreme to the other. I've been gone seven and a half months [making *Romancing the Stone*]. Diandra came to visit me several times. This summer, when Cameron finished first grade, she brought him to me in Morocco [where I was scouting sites for the sequel to *Romancing the Stone*] while she visited her mom in Spain and found us a house in St. Tropez, where we could get a bit of a break together." And, together with Diandra, he sat for an interview with Michael Gross for the *New York Times*. "I had to make a living," Michael told Gross, a way of somewhat disingenuously explaining why he worked so hard. "It was a logistical nightmare." To which Diandra icily countered, "Being young, I [found] it difficult to grow in an environment where I was always surrounded by people in one profession. It was like being surrounded by dentists for the formative years of your life."

After that interview was published, Michael agreed to move east on a trial basis, for a minimum of three years.

A YEAR EARLIER, Michael had bought a high-ceilinged four-bedroom apartment in a prewar building on Manhattan's Upper West Side. It offered twenty-four-hour doorman and butler service and a spectacular view of the park. He had purchased it for Diandra when it first appeared she was going to leave him, primarily so their child would have a comfortable place to live. Now that they were moving into it together, she agreed to let him keep the Santa Barbara house as a West Coast vacation home.

Diandra was reenergized by being back in New York. She immediately organized a fund-raiser for the American Red Cross to help the homeless. Michael, meanwhile, tried to put a happy face on the move, which had raised eyebrows all over Hollywood. To one interviewer, he sounded conciliatory, like a man trying to save his marriage. The move, he insisted, was something they had both decided was best for the family: "She [Diandra] really wasn't crazy about California. . . . I enjoyed living in Santa Barbara and Los Angeles, but we came to feel that the business was all-consuming.

"For the gift of life itself and for all our good fortune, you have to make some input into this world, I feel, and my wife feels the same way. We had different political points of view when we married, but over a period of time, those points have sort of congealed. She has very high principles and strong ideals; and she maintains them."

To another interviewer, Michael laid it on even thicker: "One of the reasons I came back here was I wanted to look into other activities. The film business becomes totally consuming, especially producing. You never get a break, it's always on your mind. I want to get a break. . . . I want to kind of get back to basics and have some roots again. I need to have a little more fun taking care of business more. It seemed like an appropriate time for everybody. My son was asking for a punk haircut because everyone in his pre-school class had one. My wife is European and has a lot of friends back here. So [the move is] for all of us."

In addition to reluctantly letting go of his Ferrari, Michael had to give away his favorite pet, Sangral, a two-year-old serval—an African feline with a body like a cheetah and spots like a leopard. He often jokingly referred to Sangral as the best personal assistant he'd ever had. The animal was really too big for the house in Santa Barbara, and out of the question for an apartment in New York City. He turned the cat over to the Charles Paddock Zoo in Atascadero, California, along with $2,000 to build her a proper cage.

Saving his marriage was important to Michael. He had already been traumatized by one divorce—his parents'—and didn't want to go through anything like that again, even if it meant giving up every-thing he'd worked for in L.A. At least he would be physically close to his mother, whom he had rarely seen while he lived on the West Coast.

No sooner had they arrived in Manhattan than Michael became involved with two new film projects. After *Romancing the Stone* he was white-hot as both actor and producer and wanted to stay hot. He knew firsthand how easy it was for a career to cool off: nobody calls you any-more or takes your calls, no one gets up from their table at a restaurant to come over and shake your hand, no new scripts arrive by messenger to your office or home.

The first was strictly an acting job, playing Zach, the director, in the screen production of the fabulously successful stage musical *A Chorus Line*. The second was *The Jewel of the Nile*, the sequel to *Romancing the Stone*.

A Chorus Line was stage director and choreographer Michael Ben-nett's semi-autobiographical performance piece about the individual lives of the auditioning hopefuls for a Broadway musical's chorus line. The power of the presentation lay in their stories, metaphors for everyone's hopes, fears, and dreams. Its bare-stage, no-name produc-tion had begun as a workshop at the Nickolaus Exercise Center and eventually moved to the Public Theater, where it was directed by Ben-nett with a book by James Kirkwood and Nicholas Dante and a score by Marvin Hamlisch. It debuted on Broadway in 1975 and became, for a time, the longest-running musical in the American theater, giving 6,137 performances.[1] It won nine Tony Awards and the 1976 Pulitzer Prize for drama.

Bennett's *A Chorus Line* takes place on a bare stage, with dancers auditioning for a spot on the chorus line. They present and respond to an unseen director, whose omnipotent voice suggests the voice of God, lifting the show to a whole other level.

Despite its enormous success on Broadway, early on *A Chorus Line*

---

1   In its first run. It was eventually passed by *Phantom of the Opera*, *Cats*, and *Les Misérables*.

was deemed untranslatable to the screen (with rare exceptions, *Hair* being one, most unconventional musicals usually are). In fact, it remained strictly a stage presentation for nine years until Joseph E. Levine's Embassy Pictures, an independent production house, bought the film rights for $5.5 million and agreed not to release the movie until five years after the current Broadway production closed.[2] Embassy then partnered with Columbia and found a producer, Cy Feuer, a notable Broadway director with three Tony Awards under his belt but only two films in his producer credits, David Butler's *Where's Charley* (1952) and Bob Fosse's *Cabaret* (1972). His Broadway forte was conventionally structured star-vehicle musicals, including *Guys and Dolls* and *How to Succeed in Business Without Really Trying*, neither of which fit the concept of *A Chorus Line*.

Film director after film director turned down *A Chorus Line*, believing, as so many did, that it would not transfer well to the screen. In addition, Feuer wanted to hire unknowns for the chorus line, and that made it an even harder sell. When Richard Attenborough agreed to direct, industry insiders saw it as one more impediment: how, they wondered, could a Brit transfer to the big screen the ultimate New York stage show?

Several name actors turned down the role of the director, Zach, before it finally came to Michael, who jumped at it, despite a crucial and ultimately disastrous script change in veteran screenwriter Arnold Schulman's adaptation. Looking to open up the stage production, Schulman made the director a visible character. By doing so he took away the original book's crucial spiritual aspect and thus destroyed the show's mystical and metaphorical reach, where all its power lay; these kids were auditioning not just for the show of their lives but to show off their lives, the confessional aspect to their songs reaching much higher and deeper than a simple audition. When the director was

---

2   Twenty percent of the film's profits had to go to the show's original producers and cast. The show was conceived as an ensemble piece, and the original cast members added much to it; in return, Bennett gave them all a piece of the show and wanted to be sure they had a piece of the movie as well. Bennett died in 1987.

made accessible, he was reduced in stature, humanized—one might say secularized—and brought down to earth. However one interpreted it, the move diminished the power of the production. Worse, in the film version, the director became something of a lech. Onstage, the show's biggest showstopper, "What I Did for Love," was about the character's love of theater; on film, it became about her relationship with Zach.

Why did Michael take the role and how did he feel about it? It was. a New York–based job. To one interviewer, Michael said he'd done it "for the joy of it, without any [producer's] responsibility." To another he said the character of Zach "is closer to a prick than what I usually play, a guy insensitive to how other people feel."

When the production began to have problems and the director asked Michael to help, he put his hands up and graciously backed away, preferring to simply enjoy the horde of half-naked girls parading around the set. As he told yet another interviewer, "And when we fell behind schedule I turned to Attenborough and said, 'I'm sorry to hear that.' . . . I've never seen so many leotards in my life. It's always been nuclear-power plants and medical equipment in the background of my pictures."

"Michael never let one leotard go by," Attenborough wryly noted.

The only problem for Michael was that, for the first time in his life, he could feel the specter of middle age looming. Off the set, the young girls in the chorus all referred to him politely as "Mr. Douglas," the way they would refer to a school principal or a friend's father.

FILMING WAS SCHEDULED to begin in January 1985 in New York City at the Mark Hellinger Theater, on the corner of Broadway and Fifty-First Street. At night, rather than going home—and despite Diandra's wanting him there every night—Michael preferred the peace and the sanctity of his office at the theater, where he could work alone and undisturbed into the night. Even as *Chorus Line* was in production, he worked on the preproduction schedule for *The Jewel of the Nile*, the sequel to *Romancing the Stone*.

Fox had made the deal for *Nile* in August 1985, before *A Chorus Line* started rehearsals and before Spielberg's *Indiana Jones and the Temple of Doom*, the sequel to *Raiders of the Lost Ark*, was breaking box office records for a sequel. Joel Douglas, one of the producers of *Romancing the Stone*, was brought back by Michael for *The Jewel of the Nile* (known jokingly to industry insiders as "Jews in Denial" and "Jews on the Nile").

A Chorus Line's shooting schedule had slowed, mostly due to Feuer and Attenborough's difficulties in getting the subtleties of the young chorus hopefuls to make sense on-screen. Attenborough especially was at a loss and again and again turned to Michael, the only non-chorus character in the production, to somehow help him make the film. To do so, he tried everything, eventually flattery. Every chance he got, Attenborough overpraised Michael's performance, to the point of comically gross exaggeration: "Michael's determination to play the 'mean and attractive' Zach—without a huge salary or star billing—represents growth in the actor's career, and the resulting performance is miraculous. He brings to the performance enormous stature and a mind. Zach doesn't work unless you believe there's a mind racing around there. . . . [I]n the deep close shots, he is, oh, so delicate, like a watercolor rather than an oil painting. But you feel behind it, as you do with all great stars, the explosion imminent. Cooper had it, and Spencer Tracy—that huge strength and power behind the gentleness."

Michael wouldn't take the bait. He resisted having any role in the production except playing the part of Zach; on the set, he was strictly a hired hand. The onus, Michael made sure, remained with Attenborough.

THE SNAIL-PACED production on *A Chorus Line* threatened to cut into the scheduled start date of *The Jewel of the Nile*, a much bigger and more important project for Michael. It didn't make things any better that both films were slated to open at Christmas 1985. That gave Michael only a year to get *Jewel* into theaters.

Fox had insisted that it have essentially the same cast, characters, writers, and director as *Romancing*. Michael didn't agree. He thought new blood was a better idea to keep the series fresh. Diane Thomas, who had some clout now, sided with Fox and insisted on writing the sequel and keeping Joan the main character. After the success of *Romancing the Stone*, offers for Thomas's services had come in fast and furious, including one that really interested her, Steven Spielberg's remake of Victor Fleming's 1943 tearjerker *A Guy Named Joe*, about an ill-fated wartime romance between Spencer Tracy (and his ghost) and Irene Dunne. The film had just enough chaste romance, with a touch of romantic fantasy to attract Spielberg, and he wanted Diane to write it. He had been impressed with *Romancing* and was confident he could get her with a two-picture deal that included the second *Indiana Jones* sequel. He was right. She eagerly accepted his offer. The remake of *Joe*, renamed *Always*, starred Richard Dreyfuss and Holly Hunter. Dreyfuss at the time was the favorite on-screen doppelganger of the director. The idea to do the remake originated with him and Spielberg while they were both struggling through what would eventually be the breakthrough for both, *Jaws*, released in 1975.

However, Diane never got to write any of these films, including *Jewel*. As a present to her after the success of *Romancing the Stone*, Michael gave the former waitress a brand-new Porsche, partly out of gratitude for her work and partly as a way to try to convince her to do the sequel. On October 21, while driving with a male friend along the Pacific Coast Highway, she let him take the wheel, even though he was drunk. He crashed, and she was killed instantly. Diane Thomas was thirty-nine years old.

When he heard about it, Michael was grief-stricken, and felt a sizable amount of guilt for having given her that car. The deadline was looming, though, and he had to get *Jewel* moving. Michael hired the television writing team of Mark Rosenthal and Lawrence Konner to somehow crank out a script. He assumed that Bob Zemeckis would direct, but Zemeckis, too, had moved on. He had signed to direct *Back to the Future* for Spielberg and his production company, Amblin, in association with Universal. Michael then chose Lewis Teague, whose direction of the 1983 film adaptation of Stephen King's *Cujo*, about a woman and her child trapped in a car by a rabid dog, had impressed Michael.

With all these mostly downward changes, it was clear now to Michael that *Jewel* was not going to be another *Stone*. Even Kathleen Turner had hesitated about signing on. She had already contracted to do two other movies, John Huston's 1985 *Prizzi's Honor*, co-starring Jack Nicholson, and Francis Ford Coppola's 1986 *Peggy Sue Got Married*, co-starring a then up-and-coming Nicolas Cage. Although she felt she owed Michael, she agreed to do his film only if she thought the script was as good as the first, which put even more pressure on Michael, who in turn put it on Rosenthal and Konner. Their first script came in while Michael was finishing up on *A Chorus Line*. He read it that night in his office, felt it didn't work, and took to rewriting it himself.

He tried to remain publicly upbeat about all the problems. "It's always difficult to try to top a very successful picture like *Romancing the Stone*," Michael said later. In an interview with the *Sunday Times* of London, he told them, "What we wanted to do was peep in on those two people who rode down West End Avenue in a sailboat . . . and pick up their relationship six months later."

He elaborated on the plot for another reporter: "We'll follow them through the south of France and they'll get into another adventure which will take them to some fictionalized North African country. I think we have a real fun story. It may even be funnier than *Romancing*."

To further sell the movie, he reminded audiences that Danny DeVito would be back, along with "some other new characters—like the Flying Karamazov Brothers and Avner the Eccentric."[3] The only principal character not returning from the original was the deliciously

---

3   Avner the Eccentric was appearing on Broadway while Michael was shooting *A Chorus Line*. He caught Avner's show one night and immediately signed him up for *Jewel*, instructing his writers to create a character for him.

evil Ira (Zack Norman), despite (or because of) Norman's having become one of Michael's best friends and future business partner.

SOMEHOW, *A Chorus Line* managed to complete filming on time. As
Michael later remembered, "We finished shooting January 31 [1985],
and next morning I ran over to England for a production meeting [for
Jewel] with the guys who had been scouting locations in five countries;
we narrowed it down to principal shooting in Morocco. . . . [W]e set
up offices in Nice, where filming was to wind up the following July."
To handle the difficult physical production he brought over fifty top
technicians and administrators hired by his new production company
created especially for the film, the Stone Group.

Even as Michael arrived in Morocco, new production problems
arose. In April, during the first few days of actual shooting, he felt a
definite lack of chemistry between Kathleen and himself (she had come
aboard at the last minute). Although offscreen they were still sexually
involved, he wasn't wrong. At one point, unhappy with the way things
were going, she threatened to pull out of the filming. With Fox backing him, Michael countered with a threat to sue for $25 million for
breach of contract. Kathleen then had an abrupt change of heart and
agreed to stay if the script could somehow be improved. In an attempt
to cool her out, Michael did to Kathleen what Attenborough had done
to him: he used flattery. He became publicly effusive about her ability to work under extremely difficult conditions. "I take my hat off to
Kathleen," he said later. "There was many a time in which we would be
doing a scene and all of a sudden someone would say, 'Excuse me one
second, the teamsters are about to strike,' and I'd have to go. She was
always wonderful about that. She could get back into it."

The locals that filled out the crew operated on a different time
clock than those Michael had imported from Hollywood. They did
not have the commitment or the expertise that Michael demanded,
resulting in a general slowdown of production. And then there was
Ramadan, a month-long religious holiday during which Muslims do

not eat, drink, smoke, and do as little work as possible during the day-light hours. That meant that work on the film could only take place at night. (Michael fired the two production managers who had not figured this into the schedule.)

The grand finale of *Jewel* had to be filmed precisely at twilight, and a solid week of action scenes had to be shot during the day, in the blistering desert city of Ouarzazate. Michael had to pull a Houdini to get all of it done.

One night, a scene was scheduled to be shot in the town square, with hundreds of extras milling beneath parapets hung with black-and-gold banners emblazoned with a falcon, the dictator Omar's symbol. It took hours to get the shot set up, and only then did someone notice there was no film in the cameras. The raw stock could not be found, and the shot was lost. "I can't fucking believe it," Michael shouted to no one, and sent everyone home. Joel quietly suggested lightening the tension by throwing a big party. Michael did not smile, and everyone close enough to hear what he told Joel about his idea turned their heads away, pretending not to have heard anything.

A while later Michael received a call saying the film stock had been found, but it was too late to reassemble everyone and shoot the scene. It had to be rescheduled.

It got worse. Two location scouts and a pilot were killed in a storm while scouting new places to shoot. Several crew members were fired when Michael felt they weren't giving enough of themselves for the film. Props often didn't work right, causing additional expensive re-shoots. The temperature in Michael's on-set tent often reached above a hundred degrees. Several crew members couldn't take the relentless heat and demanded hotel rooms. Michael's response was to threaten to release anybody who didn't like their accommodations. Several still protested, and they were all fired.

Michael summed up his experience on the film this way: "After our experiences shooting *Romancing the Stone* in Mexico, we said, 'Okay, enough of the rain and mud. Let's go somewhere where it's sandy and sunny. What I didn't realize was that in *Romancing*, you fill up the screen with a few banana trees and the rain coming down. Two people going through the jungle with a machete looks real big. You go out in the middle of the desert, though [in *Jewel*], and you look like an ass sitting there. There's nothing there. You're gonna need a lot of stuff to fill it up. Lotta toys . . . so we were constantly behind. The temperature was sometimes 140 degrees."

IN THE SUMMER of 1985, nearly eight months after he had begun, an exhausted Michael called a finish to the shooting of *Jewel on the Nile*. "Everybody knew this was gonna be a backbreaker," he said to Danny DeVito while in the back of the Mercedes stretch limo parked just outside London's Twickenham Studio, where he was feverishly working on postproduction to make the December opening. "I just need a break, man. I can't even . . . anything."

DeVito said, "You can't do it any quicker than that on a picture like this. I defy anybody to try. [You] haven't had a moment of rest. If it wasn't for the makeup they put on [you, you'd] look like a *rat* right now . . . makeup, man, I'm a sucker for makeup now."

"Makeup, man, I'm a sucker for makeup."

"Yeah, your wife says, 'Gonna go to bed with your makeup on again?'"

"*Serious* cosmetic work. Then you look in the mirror, everything's okay."

What they were talking about was cosmetic face improvements. "He's had more work done than anybody I know. Especially the eyes. He's a leading man. He's at it constantly, it's part of the gig," said a close acting friend who had appeared in *Romancing the Stone* but not *The Jewel of the Nile* and who does not wish to be identified.

BOTH *THE JEWEL OF THE NILE* and *A Chorus Line* were scheduled to open the same week. *Jewel* had the Wednesday, December 11, position, giving it a two-day jump on the rest of the still-unreleased big holiday films. *A Chorus Line* was set to open two days later, on Friday the thirteenth.

A Chorus Line had good word of mouth and was opening wide, in a thousand theaters, while *Jewel* had twelve hundred theaters guaranteed and another four hundred to be added on Christmas Day. Michael was going to be plastered over twenty-four hundred screens at one time. And because he had a lot more at stake with *Jewel* than with *A Chorus Line*, he naturally hoped that the latter didn't turn into the kind of sleeper that might seriously hurt *Jewel* at the box office.

The reviews for *The Jewel of the Nile* were mixed. The *New York Times*'s Janet Maslin dismissed the film by writing, "There's nothing in *The Jewel of the Nile* that wasn't funnier or more fanciful in *Romancing the Stone*." Roger Ebert agreed that "it is not quite the equal of *Romancing the Stone*," but at least he liked the interplay between Douglas and Turner. "It seems clear," he wrote, "that they like each other and are having fun during the parade of ludicrous situations in the movie, and their chemistry is sometimes more entertaining than the contrivances of the plot."

Two days later, *A Chorus Line* opened. The *New York Times*'s Vincent Canby observed, "Though it was generally agreed that 'Hair' would not work as a film, Miloš Forman transformed it into one of the most original pieces of musical cinema of the last 20 years. Then they said that 'A Chorus Line' couldn't be done—and this time they were right. . . . Mr. Attenborough has elected to make a more or less straightforward film version that is fatally halfhearted."

Roger Ebert of the *Chicago Sun-Times*, more of a film buff than a stage fan, sharply disagreed: "The result may not please purists who want a film record of what they saw on stage, but this is one of the most intelligent and compelling movie musicals in a long time—and the most grown up, since it isn't limited, as so many contemporary musicals are, to the celebration of the survival qualities of geriatric actresses."

Variety said, "*Chorus* often seems static and confined, rarely venturing beyond the immediate. Attenborough merely films the stage show as best he could. Nonetheless, the director and lenser Ronnie Taylor have done an excellent job working within the limitations, using every trick they could think of to keep the picture moving. More importantly, they have a fine cast, good music, and a great, popular show to work with. So if all they did was get it on film, that's not so bad."

Time Out London said, "The grit and drive of the original have been dissipated into studiously unkempt glitz as empty as plasticised pop. . . . It's too corny and unbelievable for words."

The Jewel of the Nile was the clear winner of the two, critic-proof, and grossed a whopping $96 million on a $25 million budget, giving Michael his fourth blockbuster in ten years, while *A Chorus Line* did less than $15 million on a $27 million budget. Nonetheless, *A Chorus Line* didn't hurt Michael at all; it was Attenborough who received the industrial-strength thrashing on both sides of the pond.

On the strength of the success of *The Jewel of the Nile*, Michael found himself once more at the top of his game, but he had paid a price for it. He was burned out and exhausted, facing a grueling five-month worldwide promotional tour for *Jewel on the Nile*. When that was finally over, he never wanted to see another foot of film, go to a movie theater, or even watch a TV show again. Nor did he want to have anything to do with a second sequel to *Romancing the Stone*, although the studio already had a draft finished, called *The Crimson Eagle*, written by Warren Skaaren, who had done the screenplay for Tony Scott's 1987 *Beverly Hills Cop II* (the first of two sequels). But without Michael's enthusiasm and encouragement, it proved impossible to get off the ground.

Michael knew he had made the right decision, and his days as an action star mercifully came to an end.

PART FIVE

SEX SYMBOL

With Glenn Close in 1987's water-cooler movie of the year, Fatal Attraction.
Rᴇʙᴇʟ Rᴏᴀᴅ Aʀᴄʜɪᴠᴇs

I haven't had a break in two and a half years. I'm not saying I won't produce again, but it'll be a hell of a long time and then perhaps a simple bedroom comedy. I belong right now to my wife and son.

—MICHAEL DOUGLAS

DIANDRA, THE WIFE HE "BELONGED TO," WAS LESS than pleased with an interview Kathleen Turner gave *GQ* while in Morocco filming *The Jewel of the Nile* in which she said: "He takes my breath away, like in a scene where he turns to me and says, 'God, I love you, lady.' He turns on that switch. Michael is really a man who likes women."

Or with Michael, who enjoyed being effusive about Kathleen, when he complimented her on how great she was during the making of the two difficult films: "I could never have done it with anybody else."

Diandra told friends, "I don't know how much longer I can go on living like this. When he's working, I'm never sure where he is, or when he's coming home. He eats, drinks, and sleeps movies. He has a telephone growing out of his ear."

But in reality, they were already living separate lives. Diandra had her work with the Red Cross and a growing commitment to the Metropolitan Museum of Art's Office of Film and Television, where she felt much happier and more productive than when she was stuck in Santa Barbara. "I grew up with writers and painters and archeologists," she said later. "L.A. wasn't a good place to raise children."

Only weeks into 1986, Michael, still exhausted from having to do

Chorus Line and *Jewel* back-to-back, began talking to dozens of prospective independent producing partners, and had closed in on Michael S. Phillips of the Mercury Entertainment Corporation. A decade earlier, Phillips been the hottest producer in Hollywood. He had won a Best Picture Oscar (with former wife and ex-partner Julia Phillips) for producing George Roy Hill's *The Sting* (1973), followed by a golden string of commercial and prestige hits, including Martin Scorsese's 1976 *Taxi Driver*, the film that made Robert De Niro a star, and a year later Steven Spielberg's monster *Close Encounters of the Third Kind*.

Mercury then fell in disarray following the departure of Julia Phillips, whose book *You'll Never Have Lunch in This Town Again* pulled back the curtains on the sex-and-drugs-and-dirty-deals underbelly of the business and by doing so ensured that she would never work in Hollywood again.

Michael believed he could help Michael Phillips save the company. Mercury had a development deal with Home Box Office Pictures to produce two films, and a third theatrical feature in production, *The Tender*, starring John Travolta. Michael dove into the proceedings, hoping to revive Mercury's fortunes and, along with it, make some exciting, and highly profitable, new movies.

IN 1987, the agreed-upon three years were up, and Michael asked Diandra to come back with him to Santa Barbara, where he could spread out and relax and be closer to Hollywood; an hour-and-a-half drive was far easier than a coast-to-coast flight. He suggested they could even try to have another child there. And he promised her his work would not interfere with that goal. To everyone's surprise, even Michael's, she agreed, and informed all her associates in New York she was going away for a while. Shortly thereafter, they packed up the things they needed and, with Cameron in tow, moved back to Santa Barbara.

That February, less than two months later, Sherry Lansing called

Michael. She wanted to make a new film with him, to be shot, ironically, in New York and Connecticut.[1]

"Stanley [Jaffe] and Sherry asked me to look at a short film called *Diversion*," Michael said, "At the same they were working on a project called *Fatal Attraction*." The film was about a philandering husband and what happens when he gets caught up in an extramarital affair. "I had had the same idea many years ago after reading a book called *Virgin Kisses*." Michael still owned the rights to this book by Gloria Nagy, which was about, as Michael later recalled, "a young, bored, successful psychiatrist, who cheated his way through school, had seen a hundred attractive clients, when suddenly this frumpy woman comes into his office and gives him the biggest turn-on of his life and has him breaking every ethical code of his profession." He had always liked the idea but could never figure out a way to make it. Lansing's concept was close enough to get him interested.

He talked with Diandra about the idea of working with Lansing and Jaffe on their new film. When Diandra said she was excited about returning to New York City so quickly, Michael called Lansing back and said yes. The next day he returned to New York with Diandra and Cameron, bringing an abrupt end to their make-a-baby-in-California plan—which, apparently, neither was all that committed to.

SHERRY LANSING HAD since left Fox and formed an independent production partnership with Stanley Jaffe. They had a first-look development deal at Paramount and were eagerly looking for new projects. Jaffe and Lansing had so far made only one movie together, *Firstborn* (1984), directed by Michael Apted, distributed by Paramount, starring

---

1 In an interview, Michael joked about his long association with Lansing: "I always tease, about when they used to have meetings, and she'd suggest, 'Well, what about Michael Douglas?' One day somebody said, 'Can I ask you something? Are you fucking him?' and she said, 'No.'" Michael Douglas, interviewed by Fred Schruers, *Rolling Stone*, January 14, 1988.

Teri Garr, Peter Weller, and Robert Downey Jr. It was a small-budget affair and grossed a little more than $6 million in its initial domestic release—not great, but enough to keep the Jaffe-Lansing partnership going.

"While in London," Jaffe later explained, "I had called ahead and asked agents if there was anybody they wanted me to see." One of the people was James Dearden, who had made three short films. "I loved all three, especially one about an obsessive lover."

As Dearden, a former playwright, recalled, "When I created *Diversion* in 1979, I just wanted to make an inexpensive film. . . . I was sitting at home thinking, 'What is a minimalist story that I can do?' My wife was out of town for the weekend, and I thought what would happen if a man who has just dropped his wife at the railroad station rings this girl who he's met at a party and says, 'Would you like to have dinner?' One thing of course leads to another and he has what appears to be an easy one-night-stand, but then it all gets ugly. The girl keeps calling, and finally the wife returns and the phone rings again and the wife picks it up and says hello. And that's the end of the story, a little fable about the perils of adultery."

Jaffe told Lansing about Dearden's films, and they decided to invite him to Hollywood to discuss working together. Lansing recalled, "I kept on coming back to that short film, which really ends when what would later become the Glenn Close character calls the home and the wife reaches for the phone. That's all there was, a hint of what we would later do. I became obsessed with that short, convinced there was a movie there." They optioned it and extrapolated what would eventually become *Fatal Attraction*.

After meeting with Michael, they offered him the lead, and he said yes.[2] However, despite his commitment, every studio passed.

According to Lansing, "It was a Paramount picture, it was developed at Paramount because our deal was with them, and Paramount passed on it. Even with Michael Douglas attached, the subject matter

---

2 As part of the deal, Michael was paid for the rights to *Virgin Kisses*.

was considered highly uncommercial. We then gave it to twenty-six directors and they all passed. None of the majors thought a story about adultery would find a sympathetic audience for its male lead."

It eventually came to Adrian Lyne, the British director whose previous credits included 1983's *Flashdance*, the sleeper hit of that year, about a female welder who longs to become a serious classical dancer. The hook of the film is its sleazy sex club atmospherics combined with a romantic love story (and the scene everyone remembers, where Jennifer Beals, the welder/dancer, mesmerizes her boyfriend, and audiences, when she slips out of her bra without removing her sweatshirt). In 1986 Lyne made the misguided *9½ Weeks*, a sleazy soft-core S&M film that tried to romanticize a subject that works best when it is not romanticized at all. It didn't do much at the box office, grossing about $6.7 million on a $17 million budget, but created an enormous buzz, establishing Lyne as someone who could make a film that got noticed and talked about. He was the twenty-seventh director to be offered *Fatal Attraction*, and he jumped at it.[3]

STANLEY JAFFE: "I went to see *9½ Weeks* the day after we signed Adrian, and I thought, 'Uh-oh, this isn't the film we are going to be doing.'" Jaffe met with Lyne and warned him that this could be the shortest meeting in the history of the world. But Adrian remained cool and managed to convince Jaffe that he'd done the best he could with the script he had in *9½ Weeks* and that it could have been a lot worse. Jaffe was convinced, and Lyne was officially aboard.

They spent six months rewriting, with both Michael and Dearden contributing, and eventually Lansing brought Nicholas Meyer in to help, primarily to smooth some of the dialogue and fix the ending. Meyer's previous screenplays included *The Seven-Per-Cent Solution*, his biggest success to date (he is uncredited in *Fatal Attraction*). He was able to fix some of the script's more glaring problems.

---

3   Lyne had worked with Michael for about a year on *Starman* but didn't direct the movie that was finally made (which Michael eventually co-produced but did not star in).

The next step, casting the role of the female lead, was crucial. Glenn Close was someone Sherry Lansing wanted, but Close was so nervous about getting the part she had to take Valium to calm herself down before the audition. "I had flown out from New York. I didn't know what to wear and I went to a store—Neiman Marcus or something. My hair was long and crazy. . . . I was kind of intimidated."

Later on, Close elaborated on her audition. "I walked in and the first thing I saw was a video camera, which is terrifying, and behind the video camera in the corner was Michael Douglas. I just said, 'Well, let it all go wild . . .' and it wasn't until we started shooting that I started loving working with Michael. I remember doing one scene where we go dancing, and I remember Adrian telling me to flip down my dress off-camera and expose my breast to get a reaction—and I got it!" During shooting, makeup artists worked on Close's lips, filling in the dip under her nose to make her mouth look sadder. It was subtle, but it worked.

Satisfied with the revised script, which owed more than a little to Clint Eastwood's 1971 *Play Misty for Me*, and with Michael and Lyne (and the relatively unknown Close) attached, Jaffe and Lansing once more put it back on the market. Everyone again said no.[4]

JAFFE: "We were turned down by every studio *twice*. They said basically the same thing they had the first time, 'How can you make a picture where the leading man cheats on his wife in the first ten minutes?' But eventually Paramount, which had given us a lot of money to make movies, which we weren't doing, conceded, and gave us the green light."

Michael was thrilled; this was his chance to definitively prove he could play a heated sexual character in a serious, adult movie. "For me," Michael remembers, "the appeal of *Fatal Attraction* is this very

---

4 *Misty* is a lean, dark, and cynical film—Clint's first feature-length directorial effort—dealing with a woman's can't-let-go obsession after a brief affair with a disk jockey who already has a girlfriend. The picture builds to a brutally violent climax. The premise proved a career-changer for Eastwood: it was made for $900,000 and earned $5 million in its initial theatrical release.

powerful, visceral instinct for obsessive lust amid seeming decency and normality. My character wants to go beyond the norm. I also think in a general way the film has hooked into a very deep hostility that now exists between the sexes. For some women, I know that they find themselves thinking about the guy who dumped on them and who they regret letting off too easy. For some men, let's face it, they have a lot of repressed hostility toward women. They're the ones at the end of the picture yelling 'Kill her!' "

To another interviewer, he said, "I remember [the scene where] I jumped into [my own] bed to ruffle the sheets [to make it look slept in, after returning from the weekend with Glenn Close's character], there was this laughter and I was shocked. I thought, 'My God, they've already forgiven this guy.' Whether it says something about me or the amount of adultery going on in the country, I'm not sure."

To still another, Michael added, "And something else. People kept saying to me how could you do this to your wife, the beautiful Anne Archer, and I would say yeah, but wasn't Glenn Close kind of kinky, she looked like she had something up her sleeve. Could that not happen to you?"

Nonetheless, the film's ending is a (literal) bloodbath, the result of what begins as a one-night stand between an ostensibly happily married New York City lawyer, Dan Gallagher (Michael) and an editor, Alex (Glenn Close), who works for a major publishing company. They meet for drinks to discuss business, and it leads to a passionate one-night stand while Dan's wife, Beth (Anne Archer), and daughter, Ellen (Ellen Hamilton Latzen), are away. Unfortunately for Dan, the affair continues through the entire weekend, at the end of which, as he is getting dressed and Alex is trying to get him to stay, he tells her in no uncertain terms that it's over. She grabs his shirt and rips it open. When that doesn't work, she slits her wrists. Dan, frightened by Alex's extreme behavior, stays with her, comforts and cares for her until he's sure she's safe, but when he leaves he knows and the audience knows he never wants to see her again.

Alex, however, keeps phoning him at work, and when he doesn't

return her calls, she shows up at his office. After a few weeks he reluctantly (and uncomfortably) agrees to talk to her; he remains firm and
tells her not to call him anymore, and she replies quite calmly (and
shockingly, to both Dan and the audience) that she is pregnant. He
wants her to have an abortion, but she refuses, telling him that she is
going to be in his life forever now. She keeps making his life miser-
able (to say the least), even after he moves his family out of the city
and into the suburbs.[5] Her stalking continues, becoming more intense
and to Dan (and the audience) more frightening. In one memorable
scene, she sneaks into the house when no one is there, puts the family's pet rabbit into a pot, and boils it alive. (In England after the film
was released, the phrase "bunny boiler" came to mean any woman
who was especially bitchy: "Oh, she's a real bunny boiler, that one.") In
another scene, she utters one of the most famous lines in all of eighties
cinema: "I'm not going to be ignored, Dan!" It became a rallying cry
for women who had felt they had been ignored by cheating men their
whole lives.

At that point, realizing he has no choice, Dan confesses to his wife
and moves out. While he's gone, his daughter is kidnapped by Alex,
and his wife has a serious car accident frantically searching for her.
Alex takes the child to an amusement park and afterward returns her
unharmed, but too late to prevent Beth from winding up in the hospital.

When restraining orders don't work and Dan realizes the police
don't care about the case (a nice Hitchcock touch), Dan plans to kill
Alex in her apartment, but he can't go through with it. Eventually
Alex returns once more to the Gallagher household to try to kill off
a recovering and still-fragile Beth. In one of the most tension-filled
climaxes ever filmed, Alex takes a kitchen knife to Beth in the upstairs

---

5   That year, Close and Michael were asked to present at the Oscar ceremonies.
Close: "I was very pregnant at the time, and we walked out onstage together and the
audience just fell apart! They started laughing! I'd forgotten that in the movie I say
I am pregnant. It was a great moment." From Stephen Galloway's profile of Michael
Douglas, *Hollywood Reporter*, January 23, 2004.

bathroom; Dan comes to Beth's rescue and drowns Alex, but even though Dan (and we) think she's finally dead, she's still alive. Beth then returns with a pistol and shoots Alex through the heart. After the police leave, Beth and Dan embrace, and the camera closes in on a family portrait taken during happier times, set on a piece of furniture in the hallway.

The film would touch a lot of nerves and cause extensive polarization between men and women who went to see it. Male audience members would see Dan as the victim of a woman who is obviously psychotic—out of control, desperate, and demented. Female audiences would see it differently: Alex was an innocent single and aging woman exploited and abused by a married man who sleeps with her and unceremoniously dumps her to return to his wife and child.

Several complex issues contributed to the film's eventual water-cooler appeal. Although the familiar theme of "sex is dangerous" has been around since the first foot of celluloid ever passed through a camera lens, the film was released at the height of the AIDS epidemic, and it angered those who felt that Dan's display of careless, unprotected sex sent the wrong message. (Dan does catch a psychological dose of something deadly in the form of Alex's pregnancy, something he can't get rid of that progressively destroys his marriage and in the end almost gets him killed.)

The key scene is their first sexual encounter—more violent than sexual. They rip each other's clothes off in her kitchen, and it appears they are beating each other up as much as having sex, because the scene isn't really about sex at all. It is about entrapment, control, and shared rage. Alex is enraged because she has no man who loves her, and she uses sex as her only viable weapon of allure; Dan is frustrated because the heat has gone out of his marriage. Both are needy and culpable, and so is Beth, for not recognizing her husband's sexual needs or his growing if unrecognized rage fueled by his unfulfilled desires.

Some saw the film as a parable for the Vietnam War, which had ended only a decade earlier. In a way, Dan's everyman is America, and his "conquest" of Alex echoes America's invasion of Vietnam, the assumption that he (we) can get in and out quickly and neatly, with no responsibility, and that he (we) can return home unscathed after a brief, uncommitted one-night stand, resonated with adult audiences that had spent a decade or more of their lives living through an endless, devastating, and ultimately meaningless tar-baby war.

It was also a time that saw both the rise of feminism and the first real backlash against it. The question of who was guilty in the film and who was (relatively) innocent from that point of view also polarized viewers. Some feminists saw Alex as a victim, exploited by the wealthy, married, smug Dan. Others saw Dan as the victim of a career woman with an agenda who was psychotically obsessed with the family that another woman, Dan's wife, had rightfully earned. All of it made the film the morning-after topic of the year.

MICHAEL: "The movie touched a nerve of undeclared war between the sexes."

STANLEY JAFFE: "It was not anything we could have guessed would have happened. The picture made money. . . . We set out to make a thriller with social implications, but it turned into a social phenomenon."

But cultural issues fade and the movies that raise them remain. As a pure thriller bordering on a modern monster movie, with no sociopolitical overtones, the film is a touchstone of eighties cinema and made Glenn Close, who was nominated for a Best Actress Oscar, a top-of-the-line star.

Michael was nominated for a BAFTA Best Actor Award for this film (the British equivalent of an Oscar), which was, without question, the most nuanced performance of his career. His natural likeability meshed perfectly with Close's hostile/pathetic/needy/victim/crazy-bitch performance, and each highlighted the other because of the contrast between the two.

The original ending had Glenn Close committing a *Madame Butterfly*–type suicide and Michael being arrested for murdering her, a too-neat, overly simplistic, and moralistic conclusion to a very complex story. It didn't test well, and after several tries, the ending was changed to a more confrontational resolution, based on a combination of Alfred Hitchcock's shower scene in his 1960 *Psycho* and the unforgettable bathtub climax of Clouzot's 1955 French classic, *Diabolique*.[6]

During filming, everyone had tried to figure out the proper ending. Close preferred the original, where Alex kills herself and frames Dan for her murder, while Michael wanted Alex killed off for good. According to Close, "She was a deeply disturbed woman, but not a psychopath. Once you put a knife in somebody's hand, I thought it was a betrayal of the character."

Michael disagreed. "She had been so powerful and so evil in a Machiavellian psycho way that it left the audience frustrated. The audience wanted somebody to kill her. Otherwise the picture was left—for lack of a better expression—with blue balls."

No one was sure what the film was really about, if it was about anything more than merely being an entertaining thriller. According to James Dearden: "It was all rather bizarre and not altogether comfortable. You suddenly find that a film that you see as a piece of popular entertainment is on the rack and you're being asked to account for things that weren't your decision and things that certainly were not intended to be interpreted the way they were being interpreted. My feeling was just leave it alone as a good thriller with an interesting subtext. I wasn't trying to make major philosophical statements about the human condition in 1987, nor was the film some kind of parable about AIDS. When I started the script [in 1978], AIDS was still perceived as a gay problem. I don't see that Alex symbolizes the New Woman and is therefore made to appear ghastly to sabotage the New Woman's cause. She has a career because she lives in New York, where it's difficult to survive without one. For me, it was a fable about the irrational creeping into the everyday."

Michael saw it closer to home: "I think what was a big breakthrough

---

6 Preview audiences rejected the suicide/framed-for-murder ending as unsatisfying, and at the insistence of marketing executive Joseph Farrell, Paramount Pictures had Lyne reshoot it.

for me as an actor, was that when you start preparing for a role you think about your character. And I remember having a moment when I said, 'What character? This is not about putting on the make-up, this is about wiping yourself off. I mean, I could have been a lawyer in New York, I could have had an affair, this could have happened to *me*.'" Telling words from an actor in a marriage filled with passivity who had lived a life not that far from the character he was portraying. Michael had been with other women while maintaining a marriage that on the surface seemed to the public to be idyllic. Ironically, it took a film that showed him as closer to the man he thought he really was that allowed him to break away from the type of amiable action character audiences thought he really was.

Indeed, Dan Gallagher is so difficult a part to play precisely because of the character's passivity. To find the handle, Michael called upon his father for advice. According to Michael, "The picture used to really drive me nuts. It's [Dan's] inability to act. And it was structured that way. There were places where I felt handcuffed—you want Dan to do something. I shared this with my dad, all this inability to act. . . . He said, 'Well, listen Mike, you do nothing better than anybody I know.'" *Fatal Attraction* was, if not the best, certainly the most talked-about film of the year.

WHAT *FATAL ATTRACTION* was to sex, *Wall Street* was to money.

While Michael was wrapping *Fatal Attraction*, he accepted an offer from Oliver Stone to appear as Gordon Gekko, the lizard-like Mephistophelean financier in the highly prescient if excessively overwrought *Wall Street*. Why did Stone want Michael? According to the actor, "He saw a killer." It was not the starring role, but it would prove the most memorable performance in the film. As Fox film executive Tom Rothman, whose studio made the film, said, "Mephistopheles—now there's a bad guy; but bad guys make great movies, especially if they're seductive and charming rogues bearing the promise of all you could ever desire." This deal with the devil of a movie would prove another big win for Michael.

Killer or not, Michael was not Stone's first choice to play the role, which was based in part on the lives of the iconic Wall Street names of the day—Owen Morrissey, Dennis Levine, Ivan Boesky, Carl Icahn, Asher Edelman, Michael Milken—and Stone himself. At first Fox had wanted Warren Beatty for Gordon Gekko, but Beatty said no. Stone went to Richard Gere, who also passed. Stone then thought about Michael, and was advised by some that Michael was too soft (i.e., passive) to play the killer type that the role of Gordon Gekko demanded. What Stone really needed, they said, was someone more like a younger version of Kirk. But wasn't that what Michael was? Stone offered him the role after viewing advance footage of *Fatal Attraction*.

For the leading role of Bud, Stone went to Charlie Sheen, another son of a Hollywood star, Martin Sheen, who, in an interesting bit of casting "doubling," plays Charlie's moral-high-road father in the film. It is perhaps no coincidence that Charlie played a similar role—an innocent corrupted, or brought to experience—in Stone's directorial breakthrough, 1986's *Platoon*, Stone's fourth film as a director and one of the most virulent antiwar films (or anti–Vietnam War films) ever made. In *Platoon*, Sheen played Chris, a name with significant sacrificial meaning. In *Wall Street*, he played Bud Fox—a reference to innocence (and drugs) and to a predator, which is what Fox turns into before his big fall.

Although The System was the subject, Stone originally wanted to use TV game shows for his metaphor, focusing on the notorious quiz show scandals of the 1950s. But he decided instead to tackle Wall Street. Perhaps tellingly, Stone's father had been a broker during the Great Depression, and it was to his father that Stone dedicated the making of the film. *Wall Street* comes off as Dostoyevsky's *Crime and Punishment* meets Joseph L. Mankiewicz's 1950 *All About Eve*.

The plot of *Wall Street* deals with Bud's desire to work for Gordon Gekko. A little success turns Bud's head around, and he allows himself to get involved with some dirty dealing. When he realizes that his fa-ther, a blue-collar airline worker, will go down with the bankruptcy of the airline as part of his deal done with Gekko, Bud wears a wire and gets Gekko to confess. The most memorable scene is when Michael as Gekko delivers his famous "Greed is good" speech.

The film did not qualify as a water-cooler conversation piece the way *Fatal Attraction* did, but, like *Fatal*, it arrived at the height of the Reagan finance-gone-wild administration, when money was flowing freely and everyone was invested in the stock market, with cracks in the profit facade just starting to show; two months before the film's debut the stock market crashed five hundred points, and a full-blown recession followed.

In its way, the film was not only economically prescient but was as subversive as *Platoon*, stripping away the propriety that masked crimi-nality on Wall Street at the time. In Stone's vision, the dirty playing was nothing less than an attack on the American system.

Stone was eager to begin production and pressed Michael to finish up his last dialogue-looping sessions for *Fatal Attraction* in Los Ange-les and fly back to New York City to start work on the film. Shooting began on *Wall Street* that April, and the chemistry between Stone and Michael was apparent early on. Michael had nothing but praise for Stone: "That's where I learned that a director doesn't have to be a pa-triarch. He can just be a tough director and get the best work out of all the actors. Oliver Stone tests his actors rather than console them. And as a result, you look at all of his films and in almost every film his male lead has probably given the best performance of their life."

FATAL ATTRACTION OPENED on September 18, 1987, signal-ing the start of the holiday season, when the year's most important, Oscar-bound films open. In the *Los Angeles Times*, Jack Mathews wrote that Michael's weakness as a leading man was key to the film's success: "When Douglas' Dan Gallagher ruffled the sheets in *Fatal Attraction*, audiences trusted him in a way they might not have if he were played by Richard Gere." J. Hoberman in the *Village Voice* also thought it had to do with Douglas's cinematic image but saw that image a little differently, as the "well-fed yuppie with a face that bobs and weaves around the frame, pretending to menace the camera like a kid's clenched fist. Douglas has perfected his ability to project a glowering sense of aggrieved, put-upon masculinity, taking on the defense of home, hearth, and career against a succession of castrating women. . . . [H]e is the heroic, resentful, white-guy, white-collar, heterosexual victim, the social hieroglyph and talk-show staple we might call the Mighty Kvetch."

Janet Maslin, writing in the *New York Times*: "*Fatal Attraction* is a thoroughly conventional thriller at heart, but its heart is not what will attract notice. As directed by Mr. Lyne, who also made *9½ Weeks* and *Flashdance*, it has an ingeniously teasing style that overrules substance at every turn. Mr. Lyne, who displays a lot more range this time, takes a brilliantly manipulative approach to what might have been a humdrum subject and shapes a soap opera of exceptional power. . . . Mr. Lyne is well versed in making anything—a person, a room, a pile of dishes in a kitchen sink—seem tactile, rich and sexy. . . . [I]t also offers a well-detailed, credibly drawn romantic triangle that's sure to spark a lot of cocktail-party chatter. . . . It's even difficult to tell anything about this man's inner life from Mr. Douglas's performance, and that may be the point. He doesn't understand it either."

Roger Ebert: "*Fatal Attraction* is a spellbinding psychological thriller that could have been a great movie if the filmmakers had not thrown character and plausibility to the winds in the last minutes to give us their version of a grown-up *Friday the 13th*." And J. Hoberman gave Michael his greatest review when he called the film "Douglas' *Spartacus*."

In its opening weekend, *Fatal Attraction* took in $7.6 million; it grossed $157 million in its initial domestic release ($321 million, foreign and domestic, and another $70 million including cable and video), for a picture that cost $14 million to make. Michael's salary was reportedly between $4 million and $6 million, plus percentage points, making him, at the age of forty-three, one of the highest-paid actors in

Hollywood. *Fatal Attraction* was the second-highest-grossing picture of 1987, just behind Leonard Nimoy's *Three Men and a Baby*, a modest and inexplicably successful fish-out-of-water comedy about three bachelors having to care for an infant, which grossed $168 million.[7]

WALL STREET WAS released on December 11, three months after *Fatal Attraction*, to mixed-to-good reviews. Roger Ebert: "Stone's most impressive achievement in this film is to allow all the financial wheeling and dealing to seem complicated and convincing, and yet always have it make sense. The movie can be followed by anybody, because the details of stock manipulation are all filtered through transparent layers of greed. Most of the time we know what's going on. All of the time, we know why." He also liked Michael's performance but thought Sheen was miscast. "I would have preferred a young actor who seemed more rapacious, such as James Spader, who has a supporting role in the movie. If the film has a flaw, it is that Sheen never seems quite relentless enough to move in Gekko's circle."

Vincent Canby, writing in the *New York Times*, was less enthusiastic: "Mr. Stone's heart is in the right place but, ultimately, his wit fails him. The movie crashes in a heap of platitudes that remind us that honesty is, after all, the best policy. . . . [A]t its best, 'Wall Street' is an unequal struggle. At its worst, it's a muddle." But he loved Michael's performance. "Mr. Douglas, in the funniest, canniest performance of his career, plays him with the wit and charm of Old Scratch wearing an Italian-designer wardrobe."

The rest of the important reviews pretty much followed suit: nobody really cared for the film's hackneyed plot line (the climactic, plot-

---

7   The other eight films are Tony Scott's *Beverly Hills Cop II* ($154 million), Barry Levinson's *Good Morning, Vietnam* ($124 million), Norman Jewison's *Moonstruck* ($80 million), Brian De Palma's *The Untouchables* ($76 million), Herbert Ross's *The Secret of My Success* ($67 million), John Badham's *Stakeout* ($66 million), Richard Donner's *Lethal Weapon* ($65 million), and George Miller's *The Witches of Eastwick* ($64 million).

resolving wearing of a wire is as overused a cliché as there is in film); most were so-so about Sheen; and virtually all thought Michael was the best thing in it, playing a character with echoes of Burt Lancaster's J. J. Hunsecker in Alexander Mackendrick's 1957 *Sweet Smell of Success*.

Michael, however, preferred his performance in *Fatal Attraction* to the one he gave in *Wall Street*. Regarding Dan Gallagher, he said, "If the situation . . . *if* the situation ever occurred, I'd like to think I'd have told my wife, especially after the ante got raised. But I don't know what I'd have done. That's what makes it fun to play that guy." As for Gordon Gekko: "Gekko's conduct is not in my moral vocabulary. I believe you can conduct yourself in a basically moral sense and succeed. I've always tried to conduct myself in a decent way. . . . Hollywood is a small community and your reputation is one of the few things that you have."

At Oscar time the Academy completely misread the pulse of public opinion. If any movie in recent history had stirred the interest and emotions of its audience and made a killing at the box office while doing so, *Fatal Attraction* was it and *Wall Street* wasn't, but the latter was the film that received all the attention and accolades. As for *Fatal Attraction*, the Academy tossed a few nominations its way, but gave it no coveted golden statuettes. As Gail Kinn and Jim Piazza wittily put it in their book, *The Academy Awards*, "*Fatal Attraction* couldn't manage to pull a rabbit out of [Oscar's] hat, much less out of a pot of boiling water."

THE SIXTIETH ANNUAL Academy Awards ceremonies were held on April 11, 1988, at the Shrine Auditorium, adjacent to the USC campus, where they had been moved to accommodate the award show's red carpet, which every year kept attracting larger crowds. The ceremonies, hosted by Chevy Chase, opened with a listless version of "I Hope I Get It" from *A Chorus Line* that was as dull as it was when the movie itself was released two years earlier, as it played to a half-filled venue due to a massive L.A. traffic jam.

The nominees for Best Picture of the year were Bernardo Bertolucci's *The Last Emperor*, James L. Brooks's *Broadcast News*, *Fatal Attraction*, John Boorman's *Hope and Glory*, and *Moonstruck*. The two films that dominated the awards that night were *The Last Emperor* (a box office failure, something the Academy normally shuns), which won all nine Oscars it was nominated for, including Best Picture, and *Moonstruck*, which was nominated for six and won three, including Cher for Best Actress, Olympia Dukakis for Best Supporting Actress, and John Patrick Shanley for Best Screenplay. *Fatal Attraction* received six nominations, including one for Glenn Close for Best Actress, one for Anne Archer for Best Supporting Actress, and one for Best Picture, and won none. Michael was nominated for Best Actor for *Wall Street* but not for *Fatal Attraction*.[8]

As the evening dragged on and Bertolucci's *The Last Emperor* piled up wins, both the *Fatal Attraction* people and the *Wall Street* crowd began to noticeably fidget in their seats. When it was time for the Best Actor Award to be given, Marlee Matlin, the hearing-impaired actress who had won a Best Actress Oscar the previous year for her performance in Randa Haines's *Children of a Lesser God*, did the presenting. After signing a quick introduction about the joys of acting, she vocally announced the names herself. The first belonged to William Hurt, who received a light round of applause—he was not in attendance and not especially well liked in Hollywood. The second was Michael Douglas (for *Wall Street*), to whom the audience gave a noticeably louder cheer than it had for Hurt. Dressed resplendently in black tie, with long, flowing hair neatly pushed into place and hanging over his collar, Michael smiled to the crowd and the camera. Matlin's enthusiastic

---

8   The six nominations *Fatal Attraction* received were Best Picture (Stanley Jaffe and Sherry Lansing); Best Director (Adrian Lyne); Best Actress (Glenn Close—her fourth nomination without a win); Best Supporting Actress (Anne Archer); Best Editing (Michael Kahn and Peter E. Berger); and Best Writing, Screenplay Based on Material from Another Medium (James Dearden). The other four nominees for Best Actor were William Hurt, *Broadcast News*; Marcello Mastroianni, Nikita Mikhalkov's *Dark Eyes*; Jack Nicholson, Hector Babenco's *Ironweed*; and Robin Williams, *Good Morning, Vietnam*.

reading of Robin Williams's name for *Good Morning, Vietnam* brought even louder cheers, mostly of appreciation for her struggle with this difficult-for-her title. She then announced Marcello Mastroianni, a crowd favorite who also wasn't there, and finally Jack Nicholson, for Hector Babenco's *Ironweed*. Nicholson received the loudest ovation. Dressed in a tux and wearing his signature dark glasses, Nicholson flashed his signature grin.

And then Matlin ripped open the envelope, said softly, in her special way, "Let's see," then spread her arms wide and announced, "Michael Douglas in *Wall Street!*"

The audience erupted. Michael stood up, bent over to kiss Diandra, and shook the outstretched hand of comedian and actor Albert Brooks, who minutes earlier had lost the Best Supporting Actor Oscar for his work in *Broadcast News* to Sean Connery, for *The Untouchables.* Michael then strode toward the stage while the orchestra played "Fly Me to the Moon." He was handed the Oscar by Marlee. He smiled, looked around the room, and, as the applause died down, began to speak: "Thank you . . . thank you all very much. I really want to thank the actors' branch of the Academy first, for just being a nominee with four actors I really admire, and at least one that I admire and consider a close friend." He nodded toward Jack Nicholson. "Thank you for that. And for this fellow [the Oscar] from all of the Academy I just want to share it with all the good work that was done by all the branches, whether you were nominated or not tonight. This is all with you. A large part of this award belongs to Oliver Stone. Not only as the director, but having the courage to cast me in a part that not many people thought I could play. I'll always be eternally grateful for that. And as a writer, Oliver and Stanley Weiser wrote a part that was the best part that I've ever had in my career. To Charlie and Martin Sheen, two wonderful actors who happen to be father and son, I thank them all very much for their help." After thanking a host of producers and studio people, he paused, took a breath and said, "I'd like to dedicate this award to William Darrid, Diana Douglas Darrid, Anne Douglas, and Kirk Douglas, my parents and stepparents, who have been extremely supportive and loving to me over the years. In particular to my father, who I don't think ever missed one of my college productions, for his continued support and for helping a son step out of the shadow. I'll be eternally grateful to you, Dad." At this point the audience interrupted the speech with a round of loud applause. When it died down, Michael concluded: "Finally, to my wife, Diandra, and all my old friends who are smiling with me tonight, thank you. And to all you movie buffs I just really appreciate for making this a wonderful night for me, thank you. And good night, Cameron, I love you!" With that, the music rose and Michael triumphantly left the stage, golden statuette in his hand.

Later, he reflected upon the personal impact of that night: "It was tremendous . . . there are very few second-generation actors who've succeeded at all, so that question is there. It was a lovely night."

And a game changer for Michael. It was the first time he felt he had definitively stepped out of the giant shadow of his father's fame. He could, for the first time, walk alone and like a man.

When asked later about which Oscar meant more to him, the one for Best Film for his producing work on *Cuckoo's Nest* or this one for Best Actor, he said, "They're both hugely important to me, of course, but I guess the fact that the one for *Cuckoo's Nest* came so early on in my career meant I didn't feel I'd earned it as much as the one for *Wall Street*. Actually, though, I probably had a better night the time I won the Golden Globes [earlier that year] for *Wall Street*. I was staying in the Hotel Bel-Air"—it was the Beverly Hilton—"and as I was leaving with my mother to go to the ceremony we passed George Harrison. . . . [Later that night after] I won and went through the whole press thing afterwards and came out the end of it and there was nobody there . . . I went to Trader Vic's for a drink [the Hilton's legendary bar and restaurant], then went back to the hotel, kind of excited but feeling a little sorry for myself.

"Anyway, I'm in my room around 12:30 a.m. and the phone rings and it's George Harrison saying, 'Hello, Michael. I just got back to the hotel and my mate and I thought we'd come by and say hi.' I was like, 'Wow, George Harrison's coming round!' And a couple of minutes later, there's a knock on my door and in he walks. Following him is the biggest dog I've ever seen. And following the dog was Bob Dylan. Man, that was one of the most amazing nights of my life."

AT FORTY-THREE, eleven years after *Cuckoo's Nest* swept the big four in 1976, Gordon Gekko finally gave Michael something his father had never received: a Best Actor Academy Award.

Once again, Kirk didn't attend the awards ceremony where his son was being honored, but this time he handled it with style and class. Having just returned from a European promo tour for his latest film, Jeff Kanew's *Tough Guys*, co-starring his good friend Burt Lancaster, he threw a small post-Oscar party for the entire Douglas clan at his Beverly Hills home. On this night, the patriarch of one of Hollywood's royal families graciously deferred to his son.

Everyone was there waiting to congratulate Michael: his brother, Joel, forty-one, a successful producer who often worked with his big brother; his half brother Peter, thirty-one, the eldest son of Kirk and Anne, a voting producer of the Academy, a voice dubber on several films, and the writer/director/producer of *A Tiger's Tale* (1987), starring Ann-Margret and C. Thomas Howell; and his half brother Eric, twenty-nine, the second of Kirk's sons from his second marriage, an actor who had appeared in several small roles in films, including Michael Ritchie's 1986 hit vehicle for Eddie Murphy, *Golden Child*.

When Michael and Diandra arrived, the champagne was popped, followed by hugs and kisses for all. According to someone in attendance, later that night Kirk took Michael aside and wanted to talk about, of all things, fatherhood. Kirk reportedly asked Michael what kind of father Michael thought he had been. Michael smiled and told him he was always "loopy" and uptight, never there for his family, always jumping from one picture to the other.

Kirk smiled back and said, "You mean just like you now?"

CHAPTER 14

*I'm very, very lucky. I got married relatively late in life. It
would have been a mess if it had happened earlier. I had the
usual troubled adolescence and lots of career and personal lows
in my twenties. But now I have my health. There have been no
major tragedies in my life. Like I said, life's been sort of nice this
year.*

—MICHAEL DOUGLAS

AFTER THE DOUBLE WHAMMY OF *FATAL ATTRACTION*
and *Wall Street*, Hollywood rolled over on its back for Michael.
Where once he was considered not strong or hot enough to carry a
picture on his own, he was now being offered the leadership of three
different studios, all of which he turned down. He was too smart for
that game. To Michael, running a studio had to be a losing proposition on all counts, mostly for him, because it meant he would have to
move back to Los Angeles permanently, and that was simply not possible if he wanted to stay married. Even though he and Diandra were
hanging together by a thread and everyone seemed to know it, for the
time being, at least, he was going to have to be an independent Hollywood moviemaker based in New York City.

TWO YEARS AFTER Michael joined Mercury, the partnership
had not produced a single film, and in July 1988 he and Phillips announced a "revamping." In Hollywoodese that meant that Michael

had decided to withdraw from the company.[1] His reason? According to Phillips, "We needed to introduce more flexibility in the [Mercury/Douglas] relationship so that Michael can pursue the opportunities he has now," Phillips announced to the public.

Michael split from Mercury because, after carefully studying the details of the deal and the potential of the company, he decided it wasn't going anywhere with stalled TV movies starring over-the-hill actors like John Travolta. Also, from this post-Oscar vantage point, the structure of the original deal was not right, with monies flowing the wrong way. Michael had partnered with Phillips and bought into Mercury with a percentage of rights shares from all the past films he had produced, reaching all the way back to *Cuckoo's Nest*. After the split, Michael returned 3,000,000 shares of Mercury common stock, kept about half a million (equal to a 4.6 percent interest in the company), and reacquired all the production rights to his own films.

Instead of working with Mercury, Michael told Phillips, he wanted to expand his involvement in the many liberal political causes he backed. He had already done considerable fund-raising for several charities, an interest that had begun even before the consciousness awareness he had experienced making *The China Syndrome*, reaching all the way back to his college days. The causes and the commitment were no doubt real and meaningful to Michael, but Hollywood insiders insisted the real reason for the in-and-out situation was that Michael discovered early on that personally he didn't like Phillips, or the deal, felt their chemistry didn't match, and didn't want to get in any deeper than he already was.

As if to underscore it was Mercury and not Michael, although he insisted to Phillips and everyone else he had no interest in making any more movies that year, Michael quickly and quietly took suite 719 at the Beverly Wilshire as his new production offices so he would not

---

1   Robert Harmon's *The Tender* was eventually released in 1991 on TV in America as *The Tender*; its title was later changed to *Eyes of an Angel*. After Travolta's comeback in 1994 via Quentin Tarantino's *Pulp Fiction*, the film was released on video with its original title and on DVD in 2002. Michael Douglas is listed as one of the producers.

have to spend so much time flying across the country to pursue new deals. Even the ninety-minute commute to Santa Barbara, where he stayed in his house whenever he was going to be on the West Coast for more than a few days, was exhausting him.

The Beverly Wilshire appeared to be the hotel of choice for either unhappily married movie stars or perennially single ones: both Warren Beatty and Steve McQueen kept high-floor suites there. Beatty did it because he was a bachelor; McQueen said he needed office space apart from the North Malibu home he shared with his second wife, Ali MacGraw (McQueen met his next wife in the hotel's lobby).

Not coincidentally, while Michael was in Hollywood, Jaffe and Lansing approached him about a new project, this one back at Columbia, where Dawn Steel had been elevated to its head after the studio's former top chief, David Puttnam, had resigned. At the same time, Danny DeVito wanted Michael to star in a film DeVito was going to direct. Also, Paramount and Fox wanted him to travel to Europe to promote *Fatal Attraction* and *Wall Street*, respectively. And that May, he was scheduled to make an appearance at the Cannes Film Festival in the southeast of France. Being the ever-dutiful company man, he agreed to all of the promotion necessary for both pictures. At least part of his decision was based on his wanting to sever all remaining ties with Mercury, which was proving a long and difficult separation to effect. As he was preparing to take off for the festival, he told both Jaffe and Lansing and his friend DeVito that he would think over all their offers.

At the British premiere of *Fatal Attraction*, the tabloid press surrounded Michael, firing questions at him as if he were a captured criminal—not about the film or his role in it, but about the state of his marriage to Diandra, following escalating rumors they were splitting up for real this time. After one particularly obnoxious reporter got into Michael's face, he turned the tables and asked the reporter, "How long have you been married? Do you fool around?"

The reporter declined to answer.

◈

IT WAS IN Cannes 1988 that the cracks in his marriage, which he had so vehemently denied to the press, became visible to the public for the first time.

Her name was Loredana Romito, and she was an Italian B-movie starlet, the kind that flock to the European film festival circuit in the hopes of being discovered, or at least photographed on the Croisette, preferably in as little clothing as possible. She was officially there for the out-of-competition screening of her movie, *Fatal Temptation*, a cheap rip-off of *Fatal Attraction* in which she played the Glenn Close–type character. Some called it a satire, but it was not that good; cheap exploitation, or soft-core porn, would be was a more accurate description.

At an afterparty that both had attended, she was formally introduced to Michael. She insisted they be photographed together, and Michael graciously consented. She was squeezed into a tight, low-cut black dress, and leaned into Michael for the camera. Less than twenty-four hours later, the photo showed up in American newspapers. And in Diandra's hands. She had declined to attend Cannes with Michael, and now here she was looking at her husband as he clutched some big-breasted actress tightly against him, his arm around her hips, a big fat grin on his face.

Romito later told the European press, and anybody else who cared, that she had had a brief two-day affair with Michael at the festival. Although Michael later denied any involvement with her, he was photographed with her again after Cannes in Paris, Rome, and later that year in Japan. After Cannes, he left by himself for Hawaii for a much-needed extended holiday.

Back home, Diandra suffered a miscarriage.

What especially galled her was how in every interview he had sat for during this period, such as the one he gave to the *Ladies' Home Journal* in 1988, he talked with extra-sensitive empathy about the importance of the family unit and the added pressure women faced: "It is a very difficult time for women right now. . . . The women's movement has been effective in terms of equal rights, but it puts undue pressure on women's personal lives and takes away the art of homemaking as a valid alternative."

Michael was reportedly devastated by the miscarriage—apparently not enough, though, to fly to her side. Instead he flew to Hollywood to sign the final dissolution papers with Mercury and to meet with Dawn Steel at Columbia and then with Sam Jaffe and Sherry Lansing about their new project. He never made it back east to see Diandra.

STEEL WAS ABLE to convince Michael to return to Columbia, the studio he had vowed never to work for again, by assuring him things would be different this time with her at the helm. David Begelman was old Hollywood; she was new—and so was Michael.

The key to the deal was Steel's offer of a three-picture non-exclusive producing deal that did not require him to star in any of the films but allowed him to do so if he wanted. It also didn't prohibit him from dealing separate and apart with Jaffe-Lansing. To seal the deal, Michael was made chairman of a new company, Stonebridge Productions, and given offices at Columbia's Burbank studios and, at his insistence, a branch office in New York. Additional setup costs for the New York office ran $1 million, which Columbia was happy to pay.[2] To make the deal even sweeter, Michael was allowed to take on a new partner, Rick Bieber, to handle Stonebridge's day-to-day operations; "allowed" meaning the studio would pay for his salary. Bieber had a strong pedigree, having recently been the head of Home Box Office Pictures.

---

2 Bigstick had given up producing films in favor of speculating in real estate. Michael was a canny investor. He also invested heavily in a recording company, starting up a new label and signing bands, and letting Cameron be a part of that company. As a silent partner, he also purchased at least part of the popular *L.A. Weekly*, then an alternative and free-swinging quasi-political, social, and pop-cultural rag whose back-of-the-book massage parlor ads helped keep the otherwise free newspaper financially healthy. Not all his investments panned out. Years later, he went into a complicated film development and production deal with Zack Norman, his friend and co-star in *Romancing the Stone*, that eventually wound up in litigation.

However, unlike with Phillips, it was made clear that Michael was the only one in charge.

The new deal was set to start on August 1, 1988.

Meanwhile, Sherry Lansing and Stanley Jaffe had an independent cop thriller set with Paramount they wanted Michael to star in called *Black Rain*, to be filmed on location in Japan; they would produce, he would act. He enthusiastically said yes, even if it meant giving up some creative control: "Acting is tunnel vision," he said. "Producing is 360-degree vision. To do both at once is almost a contradiction in terms. To be the producer is to be part policeman, part nanny. To be the star is to be the cherished and gifted child. Producer slash actor is very awkward for people. They don't know how to deal with you. You've hired everybody who does everything. You've signed the contracts. People don't like to applaud the employer. . . . I love being an actor for hire. No one cherishes that more than I do."

IN *BLACK RAIN,* two New York City police officers (Michael Douglas and Andy Garcia) capture a member of the yakuza, the Japanese organized crime syndicates, and have to deliver him to the Japanese police. While in Japan, the criminal escapes, and the two cops are drawn deeper into the murky nightside fringes of the Japanese underworld. It was a glossy action film, shimmery, rough, tough, neo-noir, entertaining, and utterly meaningless, set against the underbelly of Japan's neon nightlife. To prepare himself for the role, Michael rode around with the New York police in midnight patrols and worked with a trainer to build up his body for the highly physical role of the rough and tough I-don't-give-a-damn anti-Japanese detective Nick Conklin.

It was while filming *Black Rain* that Michael reconnoitered with Romito, allowing himself once again to be openly photographed with her in places and ways that did not suggest they were going to church together.

After *Black Rain*, Michael went directly into *The War of the Roses* at Fox, a film that reunited him with Kathleen Turner under the direction of his old pal Danny DeVito, the reason he had agreed to do the film. DeVito played a divorce lawyer who narrated one long argument between a couple who are in the midst of a terrible divorce but are forced to share the same house during the proceedings. The film ends, after an especially brutal battle, with a rather gruesome dénouement. (The family is named Rose, to suggest, perhaps, the magnitude of the other War of the Roses, between the Houses of York and Lancaster in fifteenth-century England.) It was supposed to be a comedy.

The film echoes one of the staples of Hollywood in the 1940s, the tragic divorce, usually handled in comic form and with a "happy" resolution to satisfy the censors (in those days the Production Code still considered couples divorcing taboo). The best of the lot was Leo McCarey's *The Awful Truth* with Cary Grant and Irene Dunne. Suffice it to say, DeVito is no McCarey, Kathleen Turner no Irene Dunne, and Michael no Cary Grant. And the film was truly awful. The physical comedy was stunt riddled and clunky, with overtones of *Romancing the Stone*—light on the romance, heavy on the stone.

It was DeVito's second feature-length directorial effort, following his 1987's *Throw Momma from the Train.* As he was much better known for his acting than for his direction, and a star nowhere near the power and box-office clout of Michael-as-producer, in order to get his films made, he also had to star in them. In *Throw Momma*, DeVito's role was essential; in *War of the Roses*, it was superfluous. Smartly, he had gone to his two good friends Michael and Kathleen and asked them to be in the picture as a personal favor to him, but as he quickly learned, favors rarely exist in Hollywood when there is a bottom line involved. The two insisted on big salaries plus healthy percentages of the gross that pushed the production budget to $50 million, which made the film a bigger risk for Twentieth Century Fox than it had anticipated, even with (or because it had) two of Hollywood's biggest stars.

BLACK RAIN OPENED on September 22, 1989, to mostly positive reviews. Michael Wilmington, writing in the *Los Angeles Times*, said,

"In *Black Rain* director Ridley Scott and his team pump in so much pyrotechnic razzle-dazzle that the movie becomes a triumph of matter over mind. It's a blast of pure sensation, shallow but scintillating, like a great rock melody, superbly produced, where the music pumps you up even as the lyrics drag you down."

Roger Ebert in the *Chicago Sun-Times*: "Even given all of its inconsistencies, implausibilities and recycled clichés, *Black Rain* might have been entertaining if the filmmakers had found the right note for the material. But this is a designer movie, all look and no heart, and the Douglas character is curiously unsympathetic. He plays it so cold and distant that the heartfelt scenes ring false. And the colors in the movie—steel grays, gloomy blues and wet concrete, occasionally illuminated by neon signs, showers of sparks and exploding automobiles— underline the general gloom. . . . The story of *Black Rain* is thin and prefabricated and doesn't stand up to much scrutiny, so Scott distracts us with overwrought visuals."

Vincent Canby, in the *New York Times*: "Mr. Douglas throws himself wholeheartedly into a role that is short on both interest and charm. He acts hard. Mr. Garcia's role is less off-putting and he's good company as long as he's in the picture. Kate Capshaw, who looks like a Vogue model, is a most unlikely Osaka bar hostess. . . . Ridley Scott's 'Black Rain,' based on an original screenplay by Craig Bolotin and Warren Lewis, plays as if it had been written in the course of production. There seems to have been more desperation off the screen than ever gets into the movie. As bad movies go, however, the American 'Black Rain' is easy to sit through, mostly because of the way Mr. Scott and his production associates capture the singular look of contemporary urban Japan."[3]

Indeed, for all its shiny, buff exterior, the film was instantly forgettable. There was nothing about it except the Mylar-like visuals that

---

3   A Japanese film also called *Black Rain*, Shohei Imamura's Japanese-language film exploring the legacy of the atomic bomb that exploded over Hiroshima on August 6, 1945, opened the same week. It was that *Black Rain* that played the New York Film Festival.

had become a trademark of Ridley Scott's vision since his 1982 futuristic thriller *Blade Runner*. (Many believed killing off Andy Garcia's character midway through the film also killed the audience's interest in it.) If Michael here was trying to combine the characters of his last two megahits, the passive/explosive Dan Gallagher from *Fatal Attraction* and the hard-as-nails Gordon Gekko, the mix didn't take—too much yeast. And on Michael's part, a notable lack of sexual intensity.

Yet, despite the Garcia misstep, audiences loved the film. It opened at number one, grossing just under $10 million its first week, stayed on top the second, and with a $30 million budget grossed nearly $43 million domestically and $88 million worldwide. *Black Rain* was a certified hit in almost every way except creatively for Michael, even though it owed its success to his star power. And for all that success, it was dwarfed at the box office by several other big movies, headed by Steven Spielberg's *Indiana Jones and the Last Crusade* ($475 million, the number one film of the year), Tim Burton's *Batman* ($411 million), and Robert Zemeckis's *Back to the Future Part II* ($331 million).

THE WAR OF THE ROSES opened on December 8, in time for the big holiday season, and proved another smash for Michael at the box office, $87 million in its initial domestic release, outgrossing *Black Rain* in the States, making it the eleventh-highest-grossing U.S. film worldwide and the twelfth-highest-earning domestically.

It was especially well received by the critics. Janet Maslin, writing in the *New York Times*, said, "Mr. DeVito happens to have more of a taste for gleeful malice than any cinematic figure this side of Freddy Kruger. . . . The film's outstanding nastiness, which is often diabolically funny until a poorly staged final battle sequence simply takes things too far, has something real and recognizable at its core. The Roses may be caricatures, but the rise and fall of their romance and the viciousness of their fighting will be elements that many viewers can understand. . . . [T]he film's tone may be slightly shaky at times, but when its humor works, it's very funny indeed. Mr. Douglas and

Ms. Turner have never been more comfortable a team, and each of them is at his or her comic best when being as awful as both are required to be here."

Roger Ebert, in the *Chicago Sun-Times*: "*The War of the Roses* stars Michael Douglas and Kathleen Turner as the doomed Roses, and although both actors also teamed with DeVito in *Romancing the Stone*, no two movies could be more dissimilar. *The War of the Roses* is a black, angry, bitter, unrelenting comedy, a war between the sexes that makes James Thurber's work on the same subject look almost resigned by comparison. . . . There are a great many funny moments in *The War of the Roses*, including one in which Turner (playing an ex-gymnast) springs to her feet from a prone position on her lawyer's floor in one lithe movement and another in which Douglas makes absolutely certain that the fish Turner is serving some of her clients for dinner will have that fishy smell." Ebert put the film in the tenth spot on his list of the best movies of the year.

The film could be taken as a fantasy extension of Michael's relationship with Diandra, perhaps one of the reasons he wanted to do it. Its themes dealt with both suppression and release. During production, it at once kept him away from Diandra and reminded him of her every day, in the guise of Kathleen Turner, who kept wanting to leave the project because she hated the script. She actually turned it down twice and agreed to make it only if the characters were made older, so she wouldn't seem even more miscast than she already was.

Both Kathleen and Michael were doing some "doubling" in this film as well, mirroring their long-standing offscreen romantic association, if somewhat darkly (one of the real reasons Turner may not have wanted to make it). And it was hard work. The final sequence, with Michael and Turner dangling from a chandelier before they fall to their unfunny deaths, took three full days to shoot.

Michael was well aware of the thematic connections the film had to his marriage. "Yes," he told one reporter, "I admit, I should align what happened to the Roses to my own situation. I could see firsthand how marital situations can just slide out of control for a succession of reasons."

When Jaffe and Lansing threw an extravagant pre-opening screening party for the film, Michael showed up without Diandra.

As an actor, he was hotter than ever. But as a husband, he was a failure. Threatening once again to file for divorce because of Michael's endless work schedule and the increasing reports in the press of his playing around, Diandra gave Michael a new ultimatum: marriage counseling or legal separation.

Michael countered this latest threat with a promise to Diandra that he would not do any more acting for a long time but would continue to wear his producing hat.

MICHAEL'S STONEBRIDGE, meanwhile, had a firm commitment to begin production on its first film, Joel Schumacher's *Flatliners*, with Julia Roberts and Kiefer Sutherland (another real-life couple "doubled" on-screen—they were engaged at the time); upon its release, on August 10, 1990, the film grossed more than $90 million, a solid moneymaker for Stonebridge and reestablished Michael as one of the most powerful producers in the industry.[4]

Michael was then drawn to two scripts he thought might be right for him to act in, despite his promise to Diandra. One was *Shining Through*, a mindless soap opera that was based on the bestselling novel by Susan Isaacs and had a plot line similar to *Romancing the Stone* but a far different feel. An ordinary American woman, in this instance a secretary, gets involved with international intrigue replete with Nazis under the table. Michael liked the part of Ed Leland, believing he could pull off the role of the lawyer/spy without breaking a sweat.

---

4   Stonebridge did not enjoy continued success. Its next three films all flopped—Sheldon Lettich's 1991 *Double Impact*, a Jean-Claude Van Damme vehicle; Craig Baxley's 1991 *Stone Cold*, starring muscle-bound hunk of the month Brian Bosworth; and Martin Davidson's 1991 *Hard Promises*, with Sissy Spacek and William Petersen. Only *Flatliners*, the only film that Michael had personally produced, ever made any money for Stonebridge. In 1992 he split with Rick Bieber and heavily cut back the staff of the company.

The other was something called *Basic Instinct*, with a role right in his wheelhouse, a detective with dual addictions—drinking and a beautiful, sexually crazy women.

Shining Through seemed an easy enough deal. Fox okayed a production budget to include on-location filming to accurately evoke the film's World War II setting. The shoot was originally intended for Budapest, but the fall of the Berlin Wall made it possible to film in East Germany. The locations were quickly changed to East and West Berlin and Potsdam, and production started in October 1990. Studio work was now scheduled to be done at DEFA Studios, the state film studios of East Germany. But because all of Berlin's great train stations had been destroyed in the war, the production had to move to the Leipzig Hauptbahnhof, the largest rail station in Europe, built in 1915.

Michael didn't complain about anything. As a producer on an acting assignment, he knew better, even when the phones didn't work. Perhaps that was a mixed blessing—being in Europe allowed Michael to rekindle his relationship with British heiress Sabrina Guinness, whom he had first met and briefly dated in London. She was the former girlfriend of Prince Charles and had more recently been seen in public with actor Steve Guttenberg. She had also dated Mick Jagger and Jack Nicholson (and after Michael, Paul McCartney). One night, on a brief furlough from shooting, Michael flew to London to meet up with Guinness, and the two were caught by a photographer from a European magazine that splayed their picture across its front pages. Soon everybody—including Diandra—knew they had been together in London while Michael was supposed to be filming and behaving himself in Germany.

WHAT MAY BE SAID of *Shining Through*, in addition to the fact that Hitler's Germany didn't make a very good backdrop for a soap opera, is that it gave soap operas a bad name. American half-Jewish blond beauty Linda Voss (played by the decidedly non-Jewish American blond beauty Melanie Griffith), spying for America in the heart

With Karl Malden in *The Streets of San Francisco*. They costarred in this series from 1972–1976. *Rebel Road Archives*

Holding his Oscar for coproducing 1975's *One Flew Over the Cuckoo's Nest*. Kirk did not show up for the presentation of the awards. He watched the ceremony at home on TV. *AP Photo*

With his new bride, Diandra, attending the 1977 Oscar ceremonies in Hollywood. *Copyright Bettmann/Corbis/AP Images*

With Geneviève Bujold in 1978's *Coma*. *Rebel Road Archives*

With Jane Fonda in *The China Syndrome*, 1979. *Rebel Road Archives*

A bearded, smiling Michael miscast as a prematurely retired baseball player who falls in and out of love with mathematics professor Jill Clayburgh in *It's My Turn*, 1980. *Rebel Road Archives*

With Hal Holbrook in *The Star Chamber*, 1983. *Rebel Road Archives*

Lobby poster for 1985's sequel to *Romancing the Stone*, *The Jewel of the Nile*. *Rebel Road Archives*

With Alyson Reed in *A Chorus Line*, 1985, made in New York City. Michael acted during the day and spent his evenings as a producer, prepping *The Jewel of the Nile*.
Rebel Road Archives

With Glenn Close in the shocking climax of 1987's *Fatal Attraction*. The film turned Michael into a sex symbol, Close into a star, and made a killing at the box office.
Rebel Road Archives

Michael's portrayal of Gordon Gekko in 1987's *Wall Street* won him his second Oscar, his first for Best Actor. *Rebel Road Archives*

Reuniting with Kathleen Turner and Danny DeVito in DeVito's *The War of the Roses*, 1989, a black comedy about a crumbling marriage, a subject Michael knew something about. *Rebel Road Archives*

With Andy Garcia in 1989's *Black Rain*, a film Michael made for Sherry Lansing and Stanley Jaffe at Paramount.
Rebel Road Archives

Doing a little publicity with Maria Shriver on the Sony Pictures lot, 1992.
Rebel Road Archives

Michael carrying Melanie Griffith to safety in the soap-opera-ish *Shining Through*, 1992. The film made no sense, but set the table for Michael's spectacular other 1992 film, *Basic Instinct*. *Rebel Road Archives*

Michael getting to know Sharon Stone in 1992's *Basic Instinct*. The film nearly ended his marriage; not long after, he entered rehab. *Rebel Road Archives*.

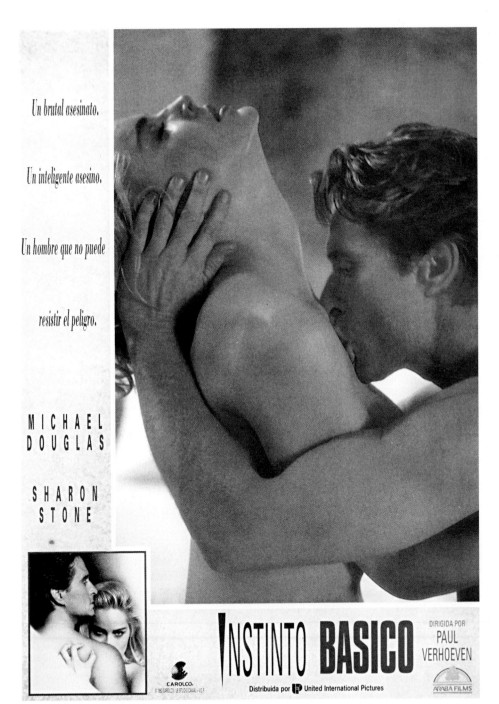

Basic Instinct created a worldwide sensation. A poster for the Spanish version.
Rebel Road Archives

A remarkably different-looking Michael Douglas in the post-rehab, off-beat *Falling Down*, 1993. *Rebel Road Archives*

Back on more familiar, sexual turf in 1994's *Disclosure*, costarring the seductive Demi Moore. *Rebel Road Archives*

With Annette Bening in the pre-Lewinsky ode to the Clinton presidency, *The American President*, 1995. *Rebel Road Archives*

In 1996's *The Ghost and the Darkness*, a film he coproduced with Michael Reuther, with a screenplay by William Goldman. The film disappeared quickly and so did the partnership between Michael and Reuther. *Rebel Road Archives*

With Gwyneth Paltrow in the Hitchcock-lite redo of *Dial M for Murder*, *A Perfect Murder*, 1998. Reportedly, the twenty-five-year-old Paltrow objected to having to play the romantic leading lady opposite the fifty-four-year-old Michael, feeling he was too old for the part. They never worked together again. *Rebel Road Archives*

With Robert Downey Jr., in *Wonder Boys*, 2000, one of Michael's best films, though it never found its audience. *Rebel Road Archives*

Father and son in 2007. *AP Photo/Adam Hunger*

Michael with his troubled son, Cameron, in 2009. *AP Photo/Chris Pizzello*

Michael, in remission after cancer treatment, with his second wife, Catherine Zeta-Jones, at the Santa Barbara Film Festival, October 13, 2011. *AP Photo/Phil Klein*

of Berlin during World War II, is somehow able to slip in and out of Germany more easily than a teenage hottie gets past security at a Justin Bieber concert. Michael, playing her boss, Ed Leland, does so as well. In one especially incredible sequence he manages to escort her by train through Germany across the border into Switzerland (at least one surmises that is the locale, although the white backgrounds look like generic Hollywood Goodguysville) dressed in full Nazi military regalia and attempting to pass through armed checkpoints manned by angry, suspicious, but none too bright Nazi officers and customs even though Leland cannot speak a word of German. (The ruse doesn't work and a shoot-out occurs.)

Rumors of an affair between Griffith and Michael quickly flared. They called enough attention to themselves to prompt Melanie and her then-husband, Don Johnson, to issue a formal statement through their publicity representative, Elliot Mintz, after principal production was completed, that "Don and Melanie are very much in love. They are together in Aspen over the holidays . . . to the best of my knowledge there is nothing wrong with their marriage." This is known in Hollywood as a non-denial denial. Michael's PR guy, Allen Burry, got into it as well. He issued a statement saying that "Michael and Griffith simply made a movie together and enjoyed each other's company. That was the extent of it." Ditto. Both statements appeared to protest too much and a bit too insistently about "nothing."

Griffith and Johnson were divorced for the second time in 1996.

THERE WAS RELATIVE peace in the uneasy valley of Diandraville for a while, until early in 1991, when Michael officially committed to *Basic Instinct*. Talks had first begun with Michael to be in the film months before he went into production in October 1990 on *Shining Through*, and if his asking price of $15 million plus points wasn't exactly agreed to, the final number, $14 million, was close enough for him to say yes. Diandra didn't want him to do it, or for that matter to work at all, except with her on saving their marriage.

❖

THEN, ON FEBRUARY 14, 1991, everything changed. Michael was notified that seventy-four-year-old Kirk had been flying over Santa Paula, California, when his helicopter collided with a stunt plane. Two nineteen-year-olds aboard were instantly killed in the crash, but Kirk somehow had survived. Also with him in the copter was Noel Blanc, who had taken over vocal duties at Warner from his father, Mel Blanc, the longtime voice of Warner Bros. cartoons. Blanc suffered a broken leg, broken ribs, and possible internal injuries. Both Kirk and Blanc were rushed to Santa Paula Memorial Hospital; both were officially listed in stable condition, with extensive cuts and bruises all over their bodies. In truth, Kirk's injuries were more serious, and he was on a life-and-death seesaw. When he was at last able to be moved, Kirk was flown from Santa Paula Memorial to Cedars-Sinai in Beverly Hills.

Michael was, understandably, badly shaken when he heard the news. He dropped everything and went directly to the hospital to see his father. There wasn't much he could do except stand by his side, which he did for hours at a time.

It marked a turning point in their relationship. When Kirk awakened in his hospital bed, he openly embraced his son and, with tears in his eyes, promised Michael that from now on things would be different between the two of them. They would be much closer than they had been, and he would try to be the father to Michael he never was. He told Michael the crash and his near-death experience had made him realize he had a lot of making up to do, and he promised they would make a picture together as soon as he was able to get around.

Kirk, being the physical fitness devotee that he was, recovered fairly quickly. And with the recovery the distance between the two quickly returned. The film he promised Michael from his hospital bed they would make together as soon as possible did happen—one stroke and twelve years later.

❖

MICHAEL, STILL SHAKEN by his father's near-fatal crash, and with his marriage hanging by a thread, began preparing for *Basic Instinct*'s April 1991 production start. He felt he had no choice: it had been four years since *Fatal Attraction* and *Wall Street*, and he needed a bigger hit than *The War of the Roses* or *Black Rain*.

He was forty-six now, and his famous dirty-blond hair was starting to turn gray. He was, for the film business, a little too old to play romantic leading men, and his last two films had situated him firmly amidst the monotony and mediocrity that engulfed most aging male movie star roués (it usually happened ten years earlier for leading ladies). He didn't need the money—he had always had deep pockets; what he did need was to do something great again, something that would reestablish his Oscar-winning stature in the world of filmmaking.

He wasn't just being paranoid. He was having trouble competing for decent scripts with the other big-name actors of the day—even the ones who, like him, and with few exceptions, were starting to show their age. Robert De Niro, exhaling after his breathtaking early run of films that had seen him compared continually to prime Brando, would be nominated for a Best Actor Oscar for his role in Martin Scorsese's 1991 *Cape Fear*. Al Pacino, also entering the twilight of his prime time, was in production for James Foley's *Glengarry Glen Ross*, which would be released in 1992; his performance would steal the show and bring him a 1993 Oscar nomination for Best Supporting Actor.[5] But Michael did not have either De Niro's edge or Pacino's swagger. Both of them were considered more actor than movie star; Michael was considered more movie star than actor. Compared to them, Michael was paper money; De Niro and Pacino were gold coins.

Michael, therefore, not only wanted *Basic Instinct*, he needed it. He knew he was chasing himself to catch up to the glory of his past, and

---

5 Pacino lost to Gene Hackman in Clint Eastwood's *Unforgiven* but won Best Actor that same year for his performance in Martin Brest's quirkily entertaining *Scent of a Woman*.

he believed this was the movie that could do it. He was both very right and very wrong. The film would be a sensation, but all the heat and attention would go to his co-star, Sharon Stone. One quick flash of her pubic hair would make her a star—if not at the morning-after water cooler, like Glenn Close in *Fatal Attraction*, then in the night-before wet dreams of the film's male viewers.

And no actor could compete with that.

CHAPTER 15

Coping stops you from much self-analysis or explanation. I hide behind my work a lot. When I talk about being a chameleon, it means basically reflecting who you are with at the time. You are always protecting yourself.

—MICHAEL DOUGLAS

"THE SEX FILM TO END ALL SEX FILMS," AS IT WAS dubbed by its promotional team, *Basic Instinct* began in the 1980s as an original screen treatment by Joe Eszterhas, who'd spent six years of his childhood in Austria in refugee camps after World War II, where the world was viewed as a cold and nasty place, murder and death were commonplace, and the wealthy were perceived as villains—a worldview he carried forward into his life as an adult. A former award-winning senior editor for *Rolling Stone*, he shared a screenwriter credit with Tom Hedley for Adrian Lyne's 1983 *Flashdance* and took solo credit for Richard Marquand's 1985 courtroom thriller *Jagged Edge*, which starred Jeff Bridges (one of the other son-of-Hollywood pretenders to the leading-man throne in the 1980s) and relative newcomer Glenn Close, that began his immersion into scripts and stories that specialized in lurid sex and violence. After a brief bidding war, Eszterhas was given $3 million based on an outline of *Basic Instinct*.

The generous payer was Mario Kassar's Carolco Pictures, an independent production company already under a crushing $180 million debt prior to its release of Paul Verhoeven's futuristic *Total Recall*, starring Arnold Schwarzenegger. (The film would eventually gross nearly $300 million and pull Carolco out of its financial hole, and the release of *Basic Instinct* would temporarily line Carolco's pockets with more gold, but neither film would prevent Carolco from going bankrupt in 1995.) Kassar was desperate to make Eszterhas's sexy, or at least sex-laden, script, originally titled *Love Hurts* (which reappears in the film as the title of one of Catherine Tramell's bestselling paperback novels), because he understood one of the most ironclad rules of Hollywood: *sex sells.*

According to Carolco's many press releases for the film, Kassar wanted Michael Douglas and *only* Michael Douglas to play the lead role of Detective Nick Curran. However, Michael was far from the only choice, and certainly not at the top of Kassar's list. Other actors who were offered it but wanted no part of Eszterhas's masturbatory screenplay were Peter Weller, Sylvester Stallone, Wesley Snipes, Denzel Washington, Kurt Russell, Mickey Rourke, Alec Baldwin, Don Johnson, Tom Cruise, and Patrick Swayze. Only Michael, whose instincts were impeccable, could see *Basic Instinct* as not just a big picture, but a phenomenon, one that would polish his slightly tarnished leading man image by allowing him to play a slightly tarnished rogue cop. The Academy, he knew, loved that kind of doubling.

Kassar eventually agreed to Michael, not necessarily for his acting abilities but because no other big name would do it. Now he hoped to pick up the dropped ball of Michael's success with *Fatal Attraction* by making another controversial film filled with sex and nudity about a damaged man who becomes emotionally entangled with a woman who may or may not be murderously psychotic.

However, the similarities between the two films ended there. Whereas *Fatal Attraction* had been written by the relatively unknown and talented James Dearden, from his original story, carefully developed over years of writing and the production of one experimental short based on his own script, Eszterhas's film slipped through the cracks of his funky, stoned, and coked-up imagination; it took him only thirteen days to write it, and played like it on-screen. The plot was confused and contradictory, the characters behaved without any obvious motivation, and bodies piled up for no apparent reason and with no visible reactions from those who killed them.

Nonetheless, Eszterhas knew Carolco was desperate to film the screenplay, which already had created a buzz around it in Hollywood, and loudly expressed his usual caveats about producers who take his precious, brilliant scripts and turn them into something conventional and mediocre (and more often than not, turn a profit). This time Eszterhas took advantage of Kassar's desperation and had written into his contract the right to approve of the choice of producer. He also made the studio head put up $1 million in escrow that would immediately go to Eszterhas if Kassar didn't keep his word.

Eszterhas's choice to produce was Irwin Winkler, who had done the inexplicably popular if hopelessly cornball *Rocky* movies, but also Martin Scorsese's 1980 *Raging Bull* and even one of Eszterhas's early and superior scripts, 1988's *Betrayed*—a vehicle for the then red-hot Debra Winger, directed by prestige-of-the-moment European director Costa-Gavras—which had done fairly well at the box office ($25 million in its initial domestic release). With all his blockbuster "serious" hit movies, Winkler had earned Eszterhas's trust. Eszterhas especially liked Winkler's ability to easily slip back and forth between literate films (which Eszterhas believed *Fatal Attraction* was) and popular pulp (which he also thought *Fatal Attraction* was).

At a July 1990 meeting, Paul Verhoeven, whom Winkler had hired off the success of *Total Recall*, clashed with Winkler over the extensive changes the producer wanted to make to Eszterhas's script; Verhoeven felt it was fine the way it was, with all its sexual deviation intact, including Catherine Tramell's ambiguous S&M preferences.

In Eszterhas's original script, Tramell is a successful detective novelist whose real-life adventures feed the plots of her novels, or perhaps vice versa. Verhoeven and Winkler nearly came to blows over one explicit lesbian love scene, which Verhoeven wanted and Winkler didn't, that required extensive nudity from its leading characters, but Kassar thought the team he had assembled, despite their differences, could make a movie that approached the edge of acceptability without going over the line.

Michael, too, had expressed concern about how his character was written, especially Detective Curran's sexual passivity. Curran seemed little more than a foil for Tramell, who was the whole show, and who was too easily able to sexually entrap men. He told Winkler there had to be more scenes that showed Curran's aggressive side; the character needed to be stronger emotionally (even though that would take away from the manipulative sway Catherine has over him). Michael was looking for major attention with this film, and he didn't want to be lost in the shadows of Catherine's broad reach.

Winkler assured him that everything would come together the way he wanted. Michael trusted him and officially signed on. What didn't come together were the divergent opinions of Verhoeven and Eszterhas. Following a few more preliminary meetings, both threatened to quit. Eszterhas didn't want his precious script changed for Michael, and Verhoeven didn't want Eszterhas or anyone else telling him how to direct. Kassar called for a break, to give both sides a chance to cool off.

Two weeks later, Winkler and Eszterhas together informed Kassar that unless Verhoeven was fired, they were leaving the project. When Kassar refused, both Winkler and Eszterhas quit, taking their guaranteed pay-or-play total of $4 million with them and leaving behind Eszterhas's script for Kassar to do with it whatever he wished.

Kassar was less than thrilled. He had by now paid out nearly $20 million and for it didn't have a polished script, a producer, or the two crucial leads.

Moreover, the gay community was now up in arms at the way lesbian behavior was being portrayed in the script, whose juicier parts had already been extensively and luridly leaked to and summarized to the gossip press that fueled the anger of Hollywood's well-organized gay community. At that point, sensing that the film might never get made, Verhoeven softened his position. After the departure of Eszterhas and Winkler, Verhoeven suggested to Kassar that he hire Gary Goldman to rework the script and reduce the amount of the straight and gay explicit sex it contained.

However, after Kassar rejected Goldman's draft, Verhoeven personally called Eszterhas to try to bring the screenwriter back into the fold. Once again they screamed, cursed, and threatened each other, but this time each was willing to cooperate for the sake of saving the film. A few modifications were made to what had been Eszterhas's original script, and that was that—the film's writer was back.[1]

The next step was crucial: finding the right leading lady to play opposite Michael, someone who was hot, young, beautiful, not afraid to show full frontal nudity, willing to expose her private parts, and not be shy about performing in explicit sex scenes that included lesbianism, bondage, and drugs. At one point the list of potential leading ladies ran to 150 names, but the line of actresses actually showing up at Carolco's door was not nearly that long. With the early negative press the film had already gotten, and the internal skirmishes that had threatened to abort the project before a single frame was shot, Verhoeven decided he had no choice but to cast the little-known Sharon Stone, who had all but stolen *Total Recall* from Arnold Schwarzenegger.

The young Pennsylvania-born former Ford model had worked on high-fashion gigs all across Europe before returning to America at the age of twenty-two to become a film actress. She quickly landed a tiny but memorable role in the last scene in Woody Allen's 1980 *Stardust Memories* as "Pretty Girl on Train." The role consisted of all of two minutes on-screen, but Allen's movie hinged upon the impact of her face and her flirtatiousness through the train window.

What followed was twelve years and seventeen features' worth of mannequin roles before Verhoeven cast her in *Total Recall*, a meatier mannequin than she had thus far been able to land, one where audiences would see her spectacular face and body for more than a couple of seconds. *Playboy* magazine quickly came calling, and she happily posed nude for it. Verhoeven liked her for Catherine and knew he could get her, no matter what the role called for her to do. At thirty-two, relatively late in the game for Stone, she would agree to make it with men *and* women, with or without clothes, appear to enjoy bondage and

---

1   Eszterhas is the only credited screenwriter for *Basic Instinct*.

discipline games, and even flash her private parts in one brief scene that sent the other characters, including Michael Douglas's, into cold sweats, as it would male audiences everywhere (and would become known as "the beaver shot heard round the world").

Michael felt he had the right to choose his leading lady and was less enthusiastic about Stone. He was concerned she wasn't a big enough star to play opposite him. "Between the hype of the [$3 million] script and the nudity, a lot of actresses we had hoped for were put off by the part. Women are often caught between politics and a particular role. But I thought that as dangerous as the film was, it was also that good of a woman's part. The irony is that for many male actors, playing a good heavy has made their careers." His personal short list included Julia Roberts (who had done an excellent job for him in *Flatliners*), Michelle Pfeiffer, Geena Davis, Ellen Barkin, Cher, Kim Basinger, and Kathleen Turner (although she was older and had put on a significant amount of weight since *The War of the Roses* and might no longer be able to pull off the role of the femme fatale as believably as she had in Lawrence Kasdan's 1981 *Body Heat*).

They all said no, saving Verhoeven the unpleasant task of saying no to them (except Turner, who briefly considered it, until Verhoeven ultimately decided not to offer her the role). Eventually, due to the process of elimination, Sharon Stone's name made it back to the top of the list. Michael then looked at her screen test again, still worried about being upstaged, but decided to green-light her.

For the crucial supporting role of an Internal Affairs therapist who had had a secret lesbian affair with Catherine in college that more or less plays into the film's central plot, such as it is, Verhoeven chose the luscious and underappreciated Jeanne Tripplehorn. Michael and Verhoeven agreed that if their leading lady was a relative unknown, the supporting female leads—Tripplehorn as Beth Garner and Leilani Sarelle as Catherine's current and crazy female lover, Roxy—had to be even bigger unknowns, in the crisscross bottom-line parlance of industrial Hollywood.

As production began again in April 1991, the director immediately focused on the sex scenes: the opening S&M-and-murder scenes with Catherine and Johnny Boz, the former rock star; the near-rape of Beth by Nick (apparently added at Michael's suggestion, to make Nick appear more twisted; the shoot went through endless retakes plus twelve pairs of panties specially made for Tripplehorn so they could be torn away by Michael); and Nick and Catherine's two lengthy and explicit sex scenes. (Doubles were reportedly used for both Stone and Michael, their bodies cleverly intercut with the stars'. Regardless, there was a lot of flesh exposed by both actors.)

And then there was *the* scene. In it, Catherine is called in for questioning following the S&M ice-pick death of her lover Boz in his own bed at his luxe manse, which the police strongly suspect she committed. Catherine, vodka in her veins, sits in a lone chair opposite half a dozen detectives. With a spotlight shining down on her, she singles out Nick: "Have you ever fucked on cocaine, Nick?" was one of Eszterhas's more poetic lines of dialogue. As she does, she uncrosses and crosses her legs, and the camera reveals not only that she is not wearing any panties but that she doesn't shave, as it gives us a clear, if momentary, view of her privates. It marks the moment, and the pathway, of Stone's entrance to stardom (after *Basic Instinct*, Stone's asking price to be in a film started at $2.5 million).

Much has been made about the scene, and both Verhoeven and Stone contradict what the other says actually happened. According to Stone, "It was Paul Verhoeven's idea. We talked about it from the beginning but it was a big surprise how it turned out. The way it was put to me was that you wouldn't see up my dress, you would just have the illusion that you could see up my dress. I was surprised when you actually could. It was a big shock to have that kind of graphic nudity." She also claimed that when she saw the rushes she slapped Verhoeven in the face. She may have been looking ahead and trying to put some distance between her and the character, with her eye, rather than other body parts, on future projects.

However, witnesses there told a different story. One person on the set during the filming and also at the screening of the dailies said, "Sharon loved it!" That sentiment was echoed by Stone herself before the film was released, when everyone was talking about what they thought (hoped) they were going to see. "At least it proves I'm a natural blonde!" she joked to anybody who would listen. (But she reportedly expressed her true priorities to the cameraman, threatening, "If I see one ounce of cellulite on the screen, you're a dead man.")

Verhoeven too dismissed what he considered her Janey-come-lately protests, claiming that every frame of the film was storyboarded and Stone knew what was expected of her. Also, as instructed, she wore no panties for the scene, and with the way it was lit and the position of the camera, it would have been impossible for her not to know what was being filmed.

The scene didn't bother Michael for its borderline pornographic explicitness as much as it confirmed his fear that Stone was, indeed, going to steal the film, which may explain why he, too, was suddenly willing to be naked in several sex scenes, as long as his privates were not seen frontally. In their penultimate sex scene together, Stone ties him up as she had Johnny Boz, leading the audience to think that Nick is either going to be killed or going to get what he later describes to his partner as "the fuck of the century."

However, as it turned out, far fewer filmgoers were interested in Michael's forty-seven-year-old slightly saggy ass than in Sharon Stone's (or her stand-in's) young and perfectly shaped one. (A British film observer noted that "there is something gruesome about Douglas' periodic bare buttock flashing . . . those pale orbs which suggest not so much Hollywood stud as 1950's British naturist film.")

The soft-core film that emerged from the febrile imagination of screenwriter/narcissist Joe Eszterhas, so in love with his own coked-up concoction, was, in essence, a series of sex scenes held together by a plot as thin as the rear strip of Catherine's thong, when she wore one. Typically, in Hollywood fake-sex scenes, actresses wear what is known as a flesh-colored "Velcro of Venus," to cover up their private parts, and actors wear a flesh-colored jock strap. For *Basic Instinct*, Stone quickly dispensed with the fake "skin" because, she said, "[e]very time you have to pee you have to unglue and reglue it, which is quite painful. Besides, Michael's a real professional, and obviously there wasn't going to be anything awkward, so I felt very safe. And of course, there isn't anything sexy about doing sex scenes."

And there was definitely no double used in the scene when Michael had oral sex with Sharon (nipple sucking and cunnilingus). It is difficult to believe any of it was simulated, given the position of the actors and the placement of the camera. In the seemingly innumerable interviews Stone gave after the film, in which virtually every questioner wanted to know about how the sex scenes were shot, Stone was always eager to elaborate: "We did nude sex scenes for two weeks! There's nothing I haven't seen about [Michael]."

The rest of the script, such as it was, went far beyond silly, with incomprehensible character twists and plot turns and at least two different endings that felt tacked on, including a brief fake fade to black shown with a soundtrack that sounds like its musicians are going to the electric chair.

Not surprisingly, the film was given the deadly X rating, the most restrictive designation of the day (the X was the equivalent of today's NC-17, now used to distinguish mainstream films from pornography). With the dreaded X, a film could not get widespread distribution or be advertised in most mainstream newspapers, making it virtually impossible to survive strictly on word of mouth. Verhoeven, at Kassar's desperate urging, made some cuts to the final theatrical version of the film, and at the last minute the rating was changed to the less restrictive R, just in time for a fresh round of protests from gays when it was confirmed that every lesbian in the film was portrayed as a psychotic multiple killer, conveying the idea that lesbianism equaled criminal insanity. Publicly the producers were nonplussed and insisted they had done nothing to offend the gay community. Michael, whose roots were in sixties protest, tried to reach out to the protesters and express some understanding, if not compassion, trying to reassure them that the film was not anti-gay.

But behind the scenes Kassar was thrilled; the demonstrations moved *Basic Instinct* from the film page to the front page and got it the kind of publicity money couldn't buy. According to Sharon Stone, "I came up with this idea that we should get the Hell's Angels for our security, and that was the beginning of the Hell's Angels doing security on movie sets."

And the "money shot" that took audiences all the way up Sharon Stone's dress set off fireworks of another kind. Hard-core porn was easily accessible by now, but showing a woman's privates was still taboo in mainstream movies—but, apparently, something everybody wanted to see, for once the film opened, the gay issue was overshadowed by Stone's frontal nudity. The only other subject that engulfed viewers was the extra wow of Michael's willingness to do extensive backside nudity.

SHINING THROUGH opened on January 31, 1992, to some of the worst reviews of Michael's career. Janet Maslin in the *New York Times* wrote that "David Seltzer's film version of *Shining Through* manages to lose the humor of Susan Isaacs's savvy novel. Even stranger than that is the film's insistence on jettisoning the most enjoyable parts of the story. There are also such memorable touches as Linda's effort to leave a secret message inside a fish, her uncanny good luck at negotiating padlocks and locating secret documents, and her startling discovery of Nazi regalia in an acquaintance's closet. When *Shining Through* has a bombshell to deliver, its touch is seldom light."

Roger Ebert, writing in the *Chicago Sun-Times*, was far less tongue-in-cheek: "I know it's only a movie, and so perhaps I should be willing to suspend my disbelief, but *Shining Through* is such an insult to the intelligence that I wasn't able to do that. Here is a film in which scene after scene is so implausible that the movie kept pushing me outside and making me ask how the key scenes could possibly be taken seriously."

The film was a modest commercial success, the popularity of its stars superseding the preposterousness of its script. The infamous Razzie Awards declared *Shining Through* the worst picture of 1992, with Melanie Griffith voted worst actress and David Seltzer worst director. There were also Razzie nominations for Michael Douglas as worst actor and for Seltzer in the category of worst screenwriter.

All of which made the upcoming opening of *Basic Instinct* that much more important to Michael. Now, after three mediocre films, he needed a big one to restore him to the A-list of Hollywood actors.

Basic Instinct opened on March 20, 1992—as it happened, Michael and Diandra's fifteenth wedding anniversary—less than two months after *Shining Through*, and with far different results. On its opening weekend *Basic Instinct* grossed more than $15 million despite mixed reviews that were, as the saying goes, good when they were good and better when they were bad. Either way, the film's advance notoriety had made it critic-proof.

Writing in the *New York Times*, Janet Maslin gave the film a soft nod—which, given the film and the fact that this was the *Times*, amounted to a rave—and for the most part ducked the sexual controversies: "*Basic Instinct* transfers Mr. Verhoeven's flair for action-oriented material to the realm of Hitchcockian intrigue, and the results are viscerally effective even when they don't make sense."

Peter Travers of *Rolling Stone*, the magazine that had published Eszterhas's earlier journalism, also liked *Basic Instinct*, calling it a "guilty pleasure" film. "Verhoeven's cinematic wet dream delivers the goods, especially when Sharon Stone struts on with enough come-on carnality to singe the screen. . . . Stone, a former model, is a knockout; *Basic Instinct* establishes Stone as a bombshell for the Nineties."

Roger Ebert of the *Chicago Sun-Times* was far less enamored of *Basic Instinct* and gave it only two out of a potential four stars: "The film is like a crossword puzzle. It keeps your interest until you solve it, by the ending. Then it's just a worthless scrap with the spaces filled in."

Newsweek's David Ansen wrote, "Funniest of all is that this who-dunit gets so tangled up in its twists that half the audience can't figure out who *did* dunit it when it's over."

As Michael feared, it became Stone's film. He was, at best, an after-thought in most reviews, if he was mentioned at all.

TO THE SURPRISE of some and the dismay of others, *Basic Instinct* was invited to be screened that spring at Cannes, giving the film an extra boost of respect among the French, who, not surprisingly, were far less shocked by the film's explicitness (and loved faux Hitchcock almost as much as they did the real thing).

At home, the film proved strong enough at the box office to make it the ninth-highest-grossing film of the year, taking in more than $117 million in its initial domestic release and $235 million worldwide.[2] It brought Michael back into the spotlight, but no one considered it any kind of acting coup for him. In fact, there were many industry insiders who thought he had made a huge mistake appearing nude in a film where the focus ultimately fell on Sharon Stone. His love scenes with her made a lot of people uncomfortable, especially the scenes where he performed cunnilingus on Stone; even if he wasn't actually giving her lip service, his face was close enough to her private parts that the difference would be splitting hairs (parts of this scene were cut from the film's first run but remained in the European release and were subsequently restored for its several DVD releases).

Why did he do it? Michael has said that he thought it was a good script, a good role for him, and that he knew it would be the big hit he was looking for. At the end of the day he walked away with $14 million in salary and additional money from his profit participation, laughing louder on the way to the bank than all those laughing at his performance.

But there was more to it than just money. To begin with, the film

---

2   BoxOfficeMojo.com and IMDb.

brought back the taunting by his father that had subsided for a while after Kirk's helicopter accident. Even from his hospital bed, Kirk, recovering quickly, continually razzed Michael for being in *Basic Instinct*. According to one observer, "Instead of compartmentalizing his wife and lovers, as his father had done, he allowed his dybbuks to cavort in public. . . . He tipped over from the self-obsessed man-on-the-edge he played so well on film, to the completely selfish man-on-the-edge he played so callously in life. After years of self-loathing and repression, he had found a way to reclaim the lost territory of the large ego."

Michael had acted out his demons on-screen. Astute film historian and critic David Thomson made the connection in a far from negative, right-on-the-money take of Michael's performance and motivation: "Imagine at the age of 16 or so, seeing your father announcing, 'I am Spartacus!'—a nearly naked gladiator fighting for his life, then leading the revolt of the slaves and ending up crucified! And being the producer of the movie! Michael may have mocked Dad's style of acting, and his total immersion in himself and his work. They may have argued and quarreled. But the fact of the matter is that Michael has the same kind of self-belief on screen, without irony or mercy. . . . The rivalry with his father had a very telling climax . . . [In *Basic Instinct*,] Douglas played a man who was a victim of his own libido and recklessness. . . . There was undeniable chemistry between the stars (Douglas is often good with strong actresses) and there was an inescapable air of sado-masochism in their bonding that was oddly reminiscent of Kirk Douglas's crazed taste for mutilation, wounding and self-abuse in *his* pictures. There's no need to build up the subtext of *Basic Instinct* unduly—give naked exploitation and sensationalism their due. . . . Douglas went a good deal further than the cool studs who are his contemporaries."

AND THEN THERE was Diandra. If Michael couldn't be the man of the house in real life, he was, if not the best actor in Hollywood during the late 1980s and early 1990s, the most overtly sexual (as opposed to the sexiest), as if what he was lacking in assertiveness at home became the fodder for what he wanted to do and be in the movies. Not surprisingly, Diandra was furious with what she saw on-screen in *Basic Instinct* and this time intended to do something about it. Really.

WHILE CONTROVERSY continued to swirl about the film, Michael took a break from crazy women and excessive nudity to appear in a small independent film produced by Studio Canal+ and Regency Enterprises and distributed by Warner Bros., Joel Schumacher's *Falling Down* (released in 1993); Michael liked Schumacher's work on *Flatliners* and wanted to work with him again. Often a Hollywood star will chose a small "artistic" film to follow a hugely successful one, to prove he is still a "serious" actor. *Falling Down* is an infinitely better film than *Basic Instinct* in almost every way, and Michael agreed to be in it for relatively little money, about half his base pay for *Basic Instinct*.[3] It is no small fact that in many ways *Falling Down* could be seen as a remake of what Kirk has always referred to as his favorite film, David Miller's 1962 *Lonely Are the Brave*, about a cowboy stuck in the modern world, out of his element, but unwilling or unable to move forward with his life.

Michael, in frightening crew-cut mode, plays William "D-Fens"

---

3   He was fine with the salary cut. The studios were on one of their drives to lower all salaries, which had gotten, to their way of thinking, out of control. Michael received $6 million for *Shining Through* before his $14 million deal with Carolco for *Basic Instinct*. Wrote J. Hoberman in the *Village Voice* (March 7, 1995): "Originally asked to play the heroic (but henpecked) cop, Douglas intuitively asked for the more fiercely self-pitying and demonstrable role of the laid-off defense worker. No less rabble-rousing than *Fatal Attraction*, *Falling Down* inspired audiences to cheer as Douglas trashed a Korean grocery, battled a bunch of Latino gang-bangers, dissed a homeless panhandler, and terrorized the robotic counter kids in a generic fast-food parlor. . . . *Falling Down*, one of the first movies to portray Los Angeles as the new behavioral sink, was in production during the 1992 riots."

Foster, a recently divorced man who cannot take the pressures of life and finally commits suicide by cop (played by Robert Duvall). A man unable to cope with the cards he'd been dealt in life was a character Michael wanted to play. Foster's inability to deal with life is best summed up by the film's tagline: "I'm the bad guy? How did that happen?" It is essentially the same question Kirk, as John W. "Jack" Burns, asks of the world in *Lonely Are the Brave.*

Joel Schumacher remembered being reluctant to ask Michael to be in his film, especially after *Basic Instinct*, not knowing where Michael was coming from. He drove himself up to the house in Santa Barbara to personally call upon his hoped-for star. "The defining moment was, Michael had this fantastic long, flowing hair, and when he committed to do it, I told him I was going to give him a buzz cut. There was about 30 seconds where he hesitated—then, when he let our hairdresser know that he was willing to have the buzz cutter go across his hair, I knew he was completely and utterly surrendering."

AFTER COMPLETING *Falling Down*, perhaps to repair his relationship with Diandra, Michael took her and Cameron to Spain to spend the summer of 1992 at their hillside retreat in Majorca. They were joined for part of the trip by Jack Nicholson and his girlfriend at the time, Rebecca Broussard. It was not a good mix.

Upon their return to the States, rumors began to spread that Michael's marriage was once again on the rocks, especially after it was reported that one night just before the trip, Diandra had found Michael in bed with another woman—a charge that was never acknowledged or denied. It was supposed to have taken place at Michael's office at the Beverly Wilshire, and the woman in question was supposed to have been one of Diandra's best friends. Whether or not it actually happened, what was undeniable was that Michael was drinking too much and taking too many drugs, and was filled with a kind of exhaustion and despair that no vacation in Spain could repair. Upon their return, with no warming between them, Diandra insisted that Michael either get professional help or get out of her life.

Whatever the actual tipping point, on September 17, 1992, while his on-screen lover Sharon Stone continued to bask in her belated but enormous fame, a grim-looking Michael, using the alias Mike Morrell, wearing a blue shirt, jeans, and sandals, checked into the Sierra Tucson Clinic, located in the foothills of the Catalina Mountains of Arizona, for a thirty-day program to treat alcohol abuse and, as it was reported by some at the time, sexual addiction.

According to John Parker: "Encouraged by his counselor, Michael [reportedly] began his program of self-discovery when he stood up, head bowed, and gave a lengthy commentary about his inner demons and the problems that had turned him into something of a Jekyll and Hyde character. He confessed to the group of eight fellow sufferers: 'Sex is just a wave that sweeps over me, an impulse that is overpowering. I'm helpless. Every time.' He also admitted to a problem with alcohol and drugs, although he denied that he was addicted to either. He also said his wife had 'kicked him out' of the bedroom, having been repulsed by his apparently uncontrollable actions."

Michael's supposed sex addiction landed all over the tabloids, and that, of course, was apparently enough proof for TV's venerable self-styled sensation-chaser Geraldo Rivera. The next day, on his TV show *Geraldo* announced that "Michael Douglas was one of several high-profile men who had used the services of prostitutes connected with Heidi Fleiss," at the time a well-known madam running a house of prostitution catering to Hollywood's rich and famous. Michael immediately threatened to sue and Rivera quickly backed down and apologized on the air, "regretting any misunderstanding or any inconvenience to Mr. Douglas." But Geraldo, a lawyer himself, well understood that once a statement is made, whether or not the jury is told to disregard it, it cannot be ignored.

Ruth Morris, a reporter for the *Independent on Sunday* in London, used a little more tact in her analysis of whether or not Michael was a sex addict: "His time in rehab at Sierra Tucson was for drugs and booze. No, for the record, Michael Douglas is not a sex addict. No, indeed. He just does it a lot."[4]

Later on, Michael had this to say about his addictions: "Despite all the information one accumulates, and despite the damage you know smoking wreaks on people, they still do it. It's the same with alcohol. Drinking has nothing to do with highs, thrills, whatever. It has to do with many other causes. Some of them inherited, as alcoholism is. Anyway, I'm not self-destructive . . . where did that sex-addiction stuff come from? . . . Some smart British editor decided to make the story about sex addiction. . . . That hung around since 1992, and that little lie that got a lot of press, affected how people looked at me."

When Kirk heard about it, he laughed and said, "What's wrong with sex addiction? I've been addicted to sex my whole life!"

After thirty days, Michael was released, and he took it easy for a while before gearing up for the February 26, 1993, scheduled release of *Falling Down*. When the film did open, it proved only a modest hit. Made for a budget of $25 million, it grossed $41 million in its initial domestic release.

DIRECTOR BARRY LEVINSON then offered Michael the lead in *Disclosure*, yet another dressed-up sexploitation film in which another aggressive woman battles another passive man.

In the film, which is set in the modern corporate world (filmed in Seattle), executive Meredith Johnson (Demi Moore) uses sex to seduce and ultimately control former lover Tom Sanders (Michael Douglas). He works for a newly merged high-tech conglomerate, DigiCom, in

---

4   While admitting to the alcohol abuse, Michael has always denied he was or has ever been treated for sex addiction (according to the clinic, sexual addiction occurs when a person has an uncontrollable urge to indulge in sexual practices without emotion). The Sierra Tucson Clinic does treat sexual maladjustment cases, although it also treats a variety of addictions, including drugs and alcohol. The actor Rob Lowe checked into Sierra Tucson in 1988 after being caught on video in a hotel room in bed with two women. Another famous alumnus is Ringo Starr.

which she has been appointed his boss. Early on, Johnson calls Sanders into her office and, in one of the film's more memorable scenes, makes it clear she expects him to resume their affair. Sanders, married now, rejects her sexual advances, and she vows revenge. She then institutes a sexual harassment lawsuit against him. He eventually comes up with evidence that helps get the lawsuit dismissed. However, there is more to it than that. The setup is actually a double double-cross, a corporate coup against Sanders. In the end, after a scene of high-tech electronic suspense that looks more like a pinball machine gone wild, Sanders manages to save his job, his career, the company, and quite possibly the universe. There is some suggestion that two "good women," his new boss and his female lawyer, helped him survive and endure. In Hollywood parlance, it was clearly an attempt to cash in on Michael's past successes—*Fatal Attraction* meets *Basic Instinct* meets *Wall Street*.

Disclosure is based on a Michael Crichton novel whose movie rights Crichton had sold to Warner Bros. for $1 million prior to publication. Miloš Forman was set to direct and very much wanted to professionally reunite with Michael. However, differences between Crichton and Forman developed, and Forman left the project. He was replaced by Barry Levinson.

For Michael, the film's real-life echoes, intentional and otherwise, are Grand Canyon deep. Here he is playing another passive man opposite another attractive, sexually aggressive woman who inflicts vengeful damage on his career and his family life when he doesn't satisfy her carnal desires. And as in *Fatal Attraction*, the seduction is ultimately not a successful one (but given the way it is presented, with Moore in high heels, black dress, and on her knees, most men would probably be quite satisfied with that failure). Overly complex and dull corporate intrigue fills out the story, and the plot that unfolds is predictable and meandering. There are more twists here than in a Philadelphia pretzel, without enough salty dialogue or action to give it any real taste. The film is helped somewhat by Donald Sutherland's nuanced performance as the outgoing corporate head, hurt by Demi Moore's unheated (and unheatable) seductress, and balanced by Michael's carefully layered if overly flat portrayal of a man caught in the middle of a battle of intrigues, on the one side sex and temptation, on the other money and position, neither of which, in the end, brings him any measure of personal satisfaction.[5]

Disclosure opened December 9, 1994, positioned as one of the big holiday films, and it didn't disappoint. Made on a budget of $55 million, it grossed $83 domestic and an additional $131 million overseas.

For Michael, it was another critic-proof release. Roger Ebert's review, one of the less vociferous, called it "a launch pad for sex scenes."

Janet Maslin, writing in the *New York Times*, said, "Meredith's subversion of old-fashioned womanly wiles is too stiffly contrived to be upsetting. But what's legitimately disturbing about *Disclosure* is its utter confusion of technology and eroticism. The computer-age products in this film easily eclipse the human players, and the sex appeal of ingenious engineering is everywhere. Ms. Moore's bold mega-cleavage, presented almost as weaponry during the story's brief, all-important seduction scene, fits in perfectly with this film's other technological marvels."

Good or bad, mediocre or marvelous, the film had given Michael one more chance to play a romantic lead. On-screen, he looked tired, almost bored as he went through his paces—certainly no match for Moore's "mega-cleavage." This would be the final role of his career in which Michael would be seen on-screen primarily as a sex partner—he had finally aged out of that type of role—but for one last time on-screen he had found a way to save himself (that is, the character he was playing) from the grip of a sexual predator (his co-star). Rob Edelson describes Michael in this period as a "contemporary, Caucasian middle-to-upper-class American male who finds himself the brunt of

5   Despite persistent rumors, Michael denied that he and Demi had had an affair during the making of the film, not that he didn't think about it: "I had a crush on her. But she was happily married [to Bruce Willis]." Michael, *People* magazine, July 6, 2009.

female anger because of real or imagined sexual slights." Familiar, if well-worn turf for Michael.

In real life, the stakes were much higher. Up next for him was not another movie role but one last real-life attempt to save his marriage.

Or save himself from it.

PART SIX

THE FLAWED
CONTEMPORARY MALE

Chapter 16

*I'm feeling a little sad today, a little sad . . . I've been packing up
my things, going through old boxes, and it brings back memories.*
— MICHAEL DOUGLAS

TWO MONTHS BEFORE *DISCLOSURE*'S DECEMBER 9,
1994, opening, Michael celebrated his fiftieth birthday, as the
cracks widened in his life's smooth exterior, especially in his marriage.
Like his father with his first wife, Michael had married a woman incompatible with the demands of the Hollywood lifestyle. Like his father, Michael had wanted to be married and single at the same time.

Even after his stint in rehab, nothing improved between him and
Diandra, and he continued to commute back and forth from Hollywood to Santa Barbara, where Diandra continued to live in their house
with Cameron. If there was any change, it was a subtle, interior one.
Michael no longer had classic rock on his car cassette player. Now he
was into Deepak Chopra's books and the audio version of John Gray's
Men Are from Mars, Women Are from Venus.

Despite this relatively late arrival of New Age sensitivity, he knew
his marriage was over. Only a month before, he had been telling
friends that he wanted to have another baby with Diandra, but when
he brought the subject up she would have none of it. Like so many of
his most memorable screen characters, he remained passive until Diandra finally let the matrimonial ax fall.

In June 1995 Diandra hired a legal team and began preparing for
a real, i.e., legal separation from Michael, citing irreconcilable differences.

Then, early in 1996, Michael and Diandra began attending mediation sessions to see if a reconciliation was possible.

PERHAPS AS A WAY of escaping his marital problems, Michael accepted a lucrative acting assignment to play the role of the president of the United States in Rob Reiner's *The American President*, opposite Annette Bening, Warren Beatty's wife, in what was intended as a cutesy homage to the pre-Lewinsky Clinton administration. To make sure he "got it right," with Clinton's permission Michael stayed a few nights at the White House and trailed the president to get down what was "presidential" about him.

According to Bening, the shoot itself had a great feel to it. "It was an incredibly warm, congenial experience. Michael is truly a professional guy. . . . I loved working with him."

Hollywood has always tried to capture the mood of the country and sell tickets with its portrayal of popular sitting presidents—FDR in Michael Curtiz's 1942 *Yankee Doodle Dandy* and Kennedy in Leslie H. Martinson's 1963 *PT 109*, the latter released earlier the same year JFK was assassinated. By the 1990s the approach had turned to fictitious scenarios that portrayed characters resembling sitting presidents. (Reiner was a big Clinton supporter and very pro-Democrat, undoubtedly one of the reasons Clinton felt safe in allowing the production to come inside the White House.)

Audiences loved the film, a testament as much to Michael's resilient star power as it was to Reiner's directing and Clinton's popularity. *The American President* also benefited from a clever script by screenwriter Aaron Sorkin, who had signed a three-picture deal with Reiner's Castle Rock Entertainment, of which this was the last. Sorkin then went on to create the TV series *The West Wing*, which bore more than a passing resemblance to *The American President*.

Made for $62 million, the film earned $108 million from its worldwide release.

WHILE MICHAEL WAS making *The American President*, his son quietly entered rehab for what had become an unshakable addiction to cocaine. An angry Diandra put the blame for Cameron's problems squarely on Michael's shoulders. While Michael had tried to bond with Cameron and help him develop his talents—knowing his son had an interest in music, in 1993 Michael invested in a new record label, the Third Stone, to help kick-start Cameron's budding music career—Diandra faulted him for not being around nearly enough to morally guide his son and set a good example for him (Michael was no Boy Scout when it came to drugs). On November 17, 1995, Diandra filed the papers she had prepared for a legal separation from Michael in Santa Barbara through her lawyer, Dennis Wasser, citing irreconcilable differences.

"It's a lot of years," Michael said not long after he was served. "We're residing in separate abodes, and we're just talking. It's eighteen years we've been married. . . . I mean we have a lot of time invested, and a lot of wonderful experiences and a lot of love . . . but at this particular time I can't say exactly what's gonna happen. We both have a son we love a lot, and hopefully we'll be able to resolve things in a positive way."

It's telling that nowhere in that public statement did Michael say he wanted the marriage to continue. There remains, in fact, some question as to who actually moved first for divorce and who wanted to remain married. Some sources claim Michael felt horse-collared by Diandra and had wanted a divorce for years, but his passivity, and his fear that he was just like Kirk when it came to women and wives, may have prevented him from taking any action. Others claim that Michael desperately wanted to stay married, if for no other reason than not having to pay Diandra a one-time settlement that could reach as high as $50 million, not counting child support.

While the financial details of their separation were slowly being worked out, Michael was careful not to be seen in public with any women. During this time he also did a series of commercials for Infiniti cars. "It was a phenomenal amount of money," he said, "and I was able to fund my charitable foundation that does lots of different things, from environmental groups to AIDS groups." Michael was pushing himself hard, as if to prove to Diana via his charitable actions that he was, after all, a good person.

Diandra, meanwhile, as if to underscore that this time she really meant it, began openly dating landscape artist Ken Slaught, who had designed the gardens of the Douglases' Santa Barbara estate.

Then, in January 1996, tragedy struck again when seventy-nine-year-old Kirk suffered a life-threatening stroke. Partially paralyzed and unable to speak clearly, he went through an epiphany about his life similar to the one he had after the helicopter crash—the way he had treated his family, the distance that had grown between him and Michael, and this time the hard fact that he would likely never act again. Now with his career gone he wanted nothing but to be surrounded by family.

Michael and the others stayed by Kirk's side throughout much of the early stages of his difficult and exhausting rehabilitation. At night, Kirk would read books about Judaism and try to reconnect with the religion he had so long ago abandoned in the name of assimilation.

The only bright spot during this period came in March, when Kirk, still barely able to walk on his own or speak, received a Lifetime Achievement Oscar. That night Michael was in the audience, and the TV cameras showed clearly the tears streaming down his face when the award was made. "You could have taken him out there in an iron lung, there was no way he was gonna miss that one. . . . [T]he buildup was difficult, because Dad was struggling with his speech at that time . . . [T]his is a moment to enjoy, I told him. Just enjoy this; let's not make this a test. For me, his Oscar was late [in] coming. My emotion was that the industry finally stood up and acknowledged him, which was long overdue."

Also long overdue was the movie Michael's father had promised they would make together. To date, nothing had occurred on either side to make it happen, and now, with Kirk partially paralyzed, it would likely never become a reality. It was tough for Michael to take, because he felt that was the only way he would ever be able to claim equal footing with his father.

Sherry Lansing saw it for as long as he knew Michael: "He went through every day of his life being compared to his father ."

Michael continued to walk a delicate path. Though Diandra was there for Kirk as much as she could be, Michael knew his marriage was unsavable. "I believe in love and marriage, [but] I'm on my own now and that's kind of exciting, [although] the thought of growing old alone scares me."

WITH HIS FILM CAREER hot after the success of *The American President*, Michael decided to throw himself into his work, and to once more try his hand at producing. To do so he partnered with former William Morris agent turned producer Steven Reuther to form Douglas/Reuther Productions. They quickly found backing and secured a domestic twelve-picture distribution deal with Paramount. The company's primary outside investor was Bodo Scriba, whose German-based Constellation Films provided $500 million in production money in return for foreign distribution rights and a 30 percent share of Douglas/Reuther stock. Several other smaller investors became minority stockholders in the company. In all instances, Douglas/Reuther maintained all copyrights and negatives for future rentals and sales.

With the money in place, Michael and Reuther announced an ambitious schedule of twelve pictures, at least three of which Michael would appear in. It was the kind of grand-scale deal only someone with Michael's credentials and Reuther's inside savvy could make. Reuther, a few years younger than Michael, was, like his new partner, something of a multitalented Hollywood player. He was tall and extremely good-looking, loved the ladies, and had a laser eye for spotting scripts that could be made into megahits.

Reuther began his career at the William Morris Agency in its legendary mailroom, like so many future Hollywood heavyweights would, including David Geffen, and quickly became the first assistant to veteran über-agent Stan Kamen. In that role Reuther got to work closely with some of the biggest stars in Hollywood. A quick learner and a smooth operator, Reuther also became an expert in film finance and structured numerous movies for the agency, and pioneered the use of Canadian tax shelters as a way to get independent films funded.

Reuther and Michael first met via Adrian Lyne. Reuther had helped develop *9½ Weeks*, the prequel, as it were, to *Basic Instinct*. What initially attracted Michael and Steve to each other was their desire to get beyond the sappy, fake-feeling love stories that were being ground out by the studios because they were cheap, easy sells at home and abroad. Michael and Steve wanted to make films that were closer to their own personalities: tough, macho movies, heavy on the action, light on the love.

The first Douglas/Reuther project was an appropriately macho true-life adventure film starring Michael, Val Kilmer, and two killer lions. *The Ghost and the Darkness*, directed by Stephen Hopkins, is based on the 1907 book *The Man-Eaters of Tsavo* by John Henry Patterson, who shot and killed two lions that had been terrorizing a railroad construction site in Kenya. The workers called the lions "The Ghost" and "The Darkness" for their stealth and nighttime attacks, which continued unabated until Patterson hunted down the animals and killed them.

The story was a good one, better because it was true, and devoid of any romantic overtones. Patterson's story had knocked around the studios for six years, with an original script by veteran screenwriter William Goldman. When it finally came to Michael's attention, he hired Goldman to revise his script and make one of the lead characters, Charles Remington, an American. Remington helps Patterson, who at this point in the script has failed in all his attempts to kill the lions.

Michael wanted the character expanded and Americanized so he could co-star in the film with Val Kilmer, who was signed to play Patterson. His reasoning had more to do with his being a producer than a movie star. Movies that take place in foreign countries with foreign lead characters do not do as well in the States as those with American characters. It is one of the reasons David Lean's 1957 *The Bridge on the River Kwai* has an American hero, played by William Holden, despite the fact that the story takes place in a Japanese POW camp for British officers held in Burma during World War II. Holden, who was a huge star at the time, accounted for a good part of the film's American success; it is the same reason John Sturges's 1963 *The Great Escape* has several American characters, although the story was originally based on a true-life escape incident in which no Americans were involved. The combined American star power of Steve McQueen and James Garner helped turn that film into a major hit.

Goldman, however, vehemently argued against Americanizing and padding the part, primarily because Remington was originally a smaller character whose mysterious nature was something Goldman thought made the story better. "In *The Ghost and the Darkness* the lions were my passion. I wanted to write about brute power and horror and fear, and at the heart of it, existence, even for nine months, and even in Tsavo, of evil moving among us. . . . [T]he producers said they will make it only if they can get one of these three stars to play Patterson, the main character: [Kevin] Costner, [Tom] Cruise, or [Mel] Gibson. . . . [T]he problem was, you don't get people like that for pictures like this." Costner had actually agreed, but when the studio hedged, hoping to get Cruise, Costner walked. Then Cruise passed, and the picture was dead until Michael and Steve Reuther came aboard as producers, with Michael agreeing to play Remington. And after his performance in 1995's *Batman Forever,* Val Kilmer was a hot commodity and Michael and Steve offered him the other lead.

The action-adventure film was shot in South Africa for tax purposes, which was right up Michael's midlife macho crisis alley. At first Goldman was thrilled to have Michael on board as an actor, but the scriptwriter quickly grew disenchanted with his choices as a producer:

"I have worked with Redford. I have been in a room with Beatty. They are brilliant men, passionate about what they produce, and boy are they not dumb. Well, Michael is their equal [as a producer]. . . .

"Who's better [as an actor]? My answer is: at what he does, no one. And just what does Douglas play so brilliantly? This: *the flawed contemporary American male.* . . .

"[Then] Michael decided to play the part himself. My initial reaction was delight. . . . But shit, as we all know, has a way of happening. The first thing that went was the name. . . . I loved 'Redbeard' [the character's original name, but] I lucked into the name Remington pretty quickly. . . . Then, sharply, I was into nightmare. Michael wanted Remington to have a history. . . .

"I did what Douglas wanted. . . . [I knew] we could cut it all out in the editing process. [But i]f you saw the movie, you know [the backstory of Remington] did not get cut out. . . .

"Michael wanted the audience *moved* when Remington died . . . [but] what he succeeded in doing was destroying him. . . .

"Guess what—when we had our first sneak, one of the questions the audience was asked was to rate the characters in order of how they liked them. And the audience rated Michael Douglas fourth [and Kilmer third, both behind the two lions]. . . .

"A lot of cuts and pads were made to be sure he was more sympathetic . . . [but] the audience wasn't buying it. . . . [W]hen your two stars are rated *below* two supporting players, do not put a down payment on that beach house in Malibu. . . .

"I also feel that if Douglas and Kilmer had been in *Butch Cassidy* [*and the Sundance Kid*, which Goldman wrote] instead of Redford and Newman, you would not remotely be listening to anything I have to say about Hollywood."

THE FILM OPENED on October 11, 1996, at a cost of $55 million and only grossed $38 million domestic, $75 million overseas. While that may seem like a clear $20 million profit, the economics of Hollywood require that a film double its cost to break even, taking into consideration advertising, promotion, prints, and other costs of post-production. In the end, *The Ghost and the Darkness* needed to make $110 million before it made any money.

That the film wasn't a big hit did not bother Paramount. They were eager to keep Douglas/Reuther Productions in-house, confident that they would eventually hit it big.

Paramount's gambit paid off when the second film of the deal, in which Michael did not appear, proved a smash. *Face/Off*, starring John Travolta and Nicolas Cage in a clever variation on the familiar switched-identities plot, with evil masked as good and good masked as evil, was a thrill ride of a motion picture. Released in 1997, directed by action stylist John Woo, *Face/Off* delivered on its premise and rein-vigorated the stalled careers of both its stars.

The script, by Mike Werb and Michael Colleary, had been knock-ing around for years, unable to find any interest from the studios, until Douglas/Reuther Productions came aboard. The original choices to play the crisscross leads were Sylvester Stallone and Arnold Schwar-zenegger, and at one point even Jean-Claude Van Damme was con-sidered. Made for $80 million, the film returned a quarter of a billion dollars (worldwide) and confirmed the status of Douglas/Reuther Pro-ductions as one of the hottest independent companies in town. Para-mount then gave them the green light to make anything else they wanted, with no prior studio approval.

They quickly signed on to do the legal thriller *The Rainmaker*, based on the novel by John Grisham and helmed by marquee director Francis Ford Coppola.

The only problem was, Michael's heart was no longer in producing that film, or any film.

Burnout had set in.

MICHAEL HAD FINALLY been worn down by his family's laundry list of problems, including Cameron's ongoing troubles with drugs,

Diandra's formal divorce proceedings, which she had begun in 1997, two years after filing for legal separation, and Kirk's stroke. All of it had wiped him out, and he didn't want to work so hard anymore producing difficult movies with difficult co-stars. Why bother? His acting salary was currently between $15 million and $20 million per picture. He would gladly surrender a lot of the behind-the-scenes power for a little more of that easy two-dimensional love and glory. "I love acting," he said simply, when asked why he was suddenly getting out of the producing business.

There was also the practical side of the business. Responsibility had taught him that if nothing else, the movie business was about numbers. If everything went completely right, which it almost never did, the twelve-picture Douglas/Reuther commitment with Paramount would not be completed until Michael was in his mid-sixties. He didn't want to work that long and that hard.

What may have prompted these stop-and-smell-the-roses midlife revelations, and another factor that prompted Michael to pull the plug, was Bodo Scriba's surprise decision to sell his shares in Douglas/Reuther to Leo Kirch, another German investor. When that deal subsequently fell through, Scriba exercised his "out" option, pulled his money, and exited the company. Its other, smaller investors, shaken by the company's sudden financial hole, followed suit until it no longer made sense to keep the company together; it would be far too difficult for Douglas/Reuther Productions to make any more films under the present distribution deal with Paramount. The only way to get out of that commitment was to dissolve the company. If Michael had been on the fence, this pushed him over, a confirmation to him that he was doing the right thing. Amidst all this, there was talk throughout Hollywood that the personal relationship between Michael and Reuther was shaky at best. In response to the rumors of internal discord and financial disarray, at a press conference, a spokesperson for the company announced, "Michael and Steven will go on to produce films." When asked if that meant they would continue to work together, the spokesperson replied, "I did not say that."

Michael elaborated and explained he was getting out of the producing business for good and that his decision had nothing to do with Reuther. "You want to spend more energy and time just looking for parts for yourself, developing material, rather than serving a company or producing. I look back a little longingly at the days when I had one or two pictures at a small company, where I could focus and enjoy acting more. . . . I became the producer as prisoner. I would come off an acting role and deal with a large number of projects that weren't in good shape and it was hard to focus on one. . . .

"Reuther and I partnered to finance our own movies and distribute through Paramount, and through the experience gained new respect for the people at studios who green-light pictures." But, in the only reference he would make to the financial mess, he added that it had made him feel "saddled with business-related problems that weren't enjoyable to solve."

Later on, he elaborated: "I had to remind myself why I was spending so much time producing when I really love acting . . . One of the mistakes I made as a producer is that I never really developed anything for myself. When you run a production company, you don't really think that way. I actually haven't made that many movies. My dad's made 84, partly because they just made movies back then, before television, but even among my generation and younger, there are a lot of actors who have made a lot more movies than I have."

In other words, good-bye hard work producing (and Reuther), and hello again easy-street acting.[1]

MICHAEL HAD FOUND two scripts he liked. The first was *The Game*, directed by David Fincher, who had made some noise with 1995's *Se7en*, a twisty thriller about a serial murder who kills according

---

1   In 1998 Reuther formed Bel-Air Productions, a co-venture with Warner Bros. and Studio Canal +, and released a number of well-received films. He died of cancer in 2010 at the age of fifty-eight.

to the tenets of the seven deadly sins; it starred Brad Pitt and Morgan Freeman.

In *The Game*, Michael plays Nicholas Van Orton, an emotionally bankrupt businessman and control freak, who receives a birthday gift that involves a series of life-threatening challenges, all part of a sophisticated game. While Michael was making the film, he logged some interviews to be used after it opened. Robert Hofler, writing for *Buzzweekly*, threw Michael a curve about his relationship with his wife (they still hadn't arrived at a financial settlement or signed the 1997 divorce agreement; neither seemed especially eager to do so). Michael didn't appear to mind being asked about it or to confirm the end of his marriage. "Diandra and I are on very good terms. Absolutely. We were married 20 years. There were a lot of loving times. Would I get married again? Sure. In a nanosecond. I'd like some more kids, too."

HIS NEXT FILM was Andrew Davis's *A Perfect Murder*, reuniting him with producer Arnold Kopelson, with whom he had worked on *Falling Down*. The film was intended to be a loose remake of Alfred Hitchcock's 1954 *Dial M for Murder*, one of the master of suspense's minor explorations of his crisscross theme, wherein one character gets another, ostensibly innocent, one, to participate in a murder for which the latter has no apparent motive. Although, as Hitchcock himself often said, *Dial M* was "a case of drained creative batteries, running for cover," it was nevertheless one of his most popular audience pleasers. It was based on a hit play by Frederick Knott, who was also credited as the screenwriter.

It is not hard to understand why Michael was attracted to this film, the first since *Wall Street* where he could play an out-and-out villain, in this case a murderer, instead of the essentially good but passive guy who is drawn into trouble. "It was fun to revisit the type. I usually think the bad guy is the most interesting character in the story." In the film, a handsome, older, and sophisticated husband (played by Michael) plots to murder his wealthy and sophisticated wife.

Hitchcock's original *Dial M* hired hand, Swann (Anthony Dawson) is blackmailed by Wendice (Ray Milland) into killing Wendice's wife, Margot (Grace Kelly). However, when Swann tries to strangle Margot, she winds up instead killing him, and the film takes off on a Hitchcock joyride. After Margot is convicted of murdering Swann, her secret American lover, mystery writer Mark Halliday (Robert Cummings), who happens to be visiting Wendice and Margot in London, figures out how and why Wendice wanted Margot dead (he wanted her money and blackmailed someone to do the dirty deed). In one of Hitchcock's more devilish touches, Margot, about to go to the gallows, is miraculously rescued; in fact, she changes places with Wendice, who, as the picture ends, is likely headed to the gallows himself, while Margot is free to marry Mark. All of it is played with speed, sophistication, wit, and scissors-sharp badinage.

In Michael's updated version, the locale is shifted from London to New York. The classic latchkey mixup remains, but even in the original it was one of the weakest aspects of the murder plot because it was so confusing; here it is utterly incomprehensible (the words "locksmith" and "duplicate keys" keep popping into the viewer's mind as simpler ways to commit the crime and get away with it). *A Perfect Murder* fails on almost every level of suspense and drama. Whereas Hitchcock knew how to twist the audience's emotions, Davis could not effectively involve the viewer to the point where any twisting is possible. In Hitchcock's version, the climax and dénouement are immensely satisfying; the capture of Wendice and the freeing of Margot suggest a restoration of law and order, the return of civilized behavior to a civilized world.

Davis's version ends in a confusing bloodbath, devoid of any obsession, compulsion, obsessive-compulsion, moral ambiguity, or emotional irresistibility. Nor is there any hint left of what the original hinged on—the crisscross. It is burning and predictable, and Michael seemed to know it, looking wan and uninvolved on-screen.

At least part of his malaise may be attributable to the bad chemistry between Michael and his co-star, Gwyneth Paltrow. She was at the front side of her career, an emerging star, who happened to be the daughter of Michael's good friend Bruce Paltrow, producer, TV director, and fellow liberal activist. Things began well enough but quickly fell apart between the two when Paltrow, then twenty-five years old, made no secret of the fact she thought Michael was too old to play opposite her romantically and was not believable as her husband. Early on she let her feelings be known to a reporter who passed them on to the public: "It's sort of creepy if in real life I'd be married to Michael Douglas. There's definitely an uncomfortable age difference."

Michael didn't appreciate her feelings or the way she had so openly expressed them. Paltrow's confession was a violation of sorts of one of the few ethical codes Hollywood has when it comes to movies: men are *never* too old to play opposite even the youngest of female co-stars. Michael believed that the stigma of his alleged sex addiction of the early 1990s was part of the reason Paltrow had publicly attacked him. In response he said, "I thought [Gwyneth's comments] were sort of silly. I was playing 48 and she [Paltrow] was playing 28. And what's the big deal? I know guys in real life who have these trophy wives who are 20 years younger . . . but it went hand-in-hand with the 'sex addict' stuff that started . . . when I went into rehab right after *Basic Instinct*."

The two would never work together again.

ON SEPTEMBER 10, Michael, looking strong and happy, accompanied by his still-frail father and a grinning Jack Nicholson in his obligatory dark glasses, put his hand- and footprints into cement alongside Kirk's in the courtyard of Mann's (Grauman's) Chinese Theatre. Kirk later joked with reporters, telling them, with a bit of sarcasm cut with bitterness, that he thought Michael's footprints should be much bigger than his. This echoed what Kirk was telling his friends every chance he got, that Michael had made more money with one picture than Kirk had made his whole career.

Two days earlier, on Monday, September 8, *The Game* had been gala-premiered with a traditional Hollywood roving-spotlight red-carpet affair, held at the same famed theater. Among the stars who attended were Michael Keaton, Anthony Edwards, and Rhea Perlman (who was married to Danny DeVito). Michael entered to a round of applause and took a seat inside, but ten minutes after the film started he slipped out and made his way across the street and up the block to the Hollywood Roosevelt Hotel, where he had arranged a suite so he could watch the Oakland Raiders play the Kansas City Chiefs on *Monday Night Football*. Made on a budget of $50 million, *The Game* did $14.3 million its first regular weekend and eventually returned $109 million (worldwide), making it a sizable hit.

The film, however, received mixed reviews. Roger Ebert, writing in the *Chicago Sun-Times*, said, "Michael is the right actor for the role. He can play smart, he can play cold, and he can play angry. He is also subtle enough that he never arrives at an emotional plateau before the film does, and never overplays the process of his inner change."

Janet Maslin, reviewing *The Game* in the *New York Times*, said, "Michael Douglas, in the film's leading role, does show real finesse in playing to the paranoia of these times."

Peter Travers, in *Rolling Stone*, criticized the film: "Fincher's effort to cover up the plot holes is all the more noticeable for being strained. . . . *The Game* has a sunny, redemptive side that ill suits Fincher and ill serves audiences that share his former affinity for loose ends hauntingly left untied."

On February 28, 1998, after being honored (along with Clint Eastwood) with an honorary César at the French film industry's annual equivalent to the Oscars, Michael traveled to the Karlovy Vary International Film Festival, in the Czech Republic, where he was once again celebrated for his contribution to world cinema. When asked to say a few words, Michael couldn't help but make a reference to Kirk and the lifelong struggle he had had to emerge from his father's

Cinemascope shadow: "Being the son or daughter of a successful person means it takes a little longer to find out who you are."[2]

On July 30, 1998, he was installed as a United Nations "Messenger of Peace" by UN Secretary-General Kofi Annan, a distinction shared at the time with few other public figures, including French-Algerian singer Enrico Macias, opera star Luciano Pavarotti, author Elie Wiesel, and basketball legend Earvin "Magic" Johnson. At the news conference following the ceremonies Michael said, "I hope to use the entertainment communications ability we have around the world to talk a little less about movies and hopefully a lot more about some of the issues pertaining to the United Nations. I'm fortunate to be able to focus on some of the issues that mean a lot to me, especially nuclear nonproliferation. . . . [T]his probably means as much to me as any of the two Oscars that I got."

A PERFECT MURDER, targeted as a summer movie, was released on June 5, 1998, for Warner Bros. in association with Kopelson Entertainment. The reviews were mixed, but James Berardinelli, a major contributor to *Rotten Tomatoes*, a film-review website, came closest to capturing the film's essence when he astutely wrote that it "has inexplicably managed to eliminate almost everything that was worthwhile about *Dial M for Murder*, leaving behind the nearly-unwatchable wreckage of a would-be '90s thriller."

Once again, as with most Michael Douglas movies, reviews didn't matter. With a budget of $60 million, the film eventually grossed $128 million worldwide despite the zero chemistry between Michael and Paltrow.

<hr>

2   Michael was being honored for his acting work in *The Jewel of the Nile*, *Wall Street*, *Basic Instinct*, and *Disclosure*.

IN THE SUMMER of 1998, on the heels of the success of *A Perfect Murder*, came Diandra's legal representatives, who presented Michael with a revised version of the divorce settlement. In addition to a reported $45 million in cash, Diandra was to keep the eight-bedroom villa in Santa Barbara and the home they had in Majorca. Michael would keep the Central Park West apartment. It was an interesting irony—Diandra had been the one who'd demanded they live in New York, while he had always loved Santa Barbara.

However, Michael was still not quite ready to sign off. "I'm just coming up for air. . . . I'm really looking forward to a little bit of reflection. I'm trying to simplify, to allow myself time to think about what I want to do."

To do so, or to avoid dealing with the present, Michael retreated into the past, revisiting his youth and embarking on a grand do-over by completely overhauling and updating the slowly deteriorating family compound in Bermuda, where he had spent so many days as a boy. But, as he was soon to learn, he had little room for looking back on a life that was relentlessly propelling itself forward. As he quickly came to realize, there were undeniable elements of freedom and renewal about all that had happened recently—Kirk's stroke, Cameron's problems, the onset of middle age, and his impending divorce.

As he prepared to return to Hollywood, he was ready, he believed, for whatever the future might bring. He was a movie star with a solid career and nothing left to prove in that area. He had all the money and creature comforts anyone could ever dream of. And he had his health. As the old song went, all he needed now was the girl.

The right one.

PART SEVEN

RADIANCE AND RADIATION

CHAPTER 17

I believe in love and marriage [but] I'm on my own now and that's kind of exciting [although] the thought of growing old alone scares me.

—MICHAEL DOUGLAS

IN 1998 MICHAEL BEGAN DATING AGAIN. HE WAS RO-mantically linked with a number of attractive, successful women, including Maureen Dowd, the flame-haired, sharp-witted star op-ed columnist for the *New York Times*; Elizabeth Vargas, the attractive network TV news personality; and the actress Minnie Driver.[1] But despite these romantic flare-ups, something remained missing in his life. He understood better now why his father had so quickly remarried after his divorce. Whether he wanted to admit it or not, Michael was on the make for something more than a one-night stand.

His noticeable weight gain and generally disheveled look were for the lead in a new film, Curtis Hanson's *Wonder Boys*. Hanson was hot, coming off his 1997 smash hit *L.A. Confidential*, based on the novel by James Ellroy. This time Hanson had chosen to adapt another book, one nothing like Ellroy's neo-noir period piece. *Wonder Boys* was based on the 1995 cult-hit novel by Michael Chabon, with a screenplay by Steve Kloves (1989's *The Fabulous Baker Boys*, screenplay and director). Kloves turned down the chance to direct, preferring to work on his new novel. *Wonder Boys* is about a middle-aged writer and educator,

---

1   At the time, unconfirmed rumors flew everywhere that the unmarried Dowd's "romance" with Michael was intended to get her to briefly stop her intense criticism of Bill Clinton.

Professor Grady Tripp, who can't finish his second novel and continues to teach English in college to pay the bills. Tripp's third wife has left him, and he's having an affair with the wife of the school's chancellor. It is not difficult to see what attracted Michael to Tripp, who is in the midst of a midlife crisis and a crumbling marriage. Tripp's character was decidedly not a leading man; that role was filled by the talented but confused student (played by Tobey Maguire) whose mentor is Professor Tripp. What they see in each other is what we see in both of them; the heart of the film is their father-son-like relationship (in which Michael gets to play the father figure).

The shabbiness of the film's overly convoluted plot—the screenplay's well-intentioned unfolding of the story's complexities goes on forever, without a clear line to hold it together—is sharpened considerably by Hanson's directing. He smartly chose to use a Bob Dylan song that perfectly set the tone for the film, and hired the late, great Dede Allen, whose razor-sharp editing kept the film moving along.[2]

Shot mostly in Pittsburgh, the film's negative was delivered in fifty-two days, but the film wasn't scheduled for release until 2000. Despite the long delay between its completion and release, Michael was extremely happy with it and was able to joke about what he believed was his successful transition to older character roles, even at the expense of his always well-groomed appearance in previous films. "He's gonna die when he sees me!" Michael told *Variety* with his tongue firmly in his cheek, referring to Kirk and his fitness-freak approach to life, which Michael had for a time made his own and used to great advantage. As for the film's unrelenting 1960s attitude, that too had an autobiographical whiff about it for Michael, as it reminded him of his days at UCSB, when he was filled with rebellious energy and still unsure of how to use it.

---

2   Dylan's song "Things Have Changed" won an Oscar for Best Song of the Year; both Dede Allen and Steve Kloves were nominated for Oscars, for Best Editing and Best Screenplay, respectively. Both lost.

◈

IN AUGUST 1998, Michael met the raven-haired, black-eyed twenty-nine-year-old Welsh-born BBC actress Catherine Zeta-Jones, who had just co-starred on the big screen opposite Antonio Banderas in Martin Campbell's 1998 *The Mask of Zorro*, the film that put her on the big-screen map. She had been a virtual unknown outside of Great Britain, where she had begun her career at the tender age of four learning tap at Hazel Johnson's Dancing School, before being enrolled by her parents in Swansea's private Dumbarton House School in 1981. Soon she was shuttling between Swansea and London to star in the West End production of *Annie*. After a few more runs on the West End, at the age of fifteen she moved permanently to London, where, at seventeen, she won a part in the chorus of the successful revival of *42nd Street*. Gorgeous, leggy, and glamorous onstage, off the boards she was still Cathy Jones from Wales who, as she described herself, "liked to chew gum—a tomboy . . . nothing prissy."

Not long afterward, she landed the starring role in the British television series *The Darling Buds of May*. The part showed off her highly appealing manner and drop-dead good looks and made her Britain's newest sweetheart. She next appeared topless in a 1992 BBC teleplay. When asked why she did it, she smiled and said, "I wanted to show there was another side of me."

In 1995 she starred in Carl Prechezer's British feature *Blue Juice*, which bombed with the public and put a halt to the upward momentum of her career in the UK. She then decided to move to Hollywood, where she quickly landed a small role in the American TV miniseries *Titanic*. Steven Spielberg saw her in it and told Campbell about her. Campbell, who at the time was looking for a fresh face to co-star opposite Banderas, checked her out and cast her in *Zorro*, in which she all but stole the film from the equally beautiful Banderas.

Michael met Catherine at the 1998 Deauville American Film Festival near Normandy, France. Film producer David Foster, who was at the August 31 party where they met, recalled that when Michael first saw Catherine in person, "his eyeballs popped out of his head. Just *Whoomp!*" However, it wasn't a chance meeting, as has always been reported.

Michael had been aware of Catherine before that night, having seen a studio screening of *The Mask of Zorro*. His reaction was visceral; afterward, he searched his body for any signs of arrows. "I first saw her up on the screen the way everybody did," he said later. "But to my mind I had not seen anybody since Julie Christie who had all that. It wasn't just her looks but a persona that came through. And I went, 'Wow,' and totally went after her. . . . [B]y the time we met at Deauville, I was looking to get involved.

"There was a whole group. She had her hairdresser, I had my [PR person]. I had finished all my Deauville promotion for the night before, so I was feeling no pain. I was celebrating, having a good time. Catherine had to work, attend a dinner that night. I waited at the bar, where I was waiting for Danny DeVito to bring her over to meet me."

Michael had come to the festival to promote *A Perfect Murder* and to be honored by the festival for his "producer-actor's contribution to world cinema." Later that night, Danny DeVito, acting as the go-between, introduced Michael to Catherine. Michael's opening line was, "I want to be the father of your children."

That got an unamused laugh from Catherine. "I've heard a lot about you," she said. "It's nice to know it's all true. Good night."

The next morning Catherine flew to Scotland's Isle of Mull to begin shooting her next film, Jon Amiel's *Entrapment*, co-starring fellow countryman Sean Connery. Waiting for her when she arrived at the hotel was a bouquet of roses from Michael, with a simple but honest note attached: "I apologize if I stepped over the line."

Catherine was impressed as much with Michael's gesture as with his determination. When she returned to the States during a break in filming, she agreed to have dinner with him. If Michael was concerned about the twenty-five-year age difference between them, he didn't show it: "My first wife was younger than me, and before that I had dated a woman [Brenda Vaccaro] who was six years older, so it's not like I had any set pattern with women. . . . [Y]eah I thought about it, but then I had heard Catherine liked older men . . . so I thought I had a shot." Later on, Michael mused, "Mike Todd was 25 years older than Elizabeth Taylor when they married in 1957."

As far as Catherine was concerned, "he was absolutely different from what I would have expected after buying my ticket to see *Basic Instinct* or *Fatal Attraction*. He [seemed a] very sensitive person, very loyal, but his sensitivity is never a weakness." They didn't begin dating seriously until the following March, 1999, and then kept their relationship as low-key as possible, which was not very possible. Their relationship quickly attracted tabloid headlines. Among the reasons Michael wanted to keep it private was that he didn't want to do anything to privately offend or publicly embarrass Diandra and threaten the delicate balance of their impending divorce and its long-worked-over agreement.

His instincts proved correct when the normally press-reticent Diandra suddenly showed up in *People* magazine. Michael's affair had set her off. She angrily voiced her opinion of Michael and Catherine's relationship, and the persistent rumors that they were about to be engaged. "Before Michael can marry," she told the magazine huffily, "he has to divorce me—or become a Muslim so he can have two wives."

If Diandra's tantrum bothered her, Catherine didn't show it publicly. Instead, she happily told interviewers she had absolutely no problem dating an older man and that she had no interest in men her own age. It was true. Before Michael she had dated director Nick Hamm, forty-one; actor Paul McGann, thirty-nine; Simply Red lead singer Mick Hucknall, thirty-nine; and *Braveheart* actor Angus Macfadyen, thirty-six, to whom she had briefly been engaged in 1995. As for Sean Connery, her co-star in *Entrapment*, she told the production designer of *The Haunting* that Sean Connery was the most fabulous thing in the world: "He's a cake. You could eat that." Moreover, it seemed karmic affirmation to Michael and Catherine when they discovered they were born twenty-five years apart on the same day, September 25.

◈

IN JUNE 1999, they vacationed together at Michael's cliffside villa on the Spanish isle of Majorca (which Michael was still able to use because the divorce had not been finalized). An ambitious photographer with a long lens managed to catch a shot of Catherine bathing topless. The photos appeared in newspapers worldwide, and she was outraged, calling them "voyeuristic" and "unnerving." She also used the opportunity to react to Mel Gibson, of all people, who had openly criticized younger women dating older men, which Catherine felt was a direct shot at Michael and her. "I don't know quite what the age thing is all about, but let's wait until Mel Gibson [then forty-three] gets to Sean Connery's age [sixty-nine] and see if he has that staying power."

On July 2, Michael accompanied Catherine to Edinburgh for the world premiere of *Entrapment*. "Michael is here tonight," she told reporters, as if to make official what everyone already knew, "because we wanted to publicly say that we are together." A beaming Michael quickly added, "I am a very lucky man." Afterward, the press had a nasty-edged field day with the relationship.

Two months later, in October 1999, twenty-year-old Cameron was arrested for attempting to buy a gram of cocaine from an undercover cop. The police had observed him leaving a black Acura outside 11 Fifth Avenue, a building in Greenwich Village. As it happened, the car was registered to him but driven that night by one Hiro Abreu, who was subsequently arrested with four bags of cocaine in his possession. Cameron later told police he was letting Abreu use the car as a form of payment for $2,000 he owed Abreu and eventually was allowed to plead down to a misdemeanor.

Michael was devastated. Despite the fact that he had once been something of a druggie himself, he could not understand why Cameron was one now. As hard as it was for Michael to admit it, this was a sad replay of the now-familiar Douglas family saga, an endless wheel-to-nowhere of struggling sons and famous fathers, with Michael playing what had once been Kirk's role.

He had, almost from the beginning, not been there for Cameron, treating the boy as an afterthought to his unhappy marriage to Diandra (as Kirk had done to him when he divorced Diana). Commenting on Cameron's legal troubles in the fall of 2000, Michael said, "My son is going to be twenty-two in December and I look back twenty-two years and my career was in an entirely different position. I was working hard and whatever shortcomings I had as a husband and a father, I'm sure they were based on ambition . . . now you don't have that." It sounded like Michael was making excuses for both Cameron and himself.

IN AUGUST MICHAEL took Catherine to meet Kirk and Anne at their home in Beverly Hills. "People used to ask me, 'Is Michael going to marry Catherine?'" Kirk told one reporter not long after meeting Michael's new love. "I would say that *I* would like to marry Catherine, but my wife won't let me . . . oh well, at least the kid is happy." To another he said, "I've never seen Michael so happy . . . She's a really intelligent woman, and I am proud."

Michael was less than thrilled with Kirk's remarks about marrying Catherine and privately told him to calm it down.

Michael and Catherine's age difference remained a headline topic, fodder for apparently endless evaluation and judgments. The *Times* of London commented on Michael's new romance with its signature combination of ironic cattiness: "Douglas must be the only 56-year-old man for whom a whirlwind romance with a throaty starlet 25 years his junior is considered a sign of slowing down."

Michael felt the need to respond: "Since the first three weeks, the age difference hasn't come up. . . . Early on, any doubts I had were because I realized that I've had it all. But the great advantage of that is nothing would make me more excited, prouder than to watch Catherine explode—something a lot of guys couldn't handle unless they've had their own success."

He was even eager to work again, especially with Catherine, and gave that tidbit to the press. The *Sunday Times* of London immediately saw this as a move by Michael to "revive his faltering career by starring opposite his girlfriend, Catherine Zeta-Jones."

Michael had indeed come up with an idea to do another sequel to *Romancing the Stone*, news of which sent Kathleen Turner into something of a public snit that smacked of both professional and personal pique. She claimed she "owned" the character of Joan Wilder and deserved at least first refusal on the project. Michael's response was quite clear, to Kathleen and to anybody else who might be listening: "I'm crazy about Catherine and want to make a movie with her. She's the only actress I want to work with right now."

To make it happen, Michael turned down a number of films being offered to him, including Frank Oz's *The Score*, a heist film that he had originally been eager to make, to search for a suitable project for himself and Catherine. Meanwhile, as the two were constantly being photographed, Diandra once again spoke publicly about the relationship, this time a bit more subdued. When asked about Michael's relationship with Catherine by the *Times* of London she said, "He can wed [now] if he wants to. Whatever Michael decides, it will be a good decision, and if he marries because he thinks it is good for him then I will accept it." The implication was that Diandra was waiting for Michael to sign the divorce papers and that she would give him no more trouble if he did.

CATHERINE SPENT Christmas 1999 with her parents in Wales because she said she was needed there for some promotional work on *Entrapment*. When she arrived without Michael, reports flew that their relationship was over. Some speculated that she had given him an ultimatum—marry or break it off—and that Michael, coming out of his long and unhappy marriage, was gun-shy. At the last minute he flew off to Wales in time to be with Catherine and her family for Christmas Eve.

From there they flew together to Aspen to spend New Year's Eve.

That evening they had showed up at a star-studded party in Aspen, where everyone was eager to ring in the new millennium. Big doings at the house were planned for the stroke of midnight, but when it came, Michael and Catherine were nowhere to be found. Instead, they had retreated to their own house, and when the clock struck midnight, Michael asked Catherine to marry him.

She said yes, and immediately called her parents in Wales to tell them the happy news.

According to a close friend, Broadway and film producer Marty Richards (who would later cast Catherine in his 2002 film version of the Kander and Ebb musical *Chicago*), "When I found out, I asked Michael, 'Why didn't you tell us [that night at the party]? All your friends have been waiting.'" The reason, Michael said, was that not even he knew. He had sat down at the party alone, amidst all the activities surrounding him, and had taken stock of his life. According to Richards, Michael said, "I put [Catherine] in comparison to everybody else, and no one compared. Then I thought about how wonderful she is. I decided at the last minute to propose that night."

To make it official, Michael had slipped on Catherine's finger a $250,000 Fred Leighton engagement ring, a ten-carat antique marquis diamond surrounded by eighteen smaller diamonds. He had picked it out in New York and had been carrying it around for some time, waiting for the right moment to give it to Catherine.

JUST AFTER the new year, Paramount, which was distributing *Wonder Boys*, announced that it was moving up the release date from early spring to February 2000, hoping to beat the rest of the Easter holiday films that year. It opened on February 25 with great fanfare and little box office, the audience apparently turned off by Michael's disheveled look, which was featured prominently in the promotion posters. Joe Morgenstern, writing for the *Wall Street Journal*, praised Douglas's acting but specifically criticized the poster, which featured a headshot of Douglas and the slug line "A raffishly eccentric role, and he's never been so appealing!" Morgenstern warned audiences not to be put off by it, which, he said, made Michael look like Michael J. Pollard from *Bonnie and Clyde*, or by the fact that the story was about campus life, a not-very-sexy subject, especially for its targeted audience, that was younger and presumably college-bound.[3]

The film, which couldn't find an audience, was not helped by the lack of enthusiasm in the major reviews. A. O. Scott complained in the *New York Times* about the film's lack of cinematic qualities: "The problem [with the film] is that everyone involved seems to have agreed that it was a great idea for a movie and pretty much left it at that." Richard Corliss, writing for *Time*, was a little more insightful but did not write a money review either: "*Wonder Boys* reminds us of a distant age (the 1970s) when bad movies were better: not stupid teen romps but sad, off-kilter studies of adults adrift. It is a rare current example of that endangered species, the honorable failure." And finally Owen Gleiberman, a post-auteurist, highly opinionated contemporary critic, said in *Entertainment Weekly*, "Curtis Hanson may have wanted to make a movie that gleamed with humanity as much as *L.A. Confidential* burned with malevolence, but he's so intent on getting us to like his characters that he didn't give them enough juice." Owen gave the film a C+ rating.

With its release coming just a week after the Academy Award nominees for the previous year's films had been announced, and the studios putting all their promotional muscle into those campaigns, *Wonder Boys* was left without a studio champion. The film died, too quickly for former studio golden boy Hanson. Michael was quick to defend Hanson and the film: "It's the most unique release experience I've ever had. *Wonder Boys* was supposed to come out this time last year, it was the reason we all cut our prices, and it didn't for whatever reason. The

---

3 Kenneth Turan of the *Los Angeles Times* also slammed the ad campaign in his review: "The film's ad poster brings Elmer Fudd to mind." Even director Curtis Hanson later criticized it, saying the poster made Douglas look "like he was trying to be Robin Williams."

person who's been most instrumental is Hanson. He insisted in his diplomatic but stubborn way that the movie deserved another look."

The film grossed $6 million its opening weekend and only $33 million total worldwide (including receipts from a second-chance November 2000 release, with an ensemble cast poster and advertising campaign). If it marked a downturn in the arc of Michael's commercial popularity, released two years after his last feature, *A Perfect Murder*, Michael didn't seem concerned. He had other matters to deal with.

In March 2000, Michael and Catherine announced they were expecting a baby and planned to be married that November, probably in Majorca. "I feel blessed," Michael said at the prospect of becoming a father again, "because I didn't think it could happen to me again. But it did."

Dylan Michael Douglas was born just before 6:00 p.m. on August 8 at Cedars-Sinai Medical Center in Los Angeles. He weighed 7 pounds, 7 ounces and was 21 inches long. Both Catherine and Michael had agreed on the name Dylan Michael Douglas: Catherine wanted her son to be named after the Welsh poet Dylan Thomas, and Michael also liked the name, not so much for the poet as for the singer-songwriter who had written the Oscar-winning song used as the theme for *Wonder Boys*.

On June 4, 2000, Michael decided it was time to quietly and officially end his twenty-three-year marriage to Diandra, who was now dating Sacha Newley, the artist son of Joan Collins and Anthony Newley. Michael signed off on the revised $45 million one-time settlement, with Diandra's original financial demands and property division remaining unchanged.[4] After twenty-three years he was officially single again.

That November, he married Catherine.

---

4   Some sources put the cash settlement as high as $60 million.

CHAPTER 18

If you have a void, you fill it with something. And love is a valuable stone that one can't necessarily find. I feel blessed.
—MICHAEL DOUGLAS

"MICHAEL IS EVERYTHING I WANTED," THE THIRTY-one-year-old bride said of her fifty-six-year-old groom on her wedding day. "I don't take any of this for granted. When I look at Michael, I run around like a little girl. I can't believe I came into his life and he came into mine."

The weekend festivities began on Friday, November 17, 2000, with a lavish buffet-style rehearsal dinner of chicken Kiev, shrimp, beluga caviar, and chocolate-covered strawberries served to 165 guests, held at the Russian Tea Room in midtown Manhattan to acknowledge Michael's Russian roots. The wedding was scheduled for the next day, Saturday, November 18, 2000, at New York's grand old Plaza Hotel on Fifth Avenue and Central Park South. It was a combination of Old World glamour and New World glitz.

The bride looked radiant as she walked down the aisle in her $100,000-plus cream-colored, diamond-encrusted gown, designed by Parisian designer Christian Lacroix. The cost of the wedding was estimated by *Celebrity Bride Guide* to be in excess of $1.5 million. One hundred fifty rooms were reserved for guests; Catherine's suite cost $5,000 a night, others considerably less.

The guest list was large. Besides her mother and father, her uncles and aunts, and her first dance teacher, Hazel Johnson, all flown in from Wales on a private jet courtesy of Michael, and his family, gathered from New York and Hollywood, the list of invitees read like a Hollywood dream casting. Among the more notable of the 350 guests were Danny DeVito and his wife, Rhea Perlman; Russell Crowe with Meg Ryan—their first date in what would be a short but impassioned relationship; Jack Nicholson and Lara Flynn Boyle; Karl Malden; Goldie Hawn (without Kurt Russell); composer Jimmy Webb; U.N. Secretary-General Kofi Annan; U.S. ambassador to the U.N. Richard Holbrooke; Martha Stewart; Anthony Hopkins; Steven Spielberg; Brad Pitt and Jennifer Aniston; Sir Michael Caine; Nick Ashford and Valerie Simpson (the singing-songwriting duo were neighbors who also owned a restaurant and bar on Seventy-Second Street, where Michael liked to hang); Oliver Stone (who proclaimed that on this night Michael was Sir Lancelot and Catherine Lady Guinevere, and threw in a Snow White reference as well); Art Garfunkel; Stephen Stills; Gladys Knight; Mick Hucknall; Barbara Walters (with whom a white-haired, stroke-impaired Kirk Douglas flirted all night); telecommunications executive George Blumenthal; Christopher Reeve, hairless and wheelchair-bound, accompanied by his wife, Dana; and Zack Norman and his wife, Nancy. Each guest received a silver Welsh love spoon engraved with the bride and groom's initials and were asked not to give gifts but, if they wished, to donate to a trust fund set up for baby Dylan. A Welsh dragon was hung above the hotel's main entrance.

The ceremony began at precisely seven thirty in the hotel's Terrace Room. A twenty-foot magnolia tree decorated with seven hundred white tulips stood at the entrance. Magnolia-shaped table assignments for the upcoming dinner hung from its branches, held there by silk ribbons. Dinner would follow the ceremony.

Down a path leading up to a raised platform, accompanied by glorious organ music, two flower girls came draped in Lacroix, followed by a ring bearer and page boy (all relatives of the couple). Four bridesmaids followed. Catherine's maid of honor was British TV host Anna Walker. Next came Michael's mother, Diana, walking down the aisle carrying baby Dylan, dressed in a sailor outfit. When Catherine appeared, the wedding march began with organ and trumpets, accompanied by a forty-member Welsh choir singing "Watching the White Wheat," a traditional Welsh song.

The altar where Michael and Catherine were about to exchange wedding vows was surrounded by grass; a garden made of lady slippers, larkspur, and delphiniums; and the aroma of twelve varieties of roses, including twenty thousand cream-colored ones beneath a twelve-foot gardenia-strewn canopy. All of it was conceived and executed by event designer David Beahm and coordinator Simone Martel, who had arrived at four o'clock that morning to begin final preparations for the elaborate setting.

Michael's best man was Cameron, twenty-one, out of rehab and looking healthy and happy.

Although Catherine had asked him not to cry when they exchanged vows and wedding rings (designed by Catherine's family jeweler in the tiny Welsh town of Aberystwyth), Michael burst into tears, and that started the waters flowing. According to one who was there, "Everyone was crying, the men even more than the women." After the twenty-five-minute nondenominational ceremony, Catherine and Michael went into in an adjacent private room to sign their marriage certificate. Chief Judge Judith Kaye gave the newlyweds her best wishes: "May they love one another forever and smile always as radiantly as they do today."

The menu included a choice of New England clam chowder or a terrine of foie gras, and then rack of roasted Welsh lamb with rosemary, or lobster. Dessert included cheesecake, apple pie, and a cheese board that included Caerphilly. The wines and beers were all picked by Michael, including Brains Mild, an ale from Cardiff, which carried the nickname "Skull Attack." Kirk, eighty-three and ever the spotlight grabber, made a special entrance with his wife, Anne, and recited a Hebrew prayer just before dinner was served. When asked how he felt about his new daughter-in-law, Kirk repeated his wince-inducing joke about wanting to marry her himself but his wife not letting him. The guests were serenaded during dinner by a dozen violinists playing classical music.

During dinner, the newlyweds made toasts declaring their love for each other, and then had their first dance to Gladys Knight singing "You're the Best Thing That Ever Happened to Me." Knight sang live for another hour, followed by Art Garfunkel, who did "Bridge over Troubled Water"; Mick Jones, of Foreigner, who did "I Want to Know What Love Is" backed by Stephen Stills and, in an incredibly civilized touch, Catherine's ex-boyfriend Mick Hucknall. Ashford and Simpson sang their hit "Solid as a Rock," and Bonnie Tyler concluded the show with a rousing version of "Total Eclipse of the Heart." The whole musical presentation was arranged by Jimmy Webb. After its conclusion, dessert was served.

The centerpiece was a six-foot, ten-tier vanilla and buttercream wedding cake created by Sylvia Weinstock, covered with thousands of edible sugar flowers. The top two tiers had to be removed to fit through the doors of the ballroom, where the cake was reassembled. After dinner, trumpets signaled it was time for everyone to move to the grand ballroom. Dance music played until five in the morning, followed by an informal early-morning sing-along in the piano bar.

The next afternoon Michael and Catherine, carrying the baby, stepped out of the hotel and were greeted by dozens of cheering fans who had been waiting since the wedding had begun for a glimpse of the new bride and groom. The newlyweds then flew by private jet to Aspen for their honeymoon, a sentimental journey back to the very site where, on New Year's Eve, Michael had proposed to Catherine.

EXCLUSIVE PHOTO RIGHTS to the wedding were sold by Michael and Catherine to Britain's *OK!* magazine, as good a way as any to pay for the wedding extravaganza, but trouble soon erupted when rival mag *Hello!* published pictures it had somehow gotten hold of, in a case that wound up in the high courts of Great Britain. After a lower court ordered the confiscation of 740,000 copies of *Hello!*, a higher one amended *Hello!*'s penalty to a full reimbursement of *OK!*'s expenses, including the full cost of the photos, with no confiscation but no right to sell any magazine containing photos of the wedding.[1]

THEY INSTANTLY BECAME Hollywood's newest "It" couple, this year's model of Elizabeth Taylor and Richard Burton, the movie capital's millennium prince and princess, occupiers of the palace of the film-going public's romantic imagination.

Later on, Catherine confirmed to *Vanity Fair* that there was a prenup. When asked for details, she would only say, "I think prenups are brilliant," and admitted that in hers with Michael, "I get taken care of very well."

---

1   To Hilary de Vries in *Los Angeles Times Magazine* (January 21, 2001) Michael defended the decision to sell the exclusive photo rights to *OK!*: "The reason we did is the control you get from it. The fact that they pay you is a luxury, but by working with an organization deciding that only one magazine in Britain and one in America [*People*] gets the photos, it stops the feeding frenzy of the paparazzi." He refused to confirm the $1.5 million price and the additional $800,000 he reportedly received from *People* for the American rights, and insisted the photo money did not pay for the wedding and that he gave much of it to charity.

CHAPTER 19

*Look, I'd love to have made more films. I know most of the
movies I've done are pretty good, but I've made many fewer
movies than everybody else. . . . [T]here's no better gig than being
the star who gets $20 million a picture and a piece of the back
end . . . but there's nothing more important than being with
Catherine.*

—MICHAEL DOUGLAS

THEY SETTLED INTO MARRIED LIFE IN NEW YORK
City. Catherine insisted they hire a nanny from her native Wales
so that young Dylan would not grow up with a New York accent, a
way of speaking Catherine particularly detested. Michael, whose familiar Connecticut accent with its broken-back *a*'s still lingered, had
no problem being surrounded by Welsh women.

The previous winter, Michael and Catherine, who was pregnant
at the time with Dylan Michael, had signed on to do *Traffic* for director Steven Soderbergh (*Sex, Lies and Videotape*, 1989; *Erin Brockovich*,
2000; and others), written by Stephen Gaghan. Soderbergh had long
wanted to make a film about the drug problem in America, but he
was not interested in doing a movie about junkies. Instead, he wanted
to explore the effects of drugs on a middle-class family. He had long
admired the British TV series *Traffik*, drawn to it because of the way
it used parallel structures to delve into the literal journey drugs take
on their way to becoming a valuable commodity, as well as to view the
victims who make the drug cartels wealthy.

Soderbergh originally had had a deal at Fox to develop the project, but the studio threatened to back away if the director didn't use

Harrison Ford as the father, a conservative Ohio judge who is appointed to head the President's Office of National Drug Control and whose teenage all-American daughter is hopelessly hooked on crack cocaine. Soderbergh, however, wanted no part of Harrison Ford, preferring Michael instead. When the studio called in its chips, Soderbergh shopped the film elsewhere and wound up making a deal with the independent USA Films, as long as he could be his own cameraman.

USA Films agreed to all of Soderbergh's conditions, even to the three-hour length of the film, the amount of time he insisted he needed to tell the story the right way. Michael initially turned down Soderbergh's offer to star in the film, perhaps feeling that playing a judge who is also the father of a drug-addicted teenager was a little too close to home. Soderbergh then offered the female lead to Catherine. Michael remembers, "When Steven presented it to me, the character on the page was kind of two-dimensional and I said, 'I love this but there's not enough here for me to do.' When he came to Catherine for her part, I looked at the [revised] script and thought, 'Hey, this has really gotten good' and I agreed to play the judge. . . . Catherine and I never actually had any scenes together—she shot down in San Diego and I was mostly in Ohio. She was supposed to have two kids in the film, but she was pregnant at the time, so I suggested to Steve that she play her character pregnant. He thought it really upped the stakes." Later on, Michael, reflecting on Soderbergh's making of the movie, said, "It was just fun to see the style it was shot in. It was a refreshing time to see how Steven [films], how quickly he could move, how mobile he was. [My role] was a small part in really a trilogy. A three-way story, and I was very proud to be part of it." Catherine's role was that of Helena Ayala, the wife of a drug dealer, who desperately tries to get the key witness to the upcoming trial killed. She is ruthless, cold, and frightening.

Made on a solid $48 million budget, *Traffic* feels like Soderbergh's Grand Guignol, filmed with myriad major cinematic influences, from D. W. Griffith's *Intolerance* (1916) to a quartet of Richard Lester films—

A Hard Day's Night (1964), *Help!* (1965), *How I Won the War* (1967), and *Petulia* (1968)—and Jean-Luc Godard's 1960 *Breathless*. One also sees touches of Gillo Pontecorvo's 1966 semidocumentary *The Battle of Algiers* and even Alan J. Pakula's 1976's *All the President's Men*.

Soderbergh elicited a terrific, unexpectedly supercharged performance from Michael as a frustrated father battling his beautiful but addicted teenage daughter, played by Erika Christensen, and a menacingly convincing one from Catherine.

The film was eventually (and sensibly) trimmed to two hours and twenty-seven minutes and given a limited run on December 27, 2000, to qualify for the Oscars, prior to a January nationwide release. It proved the biggest sleeper of the year, grossing $124 million domestically and $208 million worldwide. It received great reviews and equally strong word of mouth, which helped bring mainstream audiences to what was, essentially, a ferociously dark film about the disintegration of the American family and the government's losing battle against the international illegal drug industry.

Roger Ebert, writing in the *Chicago Sun-Times*, gave the film four out of four stars: "The movie is powerful precisely because it doesn't preach. It is so restrained that at one moment—the judge's final speech—I wanted one more sentence, making a point, but the movie lets us supply that thought for ourselves." Stephen Holden wrote in the *New York Times* that "*Traffic* is an utterly gripping, edge-of-your-seat thriller. Or rather it is several interwoven thrillers, each with its own tense rhythm and explosive payoff." Andrew Sarris, long a fan of Soderbergh, writing in the *New York Observer*, noted that "*Traffic* marks Soderbergh definitively as an enormous talent, one who never lets us guess what he's going to do next. The promise of [his debut film] *Sex, Lies and Videotape* has been fulfilled."

Entertainment Weekly gave it an A rating and praised Benicio Del Toro's performance, another member of the film's brilliant ensemble cast. Owen Gleiberman wrote, "Haunting in his understated performance, [Benicio] becomes the film's quietly awakening moral center." Desson Howe, in his review for the *Washington Post*, wrote,

"Soderbergh and screenwriter Stephen Gaghan, who based this on a British television miniseries of the same name, have created an often exhilarating, soup-to-nuts exposé of the world's most lucrative trade." In his review for *Rolling Stone*, Peter Travers wrote, "The hand-held camerawork—Soderbergh himself did the holding—provides a documentary feel that rivets attention." Richard Schickel, in *Time*, was one of the few mainstream critics who couldn't "see" the film: "There is a possibly predictable downside to this multiplicity of story lines: they keep interrupting one another. Just as you get interested in one, Stephen Gaghan's script, inspired by a British mini-series, jerks you away to another."

The film won Academy Awards for Best Director, Best Supporting Actor (Del Toro), Best Film Editing (Stephen Mirrione), and Best Adapted Screenplay. It was also nominated for Best Picture, alongside another Soderbergh film released the same year, *Erin Brockovich*, but both lost to Ridley Scott's *Gladiator*, starring Russell Crowe.[1]

After *Traffic*, a reinvigorated Michael wanted to produce again. The film he chose was a simple, inexpensive-to-make barroom drama called *One Night at McCool's*, based on a screenplay by Stan Seidel, who had spent much of his adult life as a bartender. The story focuses on the interrelated stories of the bartender and his regulars, played by Matt Dillon, Paul Reiser, John Goodman, Andrew Dice Clay (credited here as Andrew Silverstein), and, in a small part, Michael Douglas, completely out of place leching after a young knockout (Liv Tyler). As critic Sean Macaulay of the *Times* of London put it after the film opened, "Some habits die harder than others—Michael's character is obsessed with a pouting nymphet."

---

1   The film appeared on several critics' Top Ten lists, including second on A. O. Scott's *New York Times* list, third on Jami Bernard's New York *Daily News* list, second on the list of Bruce Kirkland at the *Toronto Sun*, third for Stephen Holden at the *New York Times*, third on Owen Gleiberman's list at *Entertainment Weekly*, third for Peter Travers at *Rolling Stone*, fourth for Roger Ebert at the *Chicago Sun-Times*, fourth on the list for Jack Mathews at the New York *Daily News*, and fourth for Andrew Sarris at the *New York Observer*. Several, including Sarris, also listed *Erin Brockovich*; Sarris had it at number eight.

Michael produced the film under his newly formed, solely owned Further Films. Unfortunately, Seidel died before the film went into production, leaving the entire project with an unfinished feel. The director was Harald Zwart, and *McCool's* was only his second film. Michael chose him because he had liked Zwart's first effort, *Hamilton*, a Swedish action-adventure movie, but whatever Michael saw in *Hamilton*, it did not transfer to *One Night at McCool's*. Nothing meshed as the film appeared to want to recapture some of the bartender-memoir feel that Tom Cruise did so successfully in Roger Donaldson's 1988 *Cocktail*. Made for $18 million, the film opened on April 27, 2001, and took in a total of $13.4 million. It was one of the few producing failures of Michael's career.

Almost immediately after, Michael accepted a straight acting role in Gary Fleder's *Don't Say a Word*. He played Dr. Nathan Conrad, a child psychiatrist whose daughter is kidnapped in order to pressure Nathan into getting a secret combination of numbers from a trauma-tized, catatonic young woman hospitalized and unable to speak. Un-less Nathan can somehow get the girl to give up her secret, they will kill his daughter. Despite a terrific cast, including Famke Janssen as Michael's clever and active wife, and the always entertaining Oliver Platt, the film stretched the realm of credibility, nowhere more than in its far-fetched climax. And Michael, at fifty-six, looked a bit too old to be both husband to Janssen and father to nine-year-old Skye McCole Bartusiak, who played his daughter.

WHILE MICHAEL WAS filming *Don't Say a Word*, Catherine was starring in Joe Roth's romantic comedy *America's Sweethearts* (not very romantic and hardly a comedy), about a famous couple's breakup and all the attendant clichés that come with it. Except for a cute bit where outtakes showing who the characters really are make it onto the screen, the film played off like a dud. Throughout the filming of both films, Catherine and Michael were in constant touch. Michael even took a day off to fly to California to visit Catherine.

❖

AMERICA'S SWEETHEARTS opened on July 20, 2001, and despite generally dismal ratings, had a respectable first weekend—second in box office to Joe Johnston's monster *Jurassic Park III*—based on the combined star power of Catherine and co-stars Julia Roberts, Billy Crystal, John Cusack, Hank Azaria, Stanley Tucci, and Christopher Walken. From a $48 million budget it went on to gross $94 million domestically, $138 million worldwide.

Michael couldn't have been happier with his wife's success. When *Don't Say a Word* opened that September, Catherine was cheerfully by his side at the premiere. The gala was held by Fox on September 24, 2001, and *Don't Say a Word* officially opened on September 28, although up until two weeks before it was the biggest secret in Hollywood. Fox was reluctant to put any money behind the picture because of the bath the company had taken with *One Night at McCool's*. Reportedly there were heated arguments behind the closed doors of Fox as to whether to throw good money after bad and promote what could be Michael's second bomb in a row. It wasn't until the film was tested and received great audience cards (advance ratings) that Fox hastily put together an ad campaign with full saturation—print, TV, movies.

Don't Say a Word did $17 million its first weekend and took that week's top position, ahead of the heavily favored winner, Ben Stiller's overhyped *Zoolander*, which came in at $15.7 million. *Don't Say a Word* managed to show a small profit—from its $50 million budget it grossed over $100 million worldwide. More important, it proved that at the age of fifty-six, despite the physical miscasting, Michael could still open a movie at number one.

But the real bottom line was that Michael had been able to reprioritize the things in his life that were now important to him. *Don't Say a Word*'s relative success was no more important to him than if it had been a failure. His was a glorious, glamorous profession, to be sure, but what mattered now most to him about making movies was that it allowed him the comfort and security to raise his new family the way he wanted. Dylan made Michael feel like he was reborn. He doted on the boy in a way he hadn't Cameron (and in the way Kirk hadn't with him, and Herschel hadn't Kirk). He wanted this boy, a product of his love for Catherine, to grow up happy and filled with a healthy capacity to love and be loved.

CHAPTER 20

God bless her that she likes older guys. And some wonderful enhancements have happened in the last few years—Viagra and Cialis, that can make us all feel younger.

—MICHAEL DOUGLAS

THE YEAR 2002 FOUND BOTH MICHAEL AND CATHerine busy on separate star-driven projects. In addition to a slew of fresh T-Mobile phone commercials she filmed that seemed to run every five minutes on network TV (and again in 2009), Catherine began shooting *Chicago*, produced by her old friend Marty Richards, who insisted that only she could play the part of Velma Kelly in his movie version of the musical. The original stage production had opened on Broadway in 1975 starring Chita Rivera as Velma, a vaudeville performer who murders both her husband and her sister when she finds them in bed together, with Gwen Verdon as Roxie Hart, who murders her nightclub-owner boyfriend. *Chicago* was originally directed by Verdon's real-life husband, Bob Fosse, with a score by Fred Ebb and John Kander, whose thing was to make all the world a stage and the stage the world. They had used this technique to create the musical *Cabaret* a decade earlier, a musical adaptation of John Van Druten's play *I Am a Camera*, which was, in turn, adapted from Christopher Isherwood's *Goodbye to Berlin*.

Chicago ran a little more than two years in its first run, respectable but not great. Then, when the O. J. Simpson acquittal in 1994 for a murder whose circumstances somewhat resembled the Hart murders ignited a similar firestorm of journalistic coverage that quickly turned print and TV journalists into an electronic lynch mob, a weird electronic criminal cabaret, *Chicago* was revived on Broadway in 1996 and became a smash hit. Many picked up on the similarities of both cases, and some critics felt the show was a commentary on murder and the sensational trials that turn defendants into celebrities. It was (and is) still running (five thousand-plus performances and counting) when Miramax Films, then headed by the Weinstein brothers, and Marty Richards turned it into a tent-pole film production.

Although she wasn't yet well known in America as a musical performer, Richards knew how musically talented Catherine really was, and that her performance of the song "All That Jazz" alone would surely earn her an Oscar nomination, and very likely an Academy Award.

The film version, directed by Rob Marshall, is frenetic, febrile, and a bit too faux. What worked on the stage as an extended metaphor—crime is a cabaret, old chum—came off on the screen as a messed-up musical, with too many fast cuts and breakaways that kinetically intruded on the integrity of the performances of the musical numbers.

Chicago opened in limited release in New York on December 27, 2002, one day after a massive snowstorm had shut down the city, to qualify for that year's Oscars, and nationwide on January 24. It proved a smash at the box office, eventually returning $306 million from its initial $45 million investment.[1] Its success made Catherine an international cinematic superstar. Oscar talk began opening day. She eventually got a nomination and was heavily favored to win.

---

1   Despite its huge gross and profit, *Chicago* finished out of the ten highest-grossing films of 2002 worldwide. They included, in descending order, Peter Jackson's *The Lord of the Rings: The Two Towers*, Chris Columbus's *Harry Potter and the Chamber of Secrets*, Sam Raimi's *Spider-Man*, George Lucas's *Star Wars Episode II: Attack of the Clones*, Barry Sonnenfeld's *Men in Black II*, Lee Tamahori's *Die Another Day*, M. Night Shyamalan's *Signs*, Chris Wedge and Carlos Saldanha's *Ice Age*, Joel Zwick's *My Big Fat Greek Wedding*, and Steven Spielberg's *Minority Report*. *Chicago* came in tenth domestically.

MICHAEL, MEANWHILE, was busy putting together his own long-overdue dream project, *It Runs in the Family*, a film directed by Fred Schepisi (*Six Degrees of Separation*, 1993) and executive-produced by Michael and his brother Joel. What was unique about *It Runs in the Family* is that it starred three generations of Douglases—Kirk, Michael, Cameron, and Michael's mother, Kirk's first wife, playing Kirk's wife in the movie. "We were always finding reasons not to do it," Michael said about the long-delayed project, which over the years had had many false starts. "There was a certain fear factor of working together."

For Michael, this was a life-culminating project, a wish-fulfilling screen reunion of his family, all of them playing versions of their real selves (with different names): the Nelson family (Michael's generation) meets the Kardashians (Cameron's generation). It was not a complete family get-together. Eric and Peter, Michael's two half brothers, were not asked to appear in the film. Nor was Catherine. Having just finished shooting *Chicago* and pregnant again, she didn't seem to mind not being included in the family's screen saga.

After extensive rehabilitation, Kirk had made great recuperative progress and was now able to talk relatively clearly out of one side of his mouth. And although he hadn't made a film in a while (his last effort, the first film he made after his stroke, had been John Mallory Asher's 1999 *Diamonds*, which was never commercially released), he had taken up writing as physical therapy and religion as its spiritual counterpart. In the years since he was stricken, he has written several memoirs, embraced Judaism, and finally been bar mitzvahed. For the first time, he was willing to make the project that his son had wanted him to do for so long.

Michael's film wife was played by Bernadette Peters, whom Michael preferred over Schepisi's choice, Sigourney Weaver. Clearly, Michael was the star and the producer and was going to call all the creative shots.

Everyone appeared to have a good time except Cameron, who was not used to the intensity of high-caliber professional filmmaking and felt out of place and confused on-set. While he and Michael were doing a scene together, Cameron recalled, his father "grabbed my shoulder really hard. I thought he was being supportive. Actually, he was trying to move me out of his shot."

It wasn't hard to understand. Cameron had long ago turned away from the family business in favor of contemporary music and DJing, and with little real experience in film and the daunting challenge of having to double-jump two legends to make a name for himself, he had been reluctant to be part of the film of the family he didn't feel he belonged to all that much. Drugs and music were the roadblocks he had laid down between himself and the rest of the Douglases, and they were not easy to put aside to act as someone he was not.

WITH HIS SENTIMENTAL family album of a film in the can, set for an April 2003 release, Michael turned his attention to the Academy Awards. As expected, Catherine had been nominated for Best Supporting Actress for her role as Velma in *Chicago*, and he was determined to do everything he could to see her win.

It was not going to be a shoo-in. She was up against some stiff competition, and many of the other actresses who had been nominated had far deeper Hollywood résumés than she did. *Chicago* was only Catherine's seventh Hollywood film (she had appeared in eight previously in England). What worked in Catherine's favor was that the others, with the exception of Queen Latifah, one of Catherine's co-stars, had all appeared in less-than-spectacular productions, and none of their films did anything close to *Chicago* at the box office. The nominees, besides Catherine, included Kathy Bates, for her performance in Alexander Payne's *About Schmidt*; Julianne Moore, for Stephen Daldry's *The Hours*; Queen Latifah; and Meryl Streep, for Spike Jonze's *Adaptation*.

The ceremonies were held on March 25, 2003, at Oscar's newest home, the Kodak Theater, at the corner of Hollywood Boulevard and Highland Avenue. Although 2002 was Oscar's seventy-fifth anniversary and great celebratory events had been planned, nearly all were canceled, as was almost the show itself, because of the American invasion of Iraq, which had taken place five days earlier. The presentation went on with no red carpet but still managed to create some fireworks all its own when filmmaker Michael Moore took the opportunity of winning for Best Documentary (*Bowling for Columbine*) to attack President Bush and his policies. His criticism set off a firestorm of boos, prompting host Steve Martin to come up a few minutes later with the face-saving showstopper of the evening, a joke that turned the audiences jeer's for Moore into cheers for Martin: "The Teamsters are helping Michael Moore into the trunk of his limo." In a different, nonpolitical way, however, Moore was outdone by Adrien Brody's Best Actor win (Roman Polanski's *The Pianist*): upon hearing his name announced, Brody ran up to the stage, grabbed his presenter, Halle Berry, and gave her what became known in Hollywood as "the kiss."

Chicago had been nominated for thirteen Oscars and began collecting them early in the evening, indicating a sweep. When it came time for the award for Best Supporting Actress, the room hushed as Sean Connery, dressed in what appeared to be a modified pirate outfit, read off the names of the nominees, then opened the envelope. "And the Oscar goes to . . ." He let his voice drop to bedroom level as he said simply, "Catherine."

The audience erupted. Catherine and Michael both stood up and kissed each other on both cheeks, and then the very pregnant winner made her way to the stage. Once there, she took her statuette from Connery and shouted, "Thank you so much. My Scotsman giving the Welsh! I can't believe it! Oh my gosh! This is too . . . I mean, my hormones are too out of control to be dealing with this!" After reading the traditional laundry list of thank-yous, she said, "And to my son, Dylan, watching at home, and to my husband who I love, I share this award with you . . . along with this one too," referring to her swollen belly. A look of joy flashed across his face. Now Catherine, too, was a member of the Oscar club. In its own way, it brought them even closer together.

It fell to Michael and Kirk to present the Best Picture Award together. Sensing Catherine might win, the Academy looked to enhance the expected drama of the evening. Standing together at the podium, Kirk, his speech still impaired, put his arm around his son and said, "This is my son, Michael. He has *two* awards . . . but I'm still young!" The audience laughed and applauded good-naturedly as Kirk gently prodded the Academy for having never given him an Oscar: "The seventy-fifth anniversary—oh, to be seventy-five again!" After another joke or two, Kirk finally let Michael talk, but not before admonishing him to "speak distinctly." Yet another burst of appreciation applause from the crowd. When the audience hushed, Michael responded with, "My father, who art in movies." The audience roared with appreciation.

Kirk then read the names of the Best Picture nominees: *Chicago, Gangs of New York, The Hours, Lord of the Rings—The Two Towers, The Pianist*. As Kirk fumbled with the envelope, Michael said to him, "You're supposed to say 'And the Oscar goes to . . . ,'" to which Kirk responded, "And the winner is . . ." More laughter and applause. When Kirk finally managed to open the envelope, he looked at the name of the winner, then tore the card it was written on in two, gave one half to Michael, and said into the microphone excitedly, "*Chicago!*" The film would go on to win a total of six Oscars that night, including Best Picture and Best Supporting Actress.

It was a huge night in Catherine's and Michael's lives, but hardly the biggest, not by a long shot. One month later, on April 20, 2003, Catherine gave birth to their second child, a daughter they named Carys Zeta Douglas.

MICHAEL'S GLORIFIED home movie did not do nearly as well. Released five days after the birth of Carys, *It Runs in the Family* barely opened before it disappeared from the big screen. Budget figures were not available, but the film grossed only $7 million, marking it purely as a labor of love, something for the Douglases to pull out and show to each other every Christmas.

That same year Michael made two documentaries, *Tell Them Who You Are* (released in 2004), a biographical piece about Haskell Wexler in which Wexler's friends and co-workers, including Michael, were interviewed about the revered cinematographer (Michael also narrated), and one by Scott Miller, *Direct Order* (released in 2003), about a secret army experiment during the Gulf War that had soldiers being involuntarily injected with anthrax (and dying from it) in the hopes that scientists would be able to develop a vaccine. Neither received much attention, from either critics or audiences, but Michael considered both projects highly worthwhile.

And then there were no new movies for three years, as Michael preferred to remain in the background, enjoying his new role as father and second-chance family life. Indeed, he became as close to a househusband as one could be, taking care of the chores and doting on his two young children. As he later wrote in an essay for *Newsweek*, "I adjust my schedule to my wife's, since she is in the prime of her career. The school year tells us when we are to travel. The kids know what Mommy does for a living, but they have never seen Daddy's movies (they're too young), so Mommy makes movies and Daddy makes pancakes! . . . Don't get me wrong. I still go to work, but now only on projects I really care about. . . . I love being home."

Catherine, meanwhile, coming off her Oscar win and with Michael's encouragement, cranked out five films in a row. She lent her voice to Tim Johnson's animated *Sinbad: Legend of the Seven Seas*; made Joel and Ethan Coen's *Intolerable Cruelty* (co-starring George Clooney), which grossed $120 million on a $60 million investment; and Steven Spielberg's *The Terminal*, a goofy, uninteresting film about a refugee stuck in an airport, where he lives for several months because he has no legal exit papers. *The Terminal* co-starred Tom Hanks and grossed almost $250 million off a $60 million budget. Catherine then reteamed with Steven Soderbergh for his *Ocean's Twelve*, another film with George Clooney and his modern-day version of the Rat Pack—Matt Damon, Brad Pitt, Don Cheadle, Julia Roberts, and a dozen other familiar names and faces. That one outgrossed *The Terminal*, earning $362 million off a $110 million budget. Then there was Martin Campbell's 2005 *Legend of Zorro*, the sequel to the film that had first introduced her to America.

Once again she easily stole the film. Made for $75 million, *Legend* grossed $142 million worldwide. Her successful five-film post-*Chicago* run grossed a total of just under $1 billion.

After that, feeling very much the conqueror, she too assumed a lower profile, to catch her breath, ease the risk of overexposure, and spend some quality time with her husband and children.

Their relative peace was disturbed in a fashion that holds more terror in Hollywood than perhaps anywhere else in the country because of the infamous and unforgettable Manson murders of 1969. In July 2004, an obsessed fan of Michael's was arrested and charged with stalking Catherine Zeta-Jones (a scenario that eerily echoed the plot of *Fatal Attraction*). The woman, Dawnette Knight, was arrested, and at a pretrial hearing in Los Angeles it was established that she had threatened to cut up Catherine "like meat on a bone, and feed her to the dogs"—murdered, the prosecution contended, "in the same style as Sharon Tate."

Michael testified that his wife was driven to the brink of a breakdown by the threats. "She was hysterical," Michael said under oath. "She was fainting. She could not get any air. She showed all the signs of having a nervous breakdown." Knight's defense was that she didn't mean any harm, and she wrote a letter of apology. She was sentenced to three years in prison. Michael then seriously upgraded the security for his family and decided it was best if they kept an even lower profile for a while, meaning no more movies for him or Catherine.

The only appearance they made together that year was one they had to go to, the big 2004 tribute to fifty-nine-year-old Michael at the Golden Globes (Hollywood's Batman awards to Oscar's Superman statuettes), when he was named the recipient of the 2004 Cecil B. DeMille Lifetime Achievement Award for both his acting and his producing. What made it especially meaningful to Michael was that Kirk had won the award in 1968 for the same double achievement. This time Dad would be sitting in the audience watching his son being honored.

Michael turned reflective about how far he had come. "How lucky I have been to meet my beautiful wife and start a new family," he said when he first received word of the award. "You know, at this point in my life, I certainly never anticipated having a 3½-year-old and a 7-month-old. To be able to share this award with my family during what is a very beautiful time for us just shows how my priorities have changed very dramatically. Now my wife comes first, and my family, and only then my work, and that is something I am pretty sure I couldn't have said 20 years ago."

Later on, he reflected further: "Who knows, if I hadn't met Catherine, I might be in the trenches in L.A., in my office, and focused on producing a lot more movies and television shows. But that's not—I've been fortunate. You learn to respect something of value and nurture it and treat it well."

ON JULY 6, 2004, Michael received word that his half brother Eric, forty-six years old and the youngest of Kirk's four sons, had died of a drug overdose in his one-bedroom apartment on Manhattan's East Side. His body was discovered by the housekeeper, who had come to clean. According to the coroner's report, Eric died from acute intoxication from the combined effects of alcohol, tranquilizers, and painkillers. Although Eric had always been proud of his trim physique, which he believed was part of his actor's instrument, he weighed three hundred pounds at the time of his death.

It had not been an easy life for Eric, or a successful one. Discussing his lifelong battles with drugs and alcohol, he once told New York's *Daily News* that he found it difficult being part of such a well-known family. "The pressures of being the youngest son in a famous family sometimes got to me," he said. "I used to feel I had to compare myself to them." In 1999, his speech and gait were permanently affected by an eight-day drug-related coma, and in 2003, the year before he died, he was tossed out of a North Carolina hotel after the maid, whom he had locked out along with everybody else, finally gained entrance and discovered he was drunk in a room filled with trash. It was complaints about the odor that had prompted management to check out the situation. That night, he told police he was a stand-up comedian participating in a weight-reduction program.

Michael had no public comment about Eric's death. The only statement from anyone in the Douglas family came from a joint spokesperson: "The family is very shocked and saddened by this event. We hope you will respect their privacy at this time."

THAT SAME YEAR, in a gesture that combined gratitude, satisfaction, and accomplishment, Michael donated $1 million to UC Santa Barbara for the school's new Carsey-Wolf Center for Film, Television, and New Media.

The lobby of the center was named after Michael.

CHAPTER 21

*Giving back to the planet, that's probably as close to immortality
as you can get. . . . Maybe because I'm so consumed with my
father's legacy—the honors he's receiving, the theaters that are
named after him, all of the incredible amount of impressive
things—that either I haven't dealt with mine or I just don't
think of myself in the same category. I don't know. It's sort of
the opposite side of growing up. . . . You grow up in the shadow
of somebody and then at the end, in the twilight, you have the
shadow of that somebody again.*

—MICHAEL DOUGLAS

M
ICHAEL RETURNED TO ACTIVE FILMMAKING IN
2005, via his independent production company Further Films.
The Sentinel, his first feature in three years, directed by Clark Johnson
and shot on location in Georgetown, in the northwest quadrant of
Washington, D.C. He both starred in and produced this presidential assassination movie involving rogue Secret Service men, based on
the novel by a former Secret Service agent, Gerald Petievich. Also in
the cast were Eva Longoria, Kim Basinger, and Kiefer Sutherland. In
the film, which is similar to Wolfgang Petersen's *In the Line of Fire*, a
1993 Clint Eastwood vehicle, Michael plays Pete Garrison, an aging
Secret Service agent assigned to the president's inner circle who becomes involved in an affair with the president's wife (played by Kim
Basinger), a scenario preposterous enough without the almost sixty-
one-year-old Michael Douglas in that role. Being the boss has its benefits.

Still, Michael experienced more than the usual amount of trouble raising money for this project, and it made him realize how much the business of making movies had changed. "I'm in love," he told one reporter, "and I've got a nice family, so part of [my not wanting to produce movies], you know, was saying, 'Screw it.' Now I'm trying to get my mojo back for our industry."

To another he said, "Things have changed a lot with not just me getting older. . . . The industry has changed. . . . [T]he studios are . . . companies. They are scouring their libraries to find an economical way to make movies with the least amount of profit participation, which is why we're seeing all these remakes and sequels and TV series as movies. It's depressing and difficult. If you want a certain amount of independence as a filmmaker, you're obliged to find outside financing."

And to yet another, "Studios today are just a division of an entertainment media corporation. Look, it was always a business, but there was at least the sense of a struggle between art and commerce. It's gone now . . . a tough economic climate. You're either doing big-budget studio pictures or low-budget independent films. Middle-budget films— it's Death Valley. Anyway, there are no roles at this point that I'm dying to play. . . . I can't compete with the younger men. I'm 62 years old. I'm not looking to be taking off my shirt."

Michael eventually raised the money for *The Sentinel* by partnering Further Films with another independent film company Regency Enterprises. Together they managed to get a distribution deal with Fox. With their financial backing secure, Michael felt encouraged to fill out a slate of several potential Further Films projects that included a second (unnamed) sequel to *Romancing the Stone* to star himself and Catherine.[1] At the same time, Oliver Stone was putting out feelers to bring Michael back to major name-above-the-title star status by having him reprise his Oscar-winning role as Gordon Gekko in a sequel to *Wall Street*.

Early in 2006, Michael appeared in Anthony and Joe Russo's *You*,

---

1   It never happened.

Me and Dupree, a family comedy, playing the father of Kate Hudson, and surrounded by such contemporary stars as Owen Wilson, Matt Dillon, and Seth Rogen. The films is mindless, with Michael seemingly wandering through the script looking for a place to sit down. The film was made for $54 million.

THE SENTINEL WAS released on April 21, 2006, and received almost universally negative reviews. Made for $60 million, it grossed a disappointing $78 million worldwide, opened and closed in a flash, and instantly evaporated from the consciousness of the country's moviegoers. Michael looked old and tired in it, and certainly not believable as the president's wife's lover.

After the July 2006 release of *You, Me and Dupree*, which received equally poor reviews but earned $130 million worldwide ($76 million domestic), Michael then took another break from movies and, together with Catherine, concentrated on building up their growing real-estate empire, which included homes in Barbados, Bermuda, Manhattan, Aspen, and Quebec. In 2007, Michael and Catherine decided to move full-time to Bermuda, as far from the paparazzi as possible. They built a guesthouse in Bermuda so that their parents could come and visit whenever they wanted.

Eventually, though, Michael, missing the Hollywood action, decided to take an acting job back in Hollywood in *King of California*. He read and liked the script, by first-time director-screenwriter Mike Cahill, a broken-home drama about a young girl (Evan Rachel Wood) trying to find her own identity while her father (Michael Douglas) languishes in a mental institution. Michael was sent the script directly by Cahill after it had been turned down by all the studios, and he decided to become involved simply because he thought it was a part he was well suited for. There were obvious if faint echoes of *Cuckoo's Nest* (Stephen Holden, writing in the *New York Times*, actually called the film "a sequel of sorts" to *Cuckoo's Nest*), but no one would ever mistake the two films for each other. *King of California*, shot in thirty-one days, made it to the Sundance Film Festival, an auspicious beginning, but found full theatrical distribution only in Canada; it had a very limited commercial release in the States and grossed a little over $1 million on a $10 million budget.

AND THEN THE family ghosts once more appeared. In 2007 Cameron, twenty-eight, was arrested again, in New York City, this time for felony possession of a controlled substance after police officers stopped a car he was in and found a syringe with liquid cocaine. (It was rumored but never conclusively proven that Cameron also had been detained in California on similar charges.)

For the last fifteen years Michael had been unable to prevent Cameron, if such a thing were possible, from traveling down the dead end road of drugs and booze that had killed Michael's half brother Eric. This time, when Cameron pled out to a misdemeanor and opted for rehab, Michael publicly pledged to stand by the boy, to help him by taking more of an admittedly long-overdue, direct fatherly role in his son's life. "My priorities are my marriage and my children, whereas earlier, my career was my priority. The one thing I pride myself on [with Cameron] is he could count on me. But there were big absences."

When talking about Cameron's troubles, Michael immediately recalled his own uphill climb, part of the price that came with being the son of Kirk Douglas. It was as if he were somehow trying to blame the genes he had inherited from his dad and passed along to Cameron, in an effort to absolve himself of any real responsibility. He still sounded somewhat distant and dismissive about the boy, saying, "He's really good, but acting is about creating your own identity. And the [Kirk Douglas] genes [always] come through and so it takes a little longer to establish yourself."

But when it came to talking about his second set of children, with Catherine, Michael transformed into proud papa, bursting with pride about how talented his little tykes were. Whenever he was asked about Dylan and Carys, he became the pitch-perfect adoring daddy: "The joy of raising two children includes Dylan doing a mean impersonation of Elvis and Carys memorizing all of the lyrics from *Mamma Mia!*"

Michael had put Cameron in the darkness of his own past while keeping Dylan and Carys in the brightness of his present.

In 2007, Michael accepted the personal invitation of executive producer Bob Epstein to record a new intro for his friend Brian Williams, the anchor of the broadcast, to be heard every night across America. Not long after, Oliver Stone contacted Michael about the possibility of doing a sequel to *Wall Street*. Michael jumped at the chance to make a real movie again.

To WARM UP for his reprise of the character of Gordon Gekko, his first major movie role in nearly a decade, Michael took a cameo in Mark Waters's *Ghosts of Girlfriends Past*, made in 2008 as a modern remake of Dickens's *A Christmas Carol*, starring Matthew McConaughey and Anne Archer, Michael's co-star from *Fatal Attraction* (they had no scenes together in *Ghosts*). It was only moderately successful, but it helped Michael get his acting timing back to tackle Gekko again.

Then the *Wall Street* sequel hit a series of snags, having mostly to do with Fox's dissatisfaction with the script and its feeling that the subject was dated. That allowed Michael to make two more fast films in 2008 (for release the following year). One was Peter Hyams's *Beyond a Reasonable Doubt*, an awful, phone-it-in remake of the 1956 Fritz Lang film that starred Dana Andrews and Joan Fontaine. The remake bombed big-time at the box office, taking in a total $4.3 million worldwide, not even a third of the $25 million it cost to make.[2]

Michael also made *Solitary Man* that year for two good friends, the director Brian Koppelman and producer Steven Soderbergh. It also gave him the chance to work again with Danny DeVito, who had a role in it. The film was critically well received everywhere it played, but few people went to see it. Michael described his role in it this way:

---

2   Budget: IMDB; gross: Box Office Mojo.

"I'm a car dealer who thinks he might have a medical problem and decides to go for broke. Susan Sarandon plays my wife, and Mary-Louise Parker is my girlfriend, so you can see I still get to have a good time onscreen." The film was made for $15 million and barely earned $5 million worldwide. That meant that Michael's last several films had flopped, all of which added pressure to his upcoming performance in the *Wall Street* sequel.

In 2009, Michael and Catherine experienced dual creative resurrections at approximately the same time. In June Michael received one of the highest honors Hollywood gives, the American Film Institute's Life Achievement Award, which Kirk had received in 1991. The ceremony was taped and shown as a television special that July.

In the audience for the gala presentation, to pay homage to Michael's career, were Kirk; Michael's mother, Diana; and Catherine, all sitting together. Catherine also opened the show with a sizzling performance of "One" from *A Chorus Line*. As the words "one singular sensation" came out of Catherine's mouth, she stared directly at Michael. Tears poured out of his eyes and ran down his cheeks.

When it was Kirk's turn to take the stage, he was his usual charming if heavy-handed self. "I'm a little bit confused. I'm too young to have a son getting a lifetime achievement award. I'm so proud of my son Michael. I don't tell him that much often."

Many of Michael's former co-stars showed up to pay tribute—even Bob Dylan, who still carries around the Oscar he won for "Things Have Changed" from *Wonder Boys* and displays it onstage at every concert he gives. He was a "surprise" guest and played an acoustic solo version of "Things Have Changed."

Martin Sheen took the stage to remind the audience of the night's honoree's extensive humanitarian work.

Michael was the last to speak, concluding the evening by expressing his ongoing theory of movie star science by saying he was grateful for the "great genes" his parents had blessed him with. "I want to thank you both [Kirk and Diana] and I love you both." He then made it official by announcing that he was going to star in the sequel to *Wall*

Street, to be directed once again by Oliver Stone; the news surprised the audience and brought one final standing ovation.

Wall Street: Money Never Sleeps had found renewed interest at Fox. Stone needed *Wall Street: Money Never Sleeps* to help restore him to the A-list of mainstream directors. After going through a number of writers and scenarios—one that for a time relocated the entire production to China, which neither Michael nor the Chinese government cared for—the script was restructured with the film beginning as Gekko is released from federal prison after serving an eight-year sentence. Its opening scene has him passing through the prison gates, looking older, downtrodden, and lost in the wilderness of his newly reclaimed freedom (a nice metaphor for where Stone had found himself after his career had floundered—picking up the story of Gekko is picking up his own story).

He soon discovers his daughter is engaged to Jake Moore (more money?), a young, money-hungry wanna-be reminiscent of Bud Fox (Charlie Sheen) from the original *Wall Street*, played by that week's current Hollywood hotshot Shia LaBeouf. The film's overly convoluted plot (a Stone signature) has a repentant Gekko trying to make up for his former greed-driven crimes by steering LaBeouf on the road to honest moneymaking and at the same time trying to reconcile with his daughter.

Somewhere buried among all the quick-cuts of computers and trading floors is a love story between LaBeouf's character and Winnie Gekko (Carey Mulligan), who remains angry at her father for the suicide of her brother while Gordon was in prison. Part of the drama of the film is the conflict caused between LaBeouf's emergent greed, his Gordon Gekko side, and his genuine love for Carey, who doesn't like the resemblances she sees between her boyfriend and her father, whom she stopped talking to when he went to prison. The rest of it is essentially a replay of the original—the attractive but losing game of Wall Street greed, the inevitable saving grace of redemption.

Directed by Stone from a script by TV and independent film screenwriter Allan Loeb (also a licensed stockbroker), *Wall Street:*

Money Never Sleeps was produced during the summer and early fall of 2009 for $70 million and was promoted less as Oliver Stone's than as Michael's return to mainstream moviemaking, reprising a role that had won him his Best Actor Oscar and just might cap his comeback with another one for the same role.[3]

Catherine, meanwhile, had agreed to star in the 2009 Broadway revival of Stephen Sondheim's *A Little Night Music,* a concert-style show loosely based on Ingmar Bergman's 1955 film *Smiles of a Summer Night.* As Desirée, she would have the plum song of the score, "Send in the Clowns."

Both the show and the movie were New York–based projects. Realizing they were both going to be committed to a long stay in New York, Michael and Catherine agreed to move back full-time to the Central Park West apartment and enroll the children in private schools in Manhattan. Michael began production on the film as Catherine began rehearsals for a December opening.

IN THE MIDST of all this, on July 28, 2009, Cameron, thirty years old, was arrested again, this time by the Drug Enforcement Agency, for possession of half a pound of methamphetamine and charged with the far more serious intent to distribute.

The bust was the result of a three-year sting operation. The authorities had known he was using since 2007, almost from the first time post-rehab. Using phone taps, they knew when Cameron was selling, even the code he used to disguise his transactions. He always referred to meth as "pastry" or "bath salts," as in "Did you get a chance to, like, smell any of the salts?" Before the capture, one friend who had run into him just days before said, "He came up to hug me and I didn't recognize him. He was pasty and heavy. The familiar spark was gone. . . . He had some big shoes to fill, and it haunted him. Cam-

---

3   Stephen Schiff, presumably brought in to help Loeb write the script, received co-writer credit.

eron was desperately in need of love—as if it was an out-of-reach thing for him."

The arrest gave Michael another dose of insecurity about his role in Cameron's life, and a familiar combination of denial and self-pity. Was it *his* fault that Cameron had been arrested again for drugs? Could he have done more to prevent his son from falling back into such an existence? "I'll assume whatever responsibilities I have to," Michael said at the time. "Would it have been better to have been around more? Absolutely. There were absences. I was no angel."

Cameron pled guilty, and Michael arranged bail for him for house arrest until the April 2010 sentencing. In January, Cameron was arrested again, this time for violating bail when his girlfriend was caught smuggling heroin to him inside an electric toothbrush.

COINCIDENTALLY, Michael's role in the *Wall Street* sequel involved a man full of remorse who has lost a son to suicide and is having a difficult relationship with his rebellious daughter, who can't forgive him for her brother's untimely passing. Ironically, as an acting prop, Cameron's tragedy and Eric's as well were a big help to Michael while he was making the film. But as a mirror that reflected his own perceived failures in helping to save both of them, their fates were a total emotional disaster.

And yet all of it was a mere prelude to the annus horribilis that was about to come down on Michael and Catherine.

Chapter 22

If I'd known what a big shot Michael was going to be, I'd have been nicer to him when he was a kid.

—Kirk Douglas

Hardly any second-generation people have succeeded. It's a minefield of disasters, of broken careers and self-destruction out there.

—Michael Douglas

September 25, 2009, Michael's sixty-fifth birthday and Catherine's fortieth, was the start of what each hoped would be auspicious career years. Michael had finished *Wall Street: Money Never Sleeps* and felt confident it was strong enough to mark a successful return to making big films.

On December 13, Catherine opened as Desirée in the revival of *A Little Night Music* on Broadway to glowing reviews, both for the show and for her. Ben Brantley, in his *New York Times* review, called it "a weekend in the country with Eros and Thanatos" and wrote what amounted to a love letter to Catherine. It was a Christmas season that seemed for Michael and Catherine, separately and together, drenched in snow-white perfection. With Michael back making big-time movies, and Catherine back on Broadway, everything for the moment seemed right.

In February 2010, Soderbergh asked Michael to do a cameo in *Knockout*, an ensemble action thriller to be shot mostly in Ireland. Although Catherine was still appearing in *A Little Night Music*, she encouraged him to do it, and told him that she would try to fly over as often as she could. When finished, *Knockout*'s jittery style (Soderbergh loves to shoot hand-held, holding the camera himself) and complex plot couldn't find a satisfactory distributor for the summer. Soderbergh changed the film's name to *Haywire*, made some more cuts, and planned a series of film festival releases that later helped it gain a commercial one. (*Haywire* was released in January 2012 to mixed reviews and poor box office.)

AND THEN, a few months into 2010, the darkness got darker. Cameron's defense team appeared to try to shift the emotional guilt to Michael and Kirk by describing Cameron as a lonely kid who lived in fear "of being compared to his father and his grandfather." It was not an easy thing for Michael to sit through. Then, in April 2010, he had to make the one appearance he dreaded but could not avoid, in federal court in Lower Manhattan to hear sentence passed on Cameron, who had been convicted for attempting to distribute illegal substances. The federal guidelines called for a ten-year minimum sentence.

As Michael watched, Cameron stood before U.S. District Court judge Richard Berman and told the court he was sober for the first time in his adult life and grateful for the chance to get clean. Judge Berman listened as Cameron continued: "Firstly, I would like to apologize to my family and my loved ones for putting them through this nightmare of my making—and for my behaviors that have caused a rift between us in the past. I would also like to apologize to the Court for my decisions and my actions that put me in front of you here today, Your Honor.

"But, I would like to ask you for an opportunity to be a productive family member and a good role model to my brothers and sisters during this time in their life when they're maturing from small children to young men and women so I can be there for them for whatever may occur in their lives; for advice, guidance, support, or just somebody to talk to and maybe be able to steer them in the right direction.

"Nothing, Your Honor, is more important to me than my family and the goals that I have set for myself and I feel adamant that I will not let myself be led astray by my warped thinking and false pretenses due to my long heroin addiction. I envelop my mind, instead, with the idea that I want to take the right path, the true path and the path that I know is well within my reach. And I know this because I was presented with some opportunities earlier in my life and at the time I didn't—I wasn't able to see how valuable they were and how rare they were. As a result, I squandered a lot of them, which was, you know, probably started, you know, where I am today; a lot of mistakes and missed opportunities, you know?

"I miss, so dearly, being involved in my true passion in life which brings me true happiness and fulfillment, which is being an entertainer and putting a smile on people's faces or stirring some sort of emotion inside of them; ultimately trying to inspire people in some way whether it was through dancing as a youngster or hopefully music and acting in the future.

"I believe, Your Honor, that things will be different this time because, number one, most importantly, I feel that I have the full support of my family and the people that are important in my life; number two, because obviously I know where this life can go and if I should be so fortunate to have another chance, I would never squander that opportunity because I know how fruitful my life can be; and thirdly, I will never settle for anything less than what I know myself to be capable of. I feel like it is my duty. And that's all I have to say."

It was excruciating for Michael to have to sit helplessly and listen to Cameron's splintered plea for mercy.

Before he passed sentence, Judge Berman acknowledged the thirty-seven character-reference letters he had received (not unusual in pre-sentencing, especially when celebrities or their children are involved), including an especially emotional one from Diandra, who squarely put the blame on Michael for not being there when Cameron was a boy in need of a father: "Being Michael's son and Kirk Douglas's grandson was an incredible cross for Cameron to bear. My son felt defeated before he could even get out of the gate."

In his letter, Kirk, then ninety-three, asked the judge to spare his grandson from years in prison, saying he hoped to see him rebound from his troubles "before I die. . . . I'm convinced Cameron could be a fine actor," Kirk Douglas wrote. "I hope I can see that happen before I die. I love Cameron."

In his five-page handwritten letter, which he read aloud, Michael acknowledged once more the lifelong struggle he had had to face as the son of a Hollywood star, and how he had failed to save his son from the same emotional fate. "Dear Judge Berman, I don't want to burden you with a litany of my son Cameron's rehab history, beginning at 13. He's an adult and responsible for his own life. We do know, however, that genes, family, and peer pressure are all a strong influence on a substance abuser. Many drug dealers come from families who have struggled with addiction. Few receive leniency because of it. Cameron grew up a single child in a bad marriage." Michael, in effect, blamed both himself and Diandra for Cameron's problems. Cameron had a "father whose career took him away from home, and a young mother without any parenting skills handed down from her own parents. . . . I have some idea of the pressure of finding your own identity with a famous father. I'm not sure I can comprehend it with two generations to deal with. . . . For the past eight months, I have cherished my two hour a week in person conversation with Cameron at the MCC [Metropolitan Correctional Center]. He's sober! I get to witness the wonderful young man he can be. He maintains his spirit, blames no one but himself, and recognizes his criminal activity began with his heroin use. . . . Cameron found his family in the gang mentality."

Before sentencing, Judge Berman said, "The missives indicate problematic parenting by both his mother and father in the forms of parental absence and distance, parental immaturity and drug and alcohol abuse in the immediate or extended families." He then sentenced Cameron to five years, half the ten that were expected and mandatory, and five years of close supervision, the second five the equivalent of parole, and warned him that this was his "last chance to make it."

As part of his sentence, Cameron had to forfeit $300,000, more than half of what his lawyers said was his estimated $500,000 net worth; he also had to pay another $25,000 as a fine and upon his release serve an additional 450 hours of community service.

After court, a somber Michael Douglas was overheard telling his lawyer he thought the sentence was fair. He then helped guide a bewildered-looking Diandra through a crush of photographers to a waiting car.[1]

IT TOOK SEVERAL months before Michael made one of his very few public statements about Cameron's imprisonment: "There was a deep sense of relief that as a serious substance abuser, as long as he's been, and how sick, that he was going to get clean. He's in excellent health, feeling very good and empowered. He's finally making this commitment to change. He's been dealt a few hands. He took the news fine."

As for how he was coping with his son's plight, Michael said, "Anybody who has a relative or child in substance abuse has some idea of what this feels like. This is one of those worst-case scenarios. It will ultimately be a painful lesson. . . . [M]y priorities were very similar to my father's. Career first."

THAT AUGUST, Michael revealed to the world he had been diagnosed with stage four throat cancer, the most advanced form of the disease, nearly always fatal, and was about to begin a difficult two-month regimen of radiation and chemotherapy.

Michael likely would have preferred to keep the diagnosis private, but after persistent rumors had spread throughout the entertainment

---

1   On December 21, 2011, Cameron was sentenced to an additional four and a half years for trying to smuggle drugs into prison.

industry that he might be dying, he decided to do an end run around the gossips and stop the whispers by going public with the grim news.

He had booked an appearance on the *Late Show with David Letterman* for September 1, 2010, originally to promote the September 24 release of *Wall Street: Money Never Sleeps*. Looking relaxed and happy and holding a bottle of water in one hand, Michael was dressed resplendently in a white suit with pink shirt, looking as if he had just stepped off his yacht in Bermuda. During the loud ovation that greeted him, he sat down and talked briefly with Dave about the new movie. Then, in response to Dave's question about how things were going other than that, giving Michael an easy opening to a difficult subject that everybody already knew about, Michael almost casually announced that he was indeed suffering from throat cancer. "Yeah, I've got cancer," he said. "I got cancer. . . . I found out three weeks ago. It's throat and I've just finished my first week of radiation." As for his stage four diagnosis, Michael told Letterman, "The big thing you're always worried about is it spreading, so I am head and neck. I am above the neck, so nothing's gone down, and the expectations are good."

Letterman then asked Michael if he smoked, to which Michael replied, with a weary chuckle, "This particular type of cancer is caused by alcohol and drinking." Letterman asked him about his chances for recovery, to which Michael replied, "The percentages are very good. I would hate to say, but right now, it looks like it should be 80 percent, and with certain hospitals and everything, it does improve."

Michael's appearance on Letterman made headlines around the world. He had always had an aura of youth about him, something he shared with most baby boomers (although he was born a year and a half before the official start of that generation). Now he had laid down the gauntlet, telling the world he intended to beat his cancer.

MOST AFTERNOONS, Michael sat alone in his darkened living room, staring out the window at the treetops of Central Park through a crack in the drawn curtains, sipping frequently from an aloe-based drink to soothe the sores that had developed in his mouth. As one witness reported, he was "clearly in pain."

Michael said, "The radiation kills the cancer, but it kills everything else too. The white blood cells, the red blood cells. Sores start forming in your mouth, then lesions, and then you can't swallow. People then either get fed through their stomach, or you fight it and go through it by drinking liquids. . . . I've decided to fight it.

"What I'll really be struggling with the last few weeks is the weight loss. Because you can't eat solids and you can't swallow."

When asked about his future plans, he said he wanted to play Liberace in a TV biopic to be directed by his good friend Steven Soderbergh. "'Why are you going to do that? [people ask].' And I say, 'I have no idea.' . . . [W]hat I really like and am drawn to is the unpredictable."

CATHERINE FINISHED her award-winning run on Broadway and took the children to Bermuda. Michael insisted that he and Catherine had agreed it would be better for the children this way, sparing them from having to see their father suffer from his disease and its debilitating treatment. She said Douglas told their children—Dylan, ten, and Carys, seven—the difficult news himself: he "sat them down and told them he has cancer now."

"The hardest part is seeing his fatigue, because Michael is never tired," Catherine said when asked about her husband's condition.

WALL STREET: MONEY NEVER SLEEPS had its world premiere at the 2010 Cannes Film Festival, one of Michael's old stomping grounds, and its regular commercial opening in the United States on September 24, the night before his sixty-sixth birthday. It received mixed reviews and was not a film that created a whole lot of must-see buzz, other than people's curiosity to see how Michael looked just before he got sick. On a budget of about $65 million, the film grossed $135 million worldwide—good, not great—and won no major awards.

It was a disappointment to Stone, but as far as Michael was concerned, it was a huge hit, because he was still alive to see it open on the big screen.

BEFORE RETURNING to the States from Bermuda, Catherine took the kids to Wales, where she had agreed to appear on September 30 at Cardiff's Millennium Stadium to perform as a special guest at a gala concert for the Ryder Cup golf tournament. Backstage, Prince Charles offered Catherine some words of comfort about her situation with Michael. Catherine told the audience that Michael was "doing fantastically well and the doctors could not be happier. As anyone knows, it's a grueling eight weeks and he's holding up strong. I'm very proud of him. . . . I was in love with my husband at first sight and still am. We have the most solid relationship."

After she finished her performance, she and the children were rushed by police escort to the airport, where they boarded a private jet to America, to be by Michael's side as his eight-week regimen of treatments came to an end. A spokesperson emphatically denied she was not staying for the rest of the concert because Michael's condition had taken a turn for the worse.

IN THE MIDST of all this, while he was recovering from chemotherapy and radiation treatments, Michael heard from Diandra, and not in a sympathetic fashion. The last time he'd seen her was at Cameron's sentencing. She had instituted a lawsuit against him, claiming that according to the divorce settlement, she was entitled to half of any profits from work he had done while they were together, including any spin-offs, meaning *Wall Street: Money Never Sleeps*. Michael's attorney fought the suit, claiming that there had been no plans for the film until long after the marriage was dissolved and therefore it was not a spin-off. He claimed she was not entitled to any more money.

In November 2010, a New York judge rejected Diandra's lawsuit, not on its merit but because he said it should have been brought in California, where the original divorce claim had been filed. Diandra announced through her attorneys that she intended to continue to appeal. Her motivation may not have been anything so dramatic as lasting vengeance or as pathetic as jealousy or the need to somehow remain relevant in Michael's life. Or it may have been even more practical and mundane than that. Diandra had lost a great deal of money investing separately with both Kenneth I. Starr and Bernie Madoff and, despite her inherited wealth and her huge settlement with Michael, needed cash.

After Diandra lost her appeal in the New York courts, she made one final appeal for the judge to reconsider his decision, which he said he would.[2]

Ironically, Michael, known for his generosity to friends and those who needed a helping hand, might have helped Diandra if she had simply asked him to (although friends of Michael suggest that his generosity and at times dicey business investments made to help out friends had been somewhat curtailed by Catherine, who likely would have vetoed any financial help for Diandra, believing the original settlement she had gotten from Michael was more than enough).

And there was something else. Throughout all the years in which Diandra had threatened Michael with divorce, she stayed with him; and after their separation, she made that pact with Michael about not divorcing so they wouldn't be able to marry anyone else. Michael wanted no part of that tired game. He was over her and had moved on with his life and thought she should as well.

❖

---

2   It wasn't until June 2011 that the judge announced he still could find no reason to reverse his decision, citing the clear geographical jurisdictions of the case. Diandra then announced she would continue her suit in Los Angeles.

ON JANUARY 9, 2011, Michael went on television once more to discuss his disease. This time he chose the *Today* show, where he told Matt Lauer the good news, that he believed he had beaten the cancer. "I feel good, relieved the tumor is gone. But, you know, I have to check out on a monthly basis now to maintain. I guess there's not a total euphoria. . . . But it's been a wild six-month ride . . . [My] salivary ducts have been closed down as a result of the radiation, probably for at least a year or two. So your mouth is very dry—particularly affects you at night, for sleeping. Still have the cheek factor, which will progressively go away. But that's about it . . . I'm eating like a pig. . . . I lost about 32 pounds. And I've put about 12 back. But, I mean, I got another 20, 25 to go. I can eat anything I want. They want to keep the cardio down because they want me to put some more weight on. I lost a lot of muscle mass, so I'm going to work on that. I'm going to get my fingers ready for Liberace, you know. . . . I think the odds are with the tumor gone and what I know about this particular type of cancer, which put a time line on my life, I've got it beat."

He then added, "You know, I'm fortunate I've got a mother who's 88 and my father's 94. So, you know, I feel good about those genes, but it's definitely a third act."

IN FEBRUARY 2011, as part of the Queen's birthday honors, Catherine was named a Commander of the Order of the British Empire (CBE, the third-highest rank in the Most Excellent Order of the British Empire). Michael decided he had to be by Catherine's side for that. The entire family flew to London to witness the honor. Afterward, Catherine said, "It was worth [it] to have Michael in good health to be able to enjoy it with us."

In April, back in the States, Catherine publicly admitted for the first time how hard Michael's illness had been on her: "After dealing with the stress of the past year, she made the decision to check in to a mental health facility for a brief stay to treat her bipolar II disorder," a rep said, reading from a written statement. "She's feeling great and looking forward to starting work this week on her two upcoming films."[3]

MICHAEL WAS EAGER to resume making movies, beginning with Soderbergh's Liberace biography. Michael will play the flamboyant homosexual pianist, and Matt Damon is cast as his lover. Filming was scheduled to begin the summer of 2012.

In January 2012, Michael was named the recipient of the twelfth annual Monte Cristo Award from the Eugene O'Neill Theater Center, for his career achievements and his contributions to the theater community. Catherine presented the award to Michael on April 16. As Michael had spent those three summers at the O'Neill in the '60s and been a member of its board since 1980, the award carried both an acknowledgment of his lifelong body of achievement and an appropriate third-act remembrance of how much he owed the O'Neill for the way his life turned out.

AND SO IT WENT, day by day, Michael struggling to remain optimistic, knowing that cancer was a bad loser and had a nasty habit of recurring, and that radiation therapy was an effective option but could only be used once. For the next three years, even as he continued to work, he would have to undergo monthly screenings to see if any sign of the cancer had returned. At the age of sixty-seven, checkups every month seemed a small price to pay to live. According to statistics, 85 to 90 percent of recurrences of the type of cancer Michael had take

---

3   Catherine, forty-one, spent about five days in the unidentified facility. Bipolar disorder, a mental illness marked by elevated or irritable moods alternating with periods of depression, afflicts about six million Americans. Those with bipolar II tend to have more depression, with the mood swings spread over a longer period of time and the "up" periods less elevated. The episodes can be triggered by major stress or life changes.

place within the first two years; 99 percent show up by the third year. If he made it past three years, he could optimistically declare himself completely cured.

In August 2011, *Star* magazine and others published photos of Michael puffing on a cigarette.

KIRK, OLD AND FRAIL and no longer remotely resembling Spartacus, became a regular visitor to Michael's home in New York City—to comfort his son, to commiserate on their respective fates, to enjoy the time they had left together. Each day that passed brought them even closer as it pushed them deeper into this ultimately losing competition, not just against each other but against advancing age, illness, and death.

Maybe it is worse for them, who having to grow old and weak in front of their fans who remember them as perfect gods, who continue to watch their handsome faces and strong bodies flicker across the big screen or on TV, gorgeous and timeless, living ghosts of who they once were and who they are now, and what they would all too soon become—memories instead of men.

They enjoyed watching old films together; living in the past is the kind of medicine that doctors can't prescribe. The cure for everything, Michael and Kirk knew, was right there, in high definition on that big flatscreen, where they were strong, healthy, and virile.

Where movie stars live forever.

FILMOGRAPHY, INCLUDING TELEVISION AND AWARDS

FILM

As Actor

Cast a Giant Shadow 1966—United Artists. Producer: Melville Shavelson. Director: Melville Shavelson. Screenplay: Melville Shavelson, from a novel by Ted Berkman. With Kirk Douglas, Senta Berger, Stathis Giallelis, Yul Brynner, Frank Sinatra, John Wayne, Angie Dickinson, Chaim Topol, Michael Hordern, Michael Douglas uncredited as a Jeep driver.

Hail, Hero! 1969—Cinema Center Film/Halcyon Production/National General (Warner). Producer: Harold D. Cohen. Director: David Miller. Screenplay: David Manber, from a novel by John Weston. With Michael Douglas, Peter Strauss, Arthur Kennedy, Teresa Wright.

Adam at Six a.m. 1970—National General (Warner). Producers: Robert W. Christiansen, Robert E. Relyea, Rick Rosenberg. Director: Robert Scheerer. Screenplay: Stephen Karpf and Elinor Karpf. With Michael Douglas, Lee Purcell, Joe Don Baker, Grayson Hall, Charles Aidman, Meg Foster.

Summertree 1971—A Bryna Production distributed by Columbia Pictures. Producer: Kirk Douglas. Director: Anthony Newley. Screenplay: Ron Cowen, based on his own play; Edward Hume; Stephen Yafa. With Michael Douglas, Barbara Bel Geddes, Jack Warden, Brenda Vaccaro, Kirk Callaway, Bill Vint.

When Michael Calls 1972 (for television)—Palomar Pictures/Twentieth Century-Fox. Producer: Gil Shiva. Director: Philip Leacock. Screenplay: James Bridges, from the novel by John Farris. With Ben Gazzara, Michael Douglas, Elizabeth Ashley, Karen Pearson, Albert S. Waxman.

Napoleon and Samantha 1972—Walt Disney Productions. Producer:

Winston Hibler. Director: Bernard McEveety. Screenplay: Stewart Raffill. With Michael Douglas, Jodie Foster, Henry Jones, Will Geer, Johnny Whitaker, Arch Johnson, Ellen Corby.

One Flew Over the Cuckoo's Nest 1975—Fantasy Films/United Artists. Producers: Michael Douglas, Saul Zaentz. Director: Miloš Forman. Screenplay: Lawrence Hauben, Bo Goldman, from the novel by Ken Kesey. With Jack Nicholson, Louise Fletcher, William Redfield, Brad Dourif, Danny DeVito, Christopher Lloyd, Will Sampson.

Coma 1978—MGM. Director: Michael Crichton. Producer: Martin Erlichman. Screenplay: Michael Crichton, from the novel by Robin Cook. With Geneviève Bujold, Michael Douglas, Tom Selleck, Elizabeth Ashley, Rip Torn, Richard Widmark, Lois Chiles, Lance LeGault.

The China Syndrome 1979—Columbia Pictures. Producers: Michael Douglas/IPC Films Presentation and Columbia Pictures. Director: James Bridges. Screenplay: Michael Gray, T. S. Cook, James Bridges. With Jane Fonda, Michael Douglas, Scott Brady, Jack Lemmon, James Hampton, Peter Donat, Wilford Brimley, James Karen, Diandra Luker (Douglas).

Running 1979—Universal Pictures. Producer: Ronald I. Cohen, Bob Cooper. Director: Steven Hilliard Stern. Screenplay: Steven Hilliard Stern. With Michael Douglas, Susan Anspach, Lawrence Dane, Philip Akin, Eugene Levy, Charles Shamata.

It's My Turn 1980—Columbia Pictures. Producer: Martin Elfand. Director: Claudia Weill. Screenplay: Eleanor Bergstein. With Jill Clayburgh, Michael Douglas, Beverly Garland, Charles Grodin, Steven Hill, Teresa Baxter, John Gabriel, Joan Copeland.

The Star Chamber 1983—Twentieth Century-Fox. Producer: Frank Yablans. Director: Peter Hyams. Screenplay: Roderick Taylor, Peter Hyams. With Michael Douglas, Yaphet Kotto, Hal Holbrook, Joe Regalbuto, Sharon Gless, James B. Sikking, Diana Dill, Don Calfa, Jack Kehoe.

Romancing the Stone 1984—Twentieth Century-Fox. Producer: Michael Douglas. Director: Robert Zemeckis. Screenplay: Diane Thomas. With Michael Douglas, Kathleen Turner, Danny DeVito, Alfonso Arau, Zack Norman, Holland Taylor, Manuel Ojeda.

A Chorus Line 1985—Embassy/Polygram. Producer: Cy Feuer, Ernest Martin. Director: Richard Attenborough. Screenplay: Arnold Schulman, adapted from the original stage play; concept by Michael Bennett; book by James Kirkwood Jr., Nicholas Dante. With Michael Douglas,

Alyson Reed, Terrence Mann, Gregg Burge, Cameron English, Vicki Frederick, Nicole Fosse, Audrey Landers, Janet Jones.

The Jewel of the Nile 1985—Twentieth Century-Fox. Producer: Michael Douglas. Director: Lewis Teague. Screenplay: Mark Rosenthal, Lawrence Konner. With Kathleen Turner, Michael Douglas, Danny DeVito, Avner Eisenberg, Spiros Focas, Holland Taylor, the Flying Karamazov Brothers.

Fatal Attraction 1987—Paramount Pictures. Producers: Stanley Jaffe, Sherry Lansing. Director: Adrian Lyne. Screenplay: James Dearden. With Michael Douglas, Glenn Close, Anne Archer.

Wall Street 1987—Twentieth Century Fox. Producer: Edward R. Pressman. Director: Oliver Stone. Screenplay: Stanley Weiser, Oliver Stone. With Michael Douglas, Charlie Sheen, Daryl Hannah, Martin Sheen, Terence Stamp, Sean Young, Hal Holbrook, Sylvia Miles.

Black Rain 1989—Paramount/UIP. Producers: Stanley Jaffe, Sherry Lansing. Director: Ridley Scott. Screenplay: Craig Bolotin and Warren Lewis. With Michael Douglas, Ken Takakura, Andy Garcia, Yusaku Matsuda, John Spencer, Shigeru Koyama, Stephen Root, Guts Ishimatsu, Tomisaburo Wakayama.

The War of the Roses 1989—Twentieth Century Fox. Producers: James L. Brooks, Arnon Milchan. Director: Danny DeVito. Screenplay: Michael Leeson, based on the novel by Warren Adler. With Michael Douglas, Kathleen Turner, Danny DeVito, Marianne Sagebrecht, Sean Astin, G. D. Spradlin, Heather Fairfield, Peter Donat, Dan Castellaneta, Gloria Cromwell, Susan Isaacs, Jacqueline Cassell.

Shining Through 1992—Twentieth Century Fox. Producers: Sandy Gallin, Howard Rosenman, Carol Baum. Director: David Seltzer. Screenplay: David Seltzer, based on the novel by Susan Isaacs. With Michael Douglas, Melanie Griffith, Liam Neeson, Sir John Gielgud, Joely Richardson.

Basic Instinct 1992—Carolco/Tri-Star. Producer: Alan Marshall. Director: Paul Verhoeven. Screenplay: Joe Eszterhas. With Michael Douglas, Sharon Stone, George Dzundza, Jeanne Tripplehorn, Leilani Sarelle.

Falling Down 1993—Warner Bros. Producer: Arnold Kopelson. Director: Joel Schumacher. Screenplay: Ebbe Roe Smith. With Michael Douglas, Robert Duvall, Barbara Hershey.

Disclosure 1993—Warner Bros. Producers: Michael Crichton, Barry Levinson. Director: Barry Levinson. Screenplay: Michael Crichton, Paul

Attanasio, from the novel by Michael Crichton. With Michael Douglas, Demi Moore, Donald Sutherland, Caroline Goodall.

The American President 1995—Columbia. Producers: Barbara Maltby, Charles Newirth, Rob Reiner, Jeffrey Stott. Director: Rob Reiner. Screenplay: Aaron Sorkin. With Michael Douglas, Annette Bening, Martin Sheen, Michael J. Fox, Richard Dreyfuss.

The Ghost and the Darkness 1996—Paramount. Producers: Grant Hill, Michael Douglas, Steven Reuther, Paul Radin. Director: Stephen Hopkins. Screenplay: William Goldman. With Michael Douglas, Val Kilmer, John Kani, Brian McCardie, Emily Mortimer.

The Game 1997—Polygram Filmed Entertainment. Producers: Ceán Chaffin, Steve Golin. Director: David Fincher. Screenplay: John D. Brancato, Michael Ferris, Andrew Kevin Walker (uncredited). With Michael Douglas, Sean Penn, Deborah Kara Unger, James Rebhorn, Peter Donat, Armin Mueller-Stahl.

A Perfect Murder 1998—Warner Bros. Producers: Arnold Kopelson, Anne Kopelson, Peter Macgregor-Scott, Christopher Mankiewicz. Director: Andrew Davis. Screenplay: Patrick Smith Kelly, from the play by Frederick Knott, With Michael Douglas, Gwyneth Paltrow, Viggo Mortensen, David Suchet.

Wonder Boys 2000—Paramount. Producers: Curtis Hanson, Scott Rudin. Director: Curtis Hanson. Screenplay: Steve Kloves, based on the novel *Wonder Boys* by Michael Chabon. With Michael Douglas, Tobey Maguire, Robert Downey Jr., Frances McDormand, Katie Holmes, Rip Torn.

Traffic 2000—Bedford Falls Productions, Compulsion Inc., Initial Entertainment Group (IEG), Splendid Medien AG, USA Films. Producers: Laura Bickford, Edward Zwick, Marshall Herskovitz. Director: Steven Soderbergh. Screenplay: Simon Moore (miniseries *Traffik*), Stephen Gaghan. With Michael Douglas, Catherine Zeta-Jones, Benicio Del Toro, Don Cheadle, Luis Guzmán.

Don't Say a Word 2001—Regency Enterprises, Village Roadshow Pictures, Twentieth Century Fox. Producers: Arnon Milchan, Arnold Kopelson, Anne Kopelson. Director: Gary Fleder. Screenplay: Andrew Klavan, Anthony Peckham, Patrick Smith Kelly. With Michael Douglas, Sean Bean, Brittany Murphy, Guy Torry, Jennifer Esposito, Famke Janssen, Oliver Platt.

One Night at McCool's 2001—Universal (Focus Features). Producers: Mi-

chael Douglas, Allison Lyon Segan, Veslemoey Ruud Zwart, Whitney
Green. Director: Harald Zwart. Screenplay: Stan Seidel. With Michael
Douglas, Liv Tyler, Matt Dillon, Paul Reiser, John Goodman, Andrew
Dice Clay (billed as Andrew Silverstein).

The In-Laws 2003—Warner Bros. Producers: Andrew Bergman, Bill Gerber,
Elie Samaha, Bill Todman Jr., Joel Simon. Director: Andrew Fleming.
Screenplay: Andrew Bergman, Nat Mauldin, Ed Solomon. With Mi-
chael Douglas, Albert Brooks, Candice Bergen, Ryan Reynolds.

It Runs in the Family 2003—MGM. Producers: Michael Douglas, Marcy
Drogin, Jesse Wigutow. Director: Fred Schepisi. Screenplay: Jesse
Wigutow. With Michael Douglas, Kirk Douglas, Cameron Douglas,
Diana Douglas, Rory Culkin, Bernadette Peters.

You, Me, and Dupree 2006—Universal Pictures. Producers: Mary Parent,
Scott Stuber, Owen Wilson. Director: Anthony Russo, Joe Russo.
Screenplay: Mike LeSieur. With Matt Dillon, Owen Wilson, Kate
Hudson, Michael Douglas, Seth Rogen, Amanda Detmer.

The Sentinel 2006—Twentieth Century Fox (Regency Studios). Producers:
Michael Douglas, Marcy Drogin, Arnon Milchan. Director: Clark
Johnson. Screenplay: George Nolfi, from a novel by Gerald Petie-
vich. With Michael Douglas, Kiefer Sutherland, Eva Longoria, Martin
Donovan, Kim Basinger.

King of California 2007—Millennium Films. Producers: Randall Emmett,
George Furla, Avi Lerner, Michael London, Alexander Payne, John
Thompson, Vance Owen. Director: Mike Cahill. Screenplay: Mike
Cahill. With Michael Douglas, Evan Rachel Wood, Willis Burks II.

Ghosts of Girlfriends Past 2009—New Line Cinema. Producers: Brad Ep-
stein, Jonathan Shestack, Marcus Viscidi. Director: Mark Waters.
Screenplay: Jon Lucas, Scott Moore. With Michael Douglas, Matthew
McConaughey, Jennifer Garner, Emma Stone, Noureen DeWulf,
Breckin Meyer, Lacey Chabert, Christina Milian.

Beyond a Reasonable Doubt 2009—Foresight Unlimited, RKO Pictures, Signature Pictures. Producers: Faisal S. M. Al Saud, Stephanie Caleb. Director: Peter Hyams. Screenplay: Peter Hyams, Douglas Morrow (1956
screenplay). With Michael Douglas, Jesse Metcalfe, Amber Tamblyn,
Joel David Moore, Orlando Jones.

Solitary Man 2009—Millennium Films. Producers: Steven Soderbergh,
Moshe Diamont, Danny Dimbort, Joe Gatta. Director: Brian Koppelman, David Levien. Screenplay: Brian Koppelman. With Michael

Douglas, Jenna Fischer, Jesse Eisenberg, Mary-Louise Parker, Imogen Poots, Susan Sarandon, Danny DeVito.

Wall Street: Money Never Sleeps 2010—Twentieth Century Fox. Producers: Edward R. Pressman, Eric Kopeloff. Director: Oliver Stone. Screenplay: Allan Loeb, Stephen Schiff. With Michael Douglas, Shia LaBeouf, Josh Brolin, Carey Mulligan.

Haywire 2012—Relativity Media. Producer: Gregory Jacobs. Director: Steven Soderbergh. Screenplay: Lem Dobbs. With Gina Carano, Ewan McGregor, Michael Fassbender, Channing Tatum, Michael Angarano, Antonio Banderas, Michael Douglas.

Behind the Candelabra 2013 (scheduled)—HBO Productions. Producers: Jerry Weintraub, Gregory Jacobs. Director: Steven Soderbergh. Screenplay: Richard LaGravenese. With Michael Douglas, Matt Damon.

As Executive Producer

Running 1979—Universal.
Starman 1984—Columbia.
Radio Flyer 1992—Columbia.
Eyes of an Angel 1994—Trans World Entertainment (with others).
The Ghost and the Darkness 1996—Paramount.
Face/Off 1997—Paramount.
The Rainmaker 1997—Paramount.
The Husband I Bought 2001—Hit and Run Productions/IAC Holdings.
Godspeed 2001—MGM.

As Assistant Director
(all films starring Kirk Douglas)

Lonely Are the Brave 1962—Universal.
The Heroes of Telemark 1965—Columbia.
Cast a Giant Shadow 1966—United Artists.

Other Film Work
(all films starring Kirk Douglas)

Spartacus 1960—Universal Pictures. Gofer.
Lonely Are the Brave 1962—Universal Pictures. Assistant film editor,

DOCUMENTARIES

Still Life, aka *Family Life*, 1990—Universal.

One Day in September, aka *Ein Tag im September* 1999—Sony Pictures Classics. Narrator.

Get Bruce aka *Get Bruce!* 1999—Miramax. Himself.

Forever Hollywood 1999—Esplanade Productions/American Cinémathèque. Himself.

In Search of Peace—Part One: 1948–1967, aka *In Search of Peace* 2001— Seventh Art Releasing. Narrator.

Direct Order 2003—Scott Miller and Co. Narrator.

Declaration of Independence 2003—Declaration of Independence, Inc. Himself.

Tell Them Who You Are 2005—ThinkFilm. Himself.

. . . A Father . . . A Son . . . Once Upon a Time in Hollywood 2006 (DVD release)—HBO. Directed by Lee Grant.

TELEVISION

The Experiment 1969. *CBS Playhouse*. Scientist (billed as M. K. Douglas).

The Albatross 1971. "Medical Center." CBS.

The Hitchhiker 1971. "The F.B.I." ABC.

When Michael Calls 1972. ABC. Craig.

The Streets of San Francisco. 1972–76. ABC. Inspector Steve Keller.

Will & Grace 2002. NBC. Detective Gavin Hatch.

Liberty's Kids: Est. 1776 2002. Voice of Patrick Henry.

Freedom: A History of Us 2002. Benjamin French and Benjamin Franklin.

Phineas and Ferb 2011. Voice of Waylon.

NBC Nightly News 2007–present. Announcer.

AWARDS

ACADEMY AWARDS

1976 Won Best Picture (with Saul Zaentz) for *One Flew Over the Cuckoo's Nest* (1975), the first film in forty-one years to sweep the major categories of best picture, director, actor, actress, and screenplay.

1988 Won Best Actor in a Leading Role for *Wall Street* (1987)

AMERICAN CINÉMATHÈQUE GALA TRIBUTE

1993 Won American Cinematheque Award

AMERICAN FILM INSTITUTE, USA

2009 Won Life Achievement Award

BAFTA AWARDS—BRITISH ACADEMY OF FILM AND TELEVISION ARTS

1989 Nominated for Best Actor for *Fatal Attraction* (1987)
2001 Nominated for Best Performance by an Actor in a Leading Role for *Wonder Boys* (2000)

BLOCKBUSTER ENTERTAINMENT AWARDS

1999 Nominated for Favorite Actor—Suspense—for *A Perfect Murder* (1998)
2001 Nominated for Favorite Actor—Drama—for *Traffic* (2000)

CHICAGO FILM CRITICS ASSOCIATION AWARDS

2001 Nominated for Best Actor for *Wonder Boys* (2000)

CÉSAR AWARDS (FRANCE)

1998 Won Honorary César

DALLAS FORT WORTH FILM CRITICS ASSOCIATION AWARDS

2010 Nominated for Best Actor for *Solitary Man* (2009)

DAVID DI DONATELLO AWARDS

1988 Won Best Foreign Actor for *Wall Street* (1987)
1990 Nominated for Best Foreign Actor for *The War of the Roses* (1989)

Emmy Awards

1974 Nominated for Best Supporting Actor in Drama for *The Streets of San Francisco* (ABC)

1975 Nominated for Outstanding Continuing Performance by a Supporting Actor in a Drama Series for *The Streets of San Francisco* (ABC)

1976 Nominated for Outstanding Continuing Performance by a Supporting Actor in a Drama Series for *The Streets of San Francisco* (ABC)

2002 Nominated for Outstanding Guest Actor in a Comedy Series, *Will & Grace* (NBC)

Genie Awards

1980 Nominated for Best Performance by a Foreign Actor for *Running* (1979)

Golden Globes, USA

1970 Nominated for Most Promising Newcomer—Male—for *Hail, Hero!* (1969)

1975 Nominated for Best TV Actor—Drama—for *The Streets of San Francisco* (1972)

1988 Won for Best Performance by an Actor in a Motion Picture—Drama— for *Wall Street* (1987)

1990 Nominated for Best Performance by an Actor in a Motion Picture— Comedy/Musical—for *The War of the Roses* (1989)

1996 Nominated for Best Performance by an Actor in a Motion Picture— Comedy/Musical—for *The American President* (1995)

2001 Nominated for Best Performance by an Actor in a Motion Picture— Drama—for *Wonder Boys* (2000)

2004 Won Cecil B. DeMille Lifetime Achievement Award

2011 Nominated for Best Performance by an Actor in a Supporting Role in a Motion Picture for *Wall Street: Money Never Sleeps* (2010)

Hasty Pudding Theatricals, USA

1992 Won Man of the Year

Italian National Syndicate of Film Journalists

1988 Won for Best Foreign Actor for *Wall Street* (1987)

KANSAS CITY FILM CRITICS CIRCLE AWARDS

1988 Won for Best Actor for *Wall Street* (1987)

KARLOVY VARY INTERNATIONAL FILM FESTIVAL

1998 Won Special Prize for Outstanding Contribution to World Cinema

LAS VEGAS FILM CRITICS SOCIETY AWARDS

2000 Nominated for Sierra Award for Best Actor for *Wonder Boys* (2000) and *Traffic* (2000)

LONDON CRITICS CIRCLE FILM AWARDS

2001 Nominated for ALFS Award for Actor of the Year for *Wonder Boys* (2000)

LOS ANGELES FILM CRITICS ASSOCIATION AWARDS

2000 Won for Best Actor for *Wonder Boys* (2000)

MTV MOVIE AWARDS

1992 Won Best On-Screen Duo for *Basic Instinct* (1992) with Sharon Stone
1993 Nominated for Best Male Performance for *Basic Instinct* (1992)

NATIONAL BOARD OF REVIEW, USA

1987 Won for Best Actor for *Wall Street* (1987)
2007 Won Career Achievement Award

ONLINE FILM CRITICS SOCIETY AWARDS

2001 Nominated for Best Actor for *Wonder Boys* (2000)

PGA AWARDS—PRODUCERS GUILD OF AMERICA

2009 Won Lifetime Achievement Award for Motion Pictures

People's Choice Awards, USA

1988 Won for Favorite Motion Picture Actor

Phoenix Film Critics Society Awards

2001 Nominated for Best Actor in a Leading Role for *Wonder Boys* (2000)

Razzie Awards

1993 Nominated for Worst Actor for *Basic Instinct* (1992) and *Shining Through* (1992)

San Sebastián International Film Festival

1997 Won Donostia Lifetime Achievement Award

Satellite Awards

2001 Won for Best Performance by an Actor in a Motion Picture—Comedy or Musical—for *Wonder Boys* (2000)

2010 Nominated for Best Actor in a Motion Picture—Drama—for *Solitary Man* (2009)

Screen Actors Guild Awards

2001 Won Best Actor—Outstanding Performance by the Cast of a Theatrical Motion Picture—for *Traffic* (2000), with Steven Bauer, Benjamin Bratt, James Brolin, Don Cheadle, Erika Christensen, Clifton Collins Jr., Benicio Del Toro, Miguel Ferrer, Albert Finney, Topher Grace, Luis Guzmán, Amy Irving, Thomas Milian, D. W. Moffett, Dennis Quaid, Peter Riegert, Jacob Vargas, Catherine Zeta-Jones

ShoWest Convention, USA

1979 Won Special Award for Star/Producer of the Year

Southeastern Film Critics Association Awards

2001 Won Best Actor for *Wonder Boys* (2000); tied with Javier Bardem for *Before Night Falls* (2000)

Taormina International Film Festival

2004 Won Taormina Arte Award

The Eugene O'Neill Theater Center

2012 Won Twelfth Annual Monte Cristo Award for his achievements and contributions to the American and international theater community

MICHAEL DOUGLAS'S TOP 10
DOMESTIC BOX OFFICE GROSSES

1. *Fatal Attraction* (1987) $157 million
2. *Traffic* (2000) $124 million
3. *Basic Instinct* (1992) $118 million
4. *The War of the Roses* (1989) $84 million
5. *Disclosure* (1994) $83 million
6. *Romancing the Stone* (1984) $76 million
7. *The Jewel of the Nile* (1985) $75 million
8. *You, Me and Dupree* (2006) $75 million
9. *A Perfect Murder* (1998) $68 million
10. *The American President* (1995) $60 million

MICHAEL DOUGLAS'S TOP 10
OPENING WEEKEND GROSSES (NORTH AMERICA)

		OPENING WEEKEND	TOTAL GROSS
1.	*Don't Say a Word*	$17.1 million	$102.0 million
2.	*A Perfect Murder*	$16.6 million	$67.6 million
3.	*Basic Instinct*	$15.1 million	$117.7 million
4.	*The Game*	$14.3 million	$48.3 million
5.	*Disclosure*	$10.1 million	$83.0 million
6.	*The American President*	$10.0 million	$60.1 million
7.	*The War of the Roses*	$9.68 million	$86.0 million
8.	*Black Rain*	$9.67 million	$46.2 million
9.	*The Ghost and the Darkness*	$9.2 million	$38.6 million
10.	*Falling Down*	$8.7 million	$40.9 million

BIBLIOGRAPHY

Bart, Peter. *Infamous Players: A Tale of Movies, The Mob (and Sex)*. New York: Weinstein Books, 2011.

Brode, Douglas. *The Films of Jack Nicholson*. Rev. ed. Secaucus, NJ: Citadel, 1999.

Darrid, Diana Douglas. *In the Wings: A Memoir*. New York: Barricade Books, 1999.

Douglas, Kirk. *The Ragman's Son: An Autobiography*. New York: Simon & Schuster, 1988.

Durgnat, Raymond. *The Strange Case of Alfred Hitchcock*. Cambridge, MA: MIT Press, 1982.

Edelman, Rob, and Amy L. Unterburger, eds. *International Dictionary of Films and Filmmakers*, vol. 3: *Actors and Actresses*. 3rd ed. Farmington Hills, MI: St. James Press, 1997.

Grant, Lee (director). *. . . . A Father . . . A Son . . . Once Upon a Time in Hollywood*. Produced by HBO, 2005.

Goldberg, Wendy, and Betty Goodwin. *Marry Me!: Courtships and Proposals of Legendary Couples*. Los Angeles: Angel City Press, 1994.

Goldman, William. *Which Lie Did I Tell?* New York: Random House, 2000.

Kinn, Gail, and Jim Piazza. *The Academy Awards: The Complete Unofficial History*. New York: Black Dog and Leventhal, 2002.

McDougal, Dennis. *Five Easy Decades*. Hoboken, NJ: Wiley, 2008.

New York Times. *Guide to the Best 1,000 Movies Ever Made*. New York: New York Times Company, 2004.

Parker, John. *Michael Douglas: Acting on Instinct*. London: Headline, 1994.

Phillips, Julia. *You'll Never Eat Lunch in This Town Again*. New York: Random House, 1991.

Sanello, Frank. *Naked Instinct*. Secaucus, NJ: Carol, 1997.

Thomson, David. *The New Biographical Dictionary of Film*. New York: Alfred A. Knopf, 2002.

NOTES

INTRODUCTION

ix   **"[My father] told me . . ."** Michael Douglas, quoted in Rick Lyman, "Mr. Douglas, the Younger, Comfortable in His Prime, Can Pick His Spots," *New York Times*, February 1, 2001 (quote slightly abbreviated).

ix   **"Every kid . . ."** Michael Douglas, *Playboy* interview, February 1986.

1   **"Christ, I saw my father as a gladiator . . ."** Ibid.

4   **"had some inkling . . ."** and **"Yes, I liked women . . ."** Diana Douglas and Kirk Douglas, respectively, in Grant, dir., *. . . A Father . . . A Son*.

4   **"When Diana and I were having an intense argument . . ."** Kirk Douglas, *The Ragman's Son*, 132.

5   **"I think my earliest memory . . ."** Michael Douglas in Grant, dir., *. . . A Father . . . A Son*.

5   **"Michael . . . was showing . . ."** Darrid, *In the Wings*, 153.

6   **"walked in and kissed Diana . . ."** Kirk Douglas, *The Ragman's Son*, 145.

6   **"capable of playing characters . . ."** Thomson, *New Biographical Dictionary of Film*, 247–49.

7   **"I went into theater because . . ."** Michael Douglas, in Fred Schruers, "The *Rolling Stone* Interview," *Rolling Stone*, January 14, 1988.

PART ONE: PARENTS

CHAPTER 1

11   **"As an actor, it was . . ."** Michael Douglas, in Grant, dir., *. . . A Father . . . A Son*.

12   **"I have always suspected . . ."** Kirk Douglas, *The Ragman's Son*, 15.

17   **"always with one pretty girl . . ."** Darrid, *In the Wings*, 67.

18   **"to the tinsel of Hollywood . . ."** Ibid., 72.

CHAPTER 2

21   **"I didn't grow up in Beverly Hills . . ."** Michael Douglas, quoted in Bob Thomas's syndicated column, which appeared in *Hollywood Citizen-News*, April 18, 1969.

21   **"As a child, he was very shy . . ."** Kirk Douglas, *Hollywood Reporter*, January 23, 2004.

21   **"His deep, dark Russian depressions . . ."** Darrid, *In the Wings*, 110.

24   **"No, Mommy! No, Mommy! . . . It's okay, Mikey, it's okay . . ."** Ibid., 129–30.

25   **"that was Auntie Irene . . ."** Darrid, *In the Wings*, 145.

27   **"core of sensitivity that he guarded . . ."** Diana Douglas, quoted by Sean Macaulay, *Times* (London), January 22, 2001.

28   **"I was very shocked . . ."** Michael Douglas, interviewed by Stephen Galloway, *Hollywood Reporter*, January 23, 2004.

CHAPTER 3

31   **"I was able to watch my father . . ."** Michael Douglas, interviewed by Simi Horwitz, *Back Stage West*, September 13, 2007.

31   **"Now the family is together . . ."** Kirk Douglas, *The Ragman's Son*, 205.

32   **"a talented but stubborn prick . . ."** Confidential source does not wish to be identified.

33   **"The first girl I ever kissed . . ."** Michael Douglas, quoted in Parker, *Michael Douglas*, 36.

35   **"skinny little fourteen-year-old . . ."** Darrid, *In the Wings*, 230.

36   **"took more time than . . ."** Kirk Douglas, *The Ragman's Son*, 306.

37   **"You can't sue God"** Kirk Douglas, *The Ragman's Son*, 230.

PART TWO: CONNECTICUT TO SANTA BARBARA . . .

CHAPTER 4

41   **"I think having a famous father . . ."** Kirk Douglas, quoted in *People*, April 16, 1979.

42   **"I was into hot-rods . . ."** Michael Douglas, quoted in *People*, May 5, 2003.

42   **"murderous . . ."** Kirk Douglas, *The Ragman's Son*, 336.

45   **"You were terrible . . ."** Kirk Douglas, quoted in Parker, *Michael Douglas*, 55.

45   **"There were, I suppose . . ."** David Garsite, quoted in Parker, *Michael Douglas*, 48.

47   **"On Sundays . . ."** Danny DeVito, interviewed by Charlie Rose for his syndicated PBS television program, November 24, 1994.

48   **"One night . . ."** Ibid.

48   **"I got into the Maharishi . . ."** Michael Douglas, quoted in Ben Fong-Torres, "The China Syndrome," *Rolling Stone*, April 5, 1979.

50   **"Our apartment . . ."** Danny DeVito, quoted in *People*, March 13, 2000.

51   **"which Danny drove . . ."** and **"Just go through, like Zen . . ."** Fred Schruers, "The Nineteen-Year Friendship Behind *The Jewel of the Nile*," *Us*, December 30, 1985.

51   **"This talent scout . . ."** Michael Douglas, quoted in *City of San Francisco* magazine, October 7, 1975.

CHAPTER 5

53   **"I don't think Kirk . . ."** Michael Douglas, quoted in Peer J. Oppenheimer, "Michael Douglas: Unlike Father," *Family Weekly*, May 17, 1970.

55   **"add Michael Douglas to . . ."** Bob Thomas, "More than a Smart Kid," for his column published in the *Hollywood Citizen-News*, April 18, 1969, and syndicated nationally.

56   **"I took David Miller . . ."** Kirk Douglas, *The Ragman's Son*, 310.

57   **"It's not an especially . . ."** Vincent Canby, writing in the *New York Times*, October 24, 1969.

57   **"In Hollywood, when you're a star's son . . ."** Michael Douglas, quoted in "Kirk Douglas' Son: Michael Knows What Cynics Saying," *Hollywood Citizen-News*, October 5, 1969.

58   **"Of course it's helped being . . ."** Michael Douglas, interviewed by Shaun Considine, *After Dark*, July 1971.

59   **"The director was Jules Irving . . ."** Kirk Douglas, in Grant, dir., . . . *A Father . . . A Son*.

59   **"A lot of people think that *Summertree* . . ."** Michael Douglas, in Grant, dir., . . . *A Father . . . A Son*.

60   **She is a fantastic actress . . ."** and **" 'Summertree' is a bad movie . . ."** Greenspun review of *Summertree* in the *New York Times*, June 17, 1971.

60   **"I'll keep on trying . . ."** Michael Douglas, interviewed by Shaun Considine, *After Dark*, July 1971.

61   **"I loved the role of . . ."** Kirk Douglas, *The Ragman's Son*, 341.

PART THREE: INTO THE CUCKOO'S NEST

CHAPTER 6

65   **"My producing career evolved . . ."** Michael Douglas, interviewed by Jerry Roberts, *Variety*, August 31, 1998.

66   **"a classic story . . ."** Michael Douglas, quoted by Tim Cahill, "Knocking Round the Nest," *Rolling Stone*, December 4, 1975.

66   **"I remember . . ."** Ibid.

67   **"The best work that I actually did . . ."** Michael Douglas, in Fred Schruers, "The *Rolling Stone* Interview," *Rolling Stone*, January 14, 1988.

67   **"Michael had stuck in my mind . . ."** Quinn Martin, quoted in Parker, *Michael Douglas*, 73.

68   **"Michael, you're going to learn a lot . . ."** Kirk Douglas, *The Ragman's Son*, 58.

68   **"When I started out . . ."** Michael Douglas, interviewed in *Total Film: The Modern Guide to Movies*, September 1, 2006.

68   **"I said, 'Michael, when you do crap . . .' "** Karl Malden, in Grant, dir., . . . *A Father . . . A Son*.

69   **"has fallen in love with a young actress . . ."** Dorothy Manners, *Los Angeles Times*, November 9, 1973.

69   **"*Streets* is good . . ."** Michael Douglas, interviewed in *City of San Francisco* magazine, October 7, 1975, on the occasion of his directing one episode of the show.

CHAPTER 7

73   **"Ken came in . . ."** Michael Douglas in *Playboy*, February 1986.

73   **"It was too surreal . . ."** Quoted in Ben Fong-Torres, "The China Syndrome," *Rolling Stone*, April 5, 1979.

76   **"I met with three or four directors . . ."** Michael Douglas, interviewed in *Total Film: The Modern Guide to Movies*, September 1, 2006.

76 **"we turned to each other and started crying . . ."** Ibid.

77 **"This was a Czech movie . . . about a society I lived in . . . every-thing I knew . . ."** Miloš Forman, interviewed in Tim Cahill, "Knocking Round the Nest," *Rolling Stone*, December 4, 1975.

77 **"almost incomprehensible . . ."** Kirk Douglas, *The Ragman's Son*, 401.

77 **"*I bought the book from Ken Kesey . . .*"** Kirk Douglas, Grant, dir., . . . *A Father . . . A Son.*

78 **"The director makes the casting calls . . ."** Michael Douglas, interviewed by Hilary de Vries, *Los Angeles Times Magazine*, January 21, 2001.

78 **"also fascinated with Burt Reynolds . . ."** Michael Douglas, quoted in McDougal, *Five Easy Decades*, 168.

78 **"Michael Douglas talked to me . . ."** Anjelica Huston, quoted in McDougal, *Five Easy Decades*, 167.

79 **"the starting problem with *Cuckoo* was . . ."** Jack Nicholson, quoted in Brode, *The Films of Jack Nicholson*, 185.

81 **"Michael Douglas will spend his summer hiatus . . ."** *Hollywood Reporter*, May 2, 1973.

82 **"I think the warning signs . . ."** Brenda Vaccaro, quoted in Parker, *Michael Douglas*, 78.

82 **"We were a beautiful couple . . ."** Brenda Vaccaro, quoted in Ben Fong-Torres, "The China Syndrome," *Rolling Stone*, April 5, 1979.

CHAPTER 8

83 **"It was magical . . ."** Michael Douglas, quoted by Robert Wallace, *Rolling Stone*, November 5, 1987.

83 **"We think of drooling . . ."** Miloš Forman, quoted in Tim Cahill, "Knocking Round the Nest," *Rolling Stone*, December 4, 1975.

85 **"For more than four months . . ."** Jack Nicholson, quoted in McDougal, *Five Easy Decades*, 178.

86 **"Usually, I don't have much trouble . . ."** Jack Nicholson, quoted in Brode, *The Films of Jack Nicholson*, 187.

86 **"Well, I've learned that . . ."** Michael Douglas, quoted in *City of San Francisco* magazine, October 7, 1975.

87 **"It was a really magical experience . . ."** Michael Douglas, quoted in *Playboy*, February 1986.

88   **"They took out the morality . . ."** Ken Kesey, quoted by several sources, including the *Los Angeles Times*, *Variety*, and Parker, *Michael Douglas* (who offers no further attribution).

89   **"It was a bittersweet thing . . ."** Michael Douglas, quoted in *Playboy*, February 1986.

90   **"I told you . . ."** and **"You try not to . . ."** Ibid.

90   **"I want to thank you for teaching me . . ."** Louise Fletcher's acceptance speech for winning the Academy Award, 1976.

91   **"Well . . . I guess this proves . . ."** Jack Nicholson's acceptance speech for winning the Academy Award, 1976.

91   **"It's all downhill from here . . ."** Michael Douglas, quoted by Tom Roston, *Hollywood Reporter*, June 11, 2009. In *Playboy*, February 1986, Michael remembers it was Forman who said it to him. Every other source has Michael saying it to Forman.

91   **"The dream started at the Rialto Theater . . ."** Saul Zaentz's acceptance speech for winning the Academy Award, 1976.

92   **"I think *It Happened One Night* . . ."** Michael Douglas's acceptance speech for winning the Academy Award, 1976.

92   **"It was a wonderful moment . . ."** Michael Douglas, interviewed in Richard Brown, "The Actor as Producer," *American Premiere*, Summer 1986.

CHAPTER 9

93   **"Everybody was happy to see me. . . ."** *Playboy*, February 1986.

93   **"We had a blast . . ."** Parker, *Michael Douglas*, 101.

93   **"I was single . . ."** Parker, *Michael Douglas*, 101.

95   **"He had this enormous . . ."** Diandra Douglas, quoted in Ben Fong-Torres, "The China Syndrome," *Rolling Stone*, April 5, 1979.

95   **"If my mother calls,"** Diandra Douglas, quoted in Wendy Goldberg and Betty Goodwin, *Marry Me!*, 108.

96   **"A lot of people . . ."** Michael Douglas, *Playboy*, February 1986.

98   **"a great horror movie . . ."** Ibid.

99   **"I had thought . . ."** Ibid.

103   **"Jim's reasons . . ."** Jane Fonda interviewed by Aljean Harmetz, *New York Times*, March 11, 1979.

103   **"a contemporary thriller . . ."** and **"an astonishing look . . ."** and

"monster movie with . . ." Columbia Pictures' PR book for *The China Syndrome*.

104   "Jack Lemmon was such . . ." Michael Douglas in *Parade*, July 12, 2009.

104   "blinding flash of promotion" and "time riding around . . ." Tom Buckley, *New York Times*, April 16, 1979.

105   "One of the things I . . ." Michael Douglas, quoted in *Look*, April 2, 1979.

105   "My father didn't . . ." Ibid.

106   "was well-received [at first] . . ." In *Total Film: The Modern Guide to Movies*, September 1, 2006.

107   "The first thought [for me] about the movie . . ." Michael Douglas in *Variety*, January 9, 2004.

CHAPTER 10

109   "My producing career . . ." Michael Douglas, interviewed by Jerry Roberts, *Variety*, August 31, 1998.

109   "be a bad influence . . ." Michael Douglas, quoted by Claire Safran in "The Michael Douglas Syndrome," *Redbook*, November 1979.

109   "I guess what I found out . . ." Michael Douglas, quoted in *Playgirl*, February 1981.

111   "Try to pick up a copy of . . ." Robert Vare in *Cue*, October 27, 1978.

111   "The script knocked me out . . ." Ibid.

112   "I just loved it . . ." Michael Douglas, quoted in an interview for the special DVD edition of *Romancing the Stone*, Twentieth Century Fox, 1986.

112   "I was looking . . ." Ibid.

113   "It was a bidding . . ." Ibid.

113   "The role of Jack Colton is . . ." Michael Douglas in *GQ*, December 1985.

114   "Michael's just scratched the surface . . ." Kirk Douglas in *GQ*, December 1985.

116   "I have not had . . ." Parker, *Michael Douglas*, 132.

118   "We had *Tootsie* . . ." Frank Price in *Esquire*, April 1984.

118   "What has happened to the movie business . . ." Michael Douglas in *Esquire*, April 1984.

119   "My father taught me . . ." Ibid.

PART FOUR: ACTION STAR

CHAPTER 11

125   **"*Romancing*'s script included . . ."** Michael Douglas in *Vogue*, August 1984.

128   **"At twenty-three [*sic*] his career was over . . ."** Michael Douglas quoted in an interview for the special DVD edition of *Romancing the Stone*, Twentieth Century Fox, 1986.

128   **"jaw-dropping"** Josh Green, *New York Times*, March 20, 2005.

129   **"I remember arriving on location . . ."** Michael Douglas, quoted in *Cable Guide*, April 1985.

129   **"Poor Kathleen's double . . ."** Ibid.

129   **"I remember terrible arguments . . ."** "The Last Movie Star," *Entertainment Weekly*, August 2, 1991.

130   **"Kathleen's a real trouper . . ."** Michael Douglas, quoted by Roderick Mann, *Los Angeles Times*, May 13, 1984.

130   **"Mind you, during the . . ."** Michael Douglas, in *People*, July 6, 2009.

130   **"When we were doing *Romancing* . . ."** Grant, dir., . . . *A Father . . . A Son*.

130   **"We carried on . . ."** Ibid.

132   **"I've been told that . . ."** Michael Douglas, quoted in the *Los Angeles Times*, May 13, 1984.

CHAPTER 12

133   **"My first responsibility is . . ."** Michael Douglas, interviewed by Richard Brown in *American Premiere*, Summer 1986.

134   **"To balance my family life . . ."** Michael Douglas, interviewed by Jane Ardmore in the *Sunday Times* (London), December 8, 1985.

134   **"I had to make a living . . ."** Michael Douglas in an interview by Michael Gross, *New York Times*, June 22, 1987.

134   **"Being young . . ."** Ibid.

135   **"She [Diandra] really wasn't . . ."** Michael Douglas, interviewed in the *Sunday Times* (London), June 8, 1995.

135   **"For the gift of life itself . . ."** Ibid.

135   **"One of the reasons . . ."** Michael Douglas, interviewed by David Livingston in *Cable Guide*, April 1985.

138   **"for the joy of it . . ."** Michael Douglas, interviewed by Michael Gross, *New York Times,* June 22, 1987.

138   **"is closer to a prick . . ."** Michael Douglas, interviewed in *Cable Guide,* April 1985.

138   **"And when we fell behind . . ."** Michael Douglas, interviewed by Louise Bernikow, *GQ,* December 1985.

138   **"Michael never let one leotard go by . . ."** Attenborough, interviewed by Louise Bernikow, *GQ,* December 1985.

139   **"Michael's determination . . ."** Ibid.

141   **"It's always difficult . . ."** and **"What we wanted to do . . ."** Michael Douglas, interviewed in the *Sunday Times* (London), December 8, 1985.

141   **"We'll follow them . . ."** Michael Douglas, interviewed in *Cable Guide,* April 1985.

142   **"We finished shooting . . ."** Michael Douglas, interviewed in the *Sunday Times* (London), December 8, 1985.

142   **"I take my hat off to Kathleen . . ."** Michael Douglas, interviewed by Richard Brown in *American Premiere,* summer 1986.

143   **"I can't fucking believe it"** Michael Douglas, quoted in *GQ,* December 1985.

143   **"After our experiences . . ."** Michael Douglas, interviewed by Richard Brown in *American Premiere,* summer 1986.

144   **"Everybody knew . . ."** Fred Schruers, "The Nineteen-Year Friendship Behind *The Jewel of the Nile,*" *Us,* December 30, 1985.

144   **"He's had more work done . . ."** The source wishes to remain anonymous.

PART FIVE: SEX SYMBOL

CHAPTER 13

149   **"I haven't had a break . . ."** Michael Douglas, quoted by Jane Ardmore in the *Sunday Times* (London), December 8, 1985.

149   **"He takes my breath away . . ."** Kathleen Turner, quoted in *GQ,* December 1985.

149   **"I could never have done it . . ."** Michael Douglas in *People,* June 6, 2009.

149   **"I don't know how much . . ."** Diandra, quoted in Parker, *Michael Douglas,* 173.

149   **"I grew up with writers . . ."** Diandra Douglas in the *New York Times*, June 22, 1987.

151   **"Stanley [Jaffe] and Sherry . . ."** Michael Douglas, from a short featurette called *Remembering Fatal Attraction*, made for the 2002 DVD release of the film.

151   **"I had had . . ."** Ibid.

152   **"While in London . . ."** Stanley Jaffe, from a short featurette called *Remembering Fatal Attraction*, made for the 2002 DVD release of the film.

152   **"When I created *Diversion* . . ."** James Dearden, interviewed in Myra Forsberg, "James Dearden: Life After 'Fatal Attraction,'" *New York Times*, July 24, 1988.

152   **"I kept on coming back . . ."** Sherry Lansing, from a short featurette called *Remembering Fatal Attraction*, made for the 2002 DVD release of the film.

152   **"It was a Paramount picture . . ."** Ibid.

153   **"I went to see 9½ Weeks . . ."** Ibid.

154   **"I had flown out from . . ."** Glenn Close in *Entertainment Weekly*, October 14–21, 2011. In the *Hollywood Reporter*, January 23, 2004, Close states she took Valium before the audition for *Fatal Attraction*.

154   **"I walked in and the first thing . . ."** Glenn Close in *Entertainment Weekly*, October 14–21, 2011.

154   **"We were turned down . . ."** Jaffe, from a short featurette called *Remembering Fatal Attraction*, made for the 2002 DVD release of the film.

154   **"For me . . . the appeal of . . ."** Michael Douglas, interviewed by Gene Siskel, *Daily News*, January 3, 1988.

155   **"I remember . . ."** Michael Douglas, quoted in Jack Mathews, "Playing the Bad Good Guy," *Los Angeles Times*, September 13, 1997.

155   **"And something else . . ."** Michael Douglas, in Grant, dir., . . . *A Father . . . A Son*.

158   **"The movie touched . . ."** Michael Douglas, interviewed by Patrick Pacheco in *Us* magazine, December 14, 1987.

158   **"It was not anything we . . ."** Stanley Jaffe in *Social Attraction*, 2002, a short film analyzing the social implications of *Fatal Attraction*.

159   **"She was a deeply disturbed woman . . ."** Glenn Close in *Entertainment Weekly*, October 14–21, 2011.

159   **"She had been so powerful . . ."** Michael Douglas in *Entertainment Weekly*, October 14–21, 2011.

159   **"It was all rather bizarre . . ."** Dearden, in Myra Forsberg, "James Dearden: Life After 'Fatal Attraction,'" *New York Times,* July 24, 1988.

159   **"I think what was . . ."** Michael Douglas, from a short featurette called *Remembering Fatal Attraction,* made for the 2002 DVD release of the film.

160   **"The picture used to really drive me nuts . . ."** Michael Douglas, in Fred Schruers, "The *Rolling Stone* Interview," *Rolling Stone,* January 14, 1988.

160   **"He saw a killer . . ."** Michael Douglas, interviewed by Patrick Pacheco, *Us* magazine, December 14, 1987.

160   **"Mephistopheles—now there's . . ."** Tom Rothman, quoted in *Fox Legacy,* broadcast on the Fox Movie Channel and included as extra commentary in the deluxe box set release of *Wall Street.*

162   **"That's where I learned that a director . . ."** Michael Douglas, *Variety,* January 9, 2004.

162   **"When Douglas' Dan Gallagher . . ."** Jack Mathews, "Playing the Bad Good Guy," *Los Angeles Times,* September 13, 1997.

163   **"well-fed yuppie with a face . . ."** J. Hoberman, "Victim Victorious," *Village Voice,* March 7, 1995.

165   **"If the situation . . ."** and **"Gekko's conduct . . ."** Michael Douglas, interviewed by Patrick Pacheco, *Us* magazine, December 14, 1987.

165   ***"Fatal Attraction* couldn't . . ."** Kinn and Piazza, *The Academy Awards,* 252.

167   **"Thank you . . . thank you all very much . . ."** Michael Douglas's acceptance speech, Academy Awards, 1988.

168   **"It was tremendous . . ."** Michael Douglas, interviewed by Robert Hofler, *Buzzweekly,* September 12, 2007.

168   **"They're both hugely important . . ."** Michael Douglas, interviewed in *Total Film: The Modern Guide to Movies,* September 1, 2006.

169   **later that night Kirk took Michael aside . . .** The source of this conversation wishes to remain anonymous. A similar but different version of the scene appears in Parker, *Michael Douglas,* and still another in Leslie Bennetts, "Fathers and Sons: A Movie Dynasty," *New York Times,* April 2, 1987.

CHAPTER 14

171 **"I'm very, very lucky . . ."** Michael Douglas, quoted by Gene Siskel, *Daily News* (Los Angeles), March 3, 1988.

172 **"We needed to introduce . . ."** Michael S. Phillips, reported in *Variety*, July 8, 1988.

173 **"How long have you been married?"** Michael Douglas to a reporter in London, as reported in the *Los Angeles Herald-Examiner*, April 30, 1988.

174 **"It is a very difficult time . . ."** Michael Douglas in *Ladies' Home Journal*, August 1988.

176 **"Acting is tunnel vision . . ."** Michael Douglas, interviewed by Linda Blandford, *New York Times*, December 3, 1989.

180 **"Yes . . . I admit, I should . . ."** Michael, quoted in Parker, *Michael Douglas*.

183 **"Don and Melanie are very much in love . . ."** PR statement by Elliot Mintz, who represented the couple.

183 **"Michael and Griffith simply . . ."** PR statement by Allen Burry, who represented Michael Douglas.

184 **Then, on February 14, 1991, everything changed** Details on the helicopter accident are from several sources, including the *New York Times* and the Associated Press, which both reported the accident as happening February 14, 1991.

CHAPTER 15

187 **"Coping stops you . . ."** Michael Douglas, interviewed by Linda Blandford, *New York Times*, December 3, 1989.

191 **The next step was crucial: finding the right leading lady** "The sexual content of the film helped determine the choice of its female star. Ms. Stone, who played Arnold Schwarzenegger's wife in 'Total Recall,' was cast in 'Basic Instinct' only after better-known actresses like Michelle Pfeiffer, Kim Basinger, Geena Davis, Ellen Barkin and Mariel Hemingway rejected her part, largely because it demanded so much nudity and sexual simulation." Bernard Weinraub, *New York Times*, March 15, 1992.

192 **"Between the hype . . ."** Michael Douglas, quoted in Sanello, *Naked Instinct*, 92.

193   **"It was Paul Verhoeven's idea . . ."** Sharon Stone, quoted by contact-music.com, September 15, 2002.

194   **"Sharon loved it!"** The eyewitness wishes to remain anonymous.

194   **"At least it proves . . ."** Sharon Stone, quoted in Sanello, *Naked Instinct*, 96.

194   **"If I see one ounce of cellulite . . ."** Ibid., 110.

194   **"there is something gruesome . . ."** Ruth Morris, "This Man Is Not a Sex Addict," *Independent on Sunday* (London), June 6, 1999.

195   **"[e]very time you have to pee . . ."** Sharon Stone, quoted in Sanello, *Naked Instinct*, 97.

195   **"We did nude sex scenes . . ."** Sharon Stone, *Hollywood Reporter*, January 23, 2004.

196   **"I came up with . . ."** Ibid.

199   **"Instead of compartmentalizing . . ."** Chrissy Iley in the *Sunday Times* (London), July 2, 1995.

199   **"Imagine at the age of 16 . . ."** David Thomson, "Arts," *Independent on Sunday* (London), December 3, 1995.

201   **"The defining moment was . . ."** Joel Schumacher, *Hollywood Reporter*, January 23, 2004.

202   **"Encouraged by his counselor . . ."** Parker, *Michael Douglas*, 252. Parker does not identify his source.

202   **"Michael Douglas was one of . . ."** Geraldo Rivera, *Geraldo*, September 16, 1993.

202   **"regretting any misunderstanding . . ."** Geraldo Rivera, press release, September 20, 1993.

202   **"His time in rehab at . . ."** Ruth Morris, "This Man Is Not a Sex Addict," *Independent on Sunday*, June 6, 1999.

203   **"Despite all the information . . ."** Michael Douglas, interviewed by Noreen Taylor, *Times* (London), January 29, 1997.

203   **"What's wrong with sex addiction?"** Kirk Douglas, in Grant, dir., . . . *A Father . . . A Son.*

205   **"contemporary, Caucasian middle-to-upper-class . . ."** Edelman and Unterburger, eds., 347–48.

PART SIX: THE FLAWED CONTEMPORARY MALE

CHAPTER 16

209 **"I'm feeling a little sad today . . ."** Michael Douglas, quoted in "Going the Distance," *Los Angeles* magazine, October 1997.

210 **"It was an incredibly warm . . ."** Annette Bening in the *Hollywood Reporter*, January 23, 2004.

211 **"It's a lot of years . . ."** Michael Douglas, in Grant, dir., . . . *A Father . . . A Son.*

212 **"It was a phenomenal amount . . ."** Michael Douglas, interviewed by Janet Maslin, *New York Times*, March 11, 1999.

212 **"You could have taken him . . ."** Ibid.

213 **"He went through every day . . ."** Sherry Lansing, in Grant, dir., . . . *A Father . . . A Son.*

213 **"I believe in love and marriage . . ."** Michael Douglas, in Grant, dir., . . . *A Father . . . A Son.*

215 **"In *The Ghost and the Darkness* . . ."** Goldman, *Which Lie Did I Tell?*, 52.

216 **"I have worked with Redford . . ."** Ibid., 89.

218 **"I love acting . . ."** Michael Douglas, interviewed by Nancy Griffin, *Los Angeles* magazine, October 1997.

218 **"Michael and Steven . . ."** An unidentified spokesperson for Douglas/ Reuther. The comments and other details of the situation at Douglas/ Reuther were reported by Kirk Honeycutt, *Hollywood Reporter*, July 25, 1997. According to Honeycutt, Michael had grown "disenchanted" in his partnership with Reuther.

219 **"You want to spend . . ."** Michael Douglas, *Variety*, August 31, 1998.

219 **"I had to remind myself . . ."** and **"One of the mistakes . . ."** Michael Douglas, interviewed by Hilary de Vries, *Los Angeles Times Magazine*, January 21, 2001.

220 **"Diandra and I . . ."** Michael Douglas, interviewed by Robert Hofler, *Buzzweekly*, September 12, 1997.

220 **"a case of drained creative batteries . . ."** Hitchcock, quoted in Durgnat, *The Strange Case of Alfred Hitchcock*, 234. Hitchcock's primary interest in filming what had been a hit stage play in London's West End and on Broadway was the opportunity to make it in 3-D at Warner. However, by the time the film opened, the 3-D fad had passed, and

along with it Hitchcock's interest in the film. The 3-D version was never commercially released. Hitchcock's next release, made that same year, was *Rear Window*, a spectacular return to form for the Master of Suspense.

220 **"It was fun . . ."** Michael Douglas, *Variety*, August 31, 1998.

222 **"It's sort of creepy . . ."** Gwyneth Paltrow, in *Independent on Sunday*, June 6, 1999.

222 **"I thought [Gwyneth's comments] were . . ."** Michael Douglas, in *W*, March 2000.

223 **ten minutes after the film started he slipped out** Douglas's reps at the time confirmed the story; also several other sources.

224 **"Being the son or daughter . . ."** Michael Douglas, quoted at the Karlovy Vary Film Festival by *Variety*, August 31, 1998.

224 **"I hope to use . . ."** Michael Douglas, part of his comments upon being honored as a United Nations messenger of peace at the UN, July 30, 1998.

224 **"has inexplicably managed . . ."** Berardinelli review of *A Perfect Murder* in *Rotten Tomatoes*.

225 **"I'm just coming up for air . . ."** Michael Douglas, quoted in *Los Angeles* magazine, October 1997.

PART SEVEN: RADIANCE AND RADIATION

CHAPTER 17

229 **"I believe in love and marriage . . ."** Michael Douglas, in Grant, dir., . . . *A Father . . . A Son*.

230 **"He's gonna die when . . ."** Michael Douglas, in *Variety*, March 5, 1999.

231 **"liked to chew gum . . ."** Production designer Eugenio Zanetti, quoted in *People*, January 24, 2000.

231 **"I wanted to show . . ."** Catherine Zeta-Jones, quoted in *People*, January 24, 2000.

232 **"his eyeballs popped . . ."** David Foster, interviewed by Hilary de Vries, *W*, March 2000.

232 **"I first saw her . . ."** Michael Douglas, David Foster, interviewed by Hilary de Vries, *W*, March 2000.

232 **"There was a whole group . . ."** Ibid.

232   **"I want to be the father of . . ."** Michael Douglas, quoted in the *Sunday Times* (London), October 15, 2000.

232   **"I've heard a lot about you . . ."** *AARP Magazine*, March/April 2010.

232   **"I apologize if I stepped . . ."** Michael recounted the incident in *AARP Magazine*, March/April 2010.

232   **"My first wife was younger than me . . ."** Michael Douglas, David Foster, interviewed by Hilary de Vries, *W*, March 2000.

233   **"Mike Todd was 25 years older . . ."** Michael Douglas, www.talktalk .co.uk/entertainment/film/interviews/michael_douglas.html.

233   **"he was absolutely different . . ."** Catherine Zeta-Jones, *Hollywood Reporter*, January 23, 2004.

233   **"Before Michael can marry . . ."** Diandra Douglas, several sources, including the *Times* (London), October 19, 1999.

233   **"He's a cake . . ."** Catherine Zeta-Jones, in *People*, October 13, 2010.

234   **"I don't know quite . . ."** These comments by Catherine are from *Screen International*, July 2, 1999.

234   **"Michael is here tonight . . ."** *People*, October 11, 1999.

234   **"I am a very lucky man"** Ibid.

234   **twenty-year-old Cameron was arrested** *New York Times*, October 28, 1999.

235   **"My son is going to be twenty-two . . ."** Michael Douglas, interviewed in the *Sunday Times* (London), October 15, 2000.

235   **"People used to ask . . ."** Kirk Douglas, in *People*, January 24, 2000.

235   **"I've never seen Michael so happy . . ."** Kirk Douglas, in *Variety*, January 6, 2000.

235   **"Douglas must be the only . . ."** Sean Macauley, *Times* (London), January 25, 2001.

235   **"Since the first three weeks . . ."** Ibid.

236   **"revive his faltering career . . ."** *Sunday Times* (London), December 12, 1999.

236   **"I'm crazy about Catherine . . ."** Ruth Norris, "This Man Is Not a Sex Addict," *Independent on Sunday* (London), June 6, 1999.

236   **"He can wed . . ."** Diandra, quoted in the *Times* (London), October 19, 1999.

236   **When she arrived without Michael, reports flew** According to the *Los Angeles Times* of January 7, 2000: "British tabloids had reported the relationship between Michael Douglas and Catherine Zeta-Jones was

on the rocks just last month when Zeta-Jones arrived alone in Wales shortly before Christmas, but Douglas arrived to join her for the holiday."

237 **"When I found out . . ."** Marty Richards, quoting Michael, *People*, January 24, 2000. Michael, interviewed by Hilary de Vries for *W* in March 2000, said that his "divorce from Diandra Douglas, from whom he was legally separated four years ago (1995), remains 'just a technicality,' he says. 'Everything, including the settlement, was done years ago.'" The interview took place in 1999. He signed the divorce papers in October 2000, in order to marry Catherine Zeta-Jones that November.

238 **"It's the most unique release experience . . ."** Michael Douglas, interviewed by Hilary de Vries, *Los Angeles Times Magazine*, January 21, 2001.

239 **"I feel blessed . . ."** Michael Douglas, TheTalks.com, December 7, 2011.

CHAPTER 18

241 **"If you have a void"** Michael Douglas, *Us* magazine, March 2000.

241 **"Michael is everything . . ."** *People*, December 11, 2000. Some details of the wedding are from that issue of *People*, CelebrityBrideGuide.com, and two guests who attended the wedding but do not wish to be named.

243 **"Everyone was crying . . ."** Observer wishes to remain anonymous. Many firsthand details of the wedding are from two guests I interviewed, who want to remain anonymous.

243 **"May they love one another forever . . ."** Judith Kaye in *People*, December 11, 2000.

243 **Kirk repeated his wince-inducing joke** *Times* (London), November 26, 2000.

245 **Later on, Catherine confirmed to *Vanity Fair*** Various sources, including *Vanity Fair*, December 2000, interviewed by Leslie Bennetts. Catherine's interview was the cover story.

CHAPTER 19

247 **"Look, I'd love to have . . ."** Michael Douglas, *Us* magazine, March 2000.

248 **"When Steven presented it to me . . ."** Sean Macauley, *Times* (London), January 25, 2001.

248 **"It was just fun . . ."** Michael Douglas, *Variety*, January 9, 2004.

CHAPTER 20

255 **"God bless her that . . ."** Michael Douglas, in *AARP Magazine*, March/April 2010.

257 **"We were always finding . . ."** Michael Douglas, in *People*, May 5, 2003.

258 **"grabbed my shoulder . . ."** Cameron Douglas, quoted in *People*, May 5, 2003.

259 **"The Teamsters are helping . . ."** Steve Martin, Academy Awards, 2003.

259 **"Thank you so much. My Scotsman . . ."** Catherine Zeta-Jones's acceptance speech, Academy Awards, 2003.

260 **"This is my son, Michael"** and **"My father, who art in movies"** Kirk and Michael, respectively, presenting at the seventy-fifth Academy Awards, 2003.

261 **"I adjust my schedule to my wife's . . ."** Michael Douglas, "The Role of a Lifetime," *Newsweek*, September 17, 2007.

262 **"like meat on a bone . . ."** Quote from the *Times* (London), January 29, 2004.

262 **"She was hysterical . . ."** Michael Douglas, in the *Times* (London), January 29, 2004.

263 **"How lucky I have been . . ."** Michael Douglas, *Los Angeles Times*, January 25, 2004.

263 **"Who knows . . ."** Michael Douglas, quoted in Marie Laskas, "The Aging Casanova," GQ.com, April 2006.

263 **On July 6, 2004, Michael received word** Information about the death of Eric Douglas is from *People*, July 7, 2004; and "Douglas Son 'Died Accidentally,'" bbc.co.uk, August 10, 2004.

CHAPTER 21

265 **"Giving back to the planet . . ."** Michael Douglas, quoted in Marie Laskas, "The Aging Casanova," GQ.com, April 2006.

266 **"I'm in love . . .and I've got a nice family . . ."** Ibid.

266   **"Things have changed a lot . . ."** Michael Douglas, in *Screen International*, September 23, 2005.

266   **"Studios today are just . . ."** Michael Douglas, interviewed by Simi Horwitz, *Back Stage West*, September 13, 2007.

268   **"My priorities are my marriage . . ."** Michael Douglas, *People*, May 5, 2003.

268   **"He's really good, but acting . . ."** from Tom Roston, *Hollywood Reporter*, June 11, 2009.

269   **"The joy of raising two children . . ."** Ibid.

270   **"I'm a car dealer who . . ."** Michael Douglas, *Parade*, July 12, 2009.

270   **American Film Institute's Life Achievement Award** *Los Angeles Times*, June 13, 2009.

272   **"He came up to hug me . . ."** Steve Lewis, quoted in *People*, August 24, 2009.

273   **"I'll assume whatever responsibilities . . ."** Michael Douglas in *AARP Magazine*, March/April 2010.

CHAPTER 22

275   **"If I'd known what a big shot . . ."** and **"Hardly any second-generation . . ."** Kirk Douglas and Mike Douglas, respectively, quoted by Paul Harris, *Observer*, April 24, 2010.

276   **Cameron stood before U.S. District Court . . .** Various sources, including publicly available court records, *New York Post*, and *Crimesider*, a website devoted to crime (several entries consulted, including those by Edacio Martinez, April 20, 2010, and Caroline Black, April 21, 2010); *Hello!*, March 3, 2010.

279   **After court, a somber Michael Douglas** New York *Daily News*, April 20, 2010.

279   **"There was a deep sense of relief . . ."** Michael Douglas, in *People*, September 13, 2010.

279   **"Anybody who has a relative or child . . ."** Michael Douglas, interviewed by Evgenia Peretz, *Vanity Fair*, April 2010.

280   **He had booked an appearance on the *Late Show*** Details are from the broadcast and David Itzkoff, "Michael Douglas Discusses His Throat Cancer with David Letterman," *New York Times*, September 1, 2010.

281   **"clearly in pain"** This quote and other details about Michael's

condition are from Rebecca Asher-Walsh in the *Los Angeles Times*, September 19, 2010.

281   **"The radiation kills the cancer, but . . ."** Ibid.

281   **"sat them down . . ."** and **"The hardest part . . ."** Catherine Zeta-Jones, *People*, September 13, 2010.

282   **"doing fantastically well . . ."** Catherine Zeta-Jones, quoted in *Hello!*, October 11, 2010.

283   **Diandra had lost a great deal of money** *Huffington Post*, July 3, 2011.

284   **"I feel good, relieved the tumor is gone . . ."** Michael Douglas, interviewed by Matt Lauer on *Today*, January 9, 2011, with additional reporting in the *Hollywood Reporter*, January 10, 2011.

284   **"You know, I'm fortunate . . ."** Michael Douglas, quoted by a staff writer, cnn.com, January 10, 2011.

286   **In August 2011, *Star* magazine** The *Star* published a long-lens photos of Michael smoking on August 8, 2011.

AUTHOR'S NOTE AND
ACKNOWLEDGMENTS

I saw Michael Douglas a few times in the nineties while I was living and writing in Los Angeles. We ran into each other mostly at the private, membership-only Foundation Room of the House of Blues on Sunset Boulevard. Zack Norman had remained friends with Michael after the movie and sometimes traveled with him to Germany and various film festivals (I guessed he might have actually been Michael's beard on some of those all-male excursions to Cannes). A few years later Zack brought Michael a film-related business venture that he invested in. I always felt that, from what I knew of the deal's structure, it didn't make a lot of sense, but I figured it was a way for the always generous Michael to help out a friend and, if possible, make a few dollars. Eventually the company ran into problems, the principals wound up in court, and, as I understand it, Zack was eventually edged out.

Zack and I first met at the height of O.J. mania. I had written a 1995 bestseller about my reluctant involvement in that case (*The Whole Truth*). I had been subpoenaed as a witness for the prosecution but never testified. It was a State trial. While they were looking for me in California, I was hiding out at my lawyer's home in New York. At one point, although I was certain O.J. had killed his wife and the unfortunate Ronald Goldman, it looked as if I was the only one who might go to jail—for contempt.

Zack was also connected to the O.J. madness. He had produced an expensive one-hour video about the defendant. Zack then approached me to work with him on another, undefined O.J. project he was trying to put together. Nothing came out of that except our friendship. Zack is genuinely likable with a natural hustler's instinct and a heart of gold. We often went to the Foundation Room together, and because of the frequency of our visits, I agreed to share the membership fees. That is when I became a regular "waver" to Michael—in Hollywood, a "waver" is someone who waves hello to a celebrity and gets a friendly maybe-I-know-you-maybe-I-don't-but-just-in-case-I-do wave back. I often wondered whether seeing me with Zack made Michael want to come over and say hello or to run the other way as fast as he could.

One time at the club I found myself in the private elevator with Michael. I smiled and said, "You and I have a female friend in common." I knew the subject of women was a touchy one for Michael. I could see him snap to attention, the smile on his face morph to a set of pursed lips, and his eyes slightly squint.

"Oh yeah?" he said. "Who might that be?"

"Dede Allen." Dede had edited *Wonder Boys*.

His face melted back into the smile. "She's a great lady," he said. "She's got a great bullshit detector." The elevator came to a halt on the ground level. He gave me a take-care wave and ran out.

A few weeks later I happened to be having dinner in Hollywood with Dede, who was a longtime friend. She had been kept out of the world of directing when she was young by Hollywood's notorious glass ceiling (she did the cutting on Arthur Penn's 1967 *Bonnie and Clyde*, which many consider the film's saving grace and which established her credentials as one of the premier editors in the business). She was also one of the executive producers on Warren Beatty's 1980 *Reds*, though working with Beatty literally drove her crazy. After completing the film she had a nervous breakdown. By the time she got to work with Michael on Curtis Hanson's 2000 film, she had become a wise, talented, and patient mother figure to everyone aboard, including Michael.

Anyway, at that dinner I told her what Michael had said. She laughed and replied, "He's a wonderful guy to work with." When I asked her what that meant, she referred first to his on-set "sanity," and to his ability to work with talented people to both his and their best advantage. This was rare in narcissism-driven Hollywood, she said, where ego outruns integrity ten times out of ten. She also admired Michael's courage to be daringly political, both in real life and in movies such as *The China Syndrome*. This was particularly significant to Dede. In her earlier years she was forced to live in New York because her husband, a TV journalist, had been blacklisted.

When Dede did *Wonder Boys*, she told me the story of the day Bob Dylan showed up at her office to watch some rushes before he wrote (or pulled out of his trunk) the song "Things Have Changed," which would become the movie's theme and eventually earn him an Oscar. She said he was quiet and polite, spoke little, watched the scenes on an edit screen, disappeared, and returned the next day with the completed song. I've always loved the thought of Dede and Dylan as a team. And I have to say, "Things Have Changed" is one of the better late-Dylan tunes.

Whenever a biography I had written was published, Dede, like a good mother should, always gushed about it, while Steve, her husband, who was a bit on the cranky side, would talk to me out of the side of his mouth and say, "Another one of those books about lousy fathers and great sons?" Steve recently passed away. I wish he were still alive for a lot of reasons, not the least of which is that this time I could say to him, "Yes, Steve, this really is one of those books about lousy fathers and great sons!"

Sad to say, Dede passed away before Steve, in 2010. She was a good friend of Michael's, a good friend and unofficial surrogate mother to me, and a neighbor on both coasts. She is missed.

Michael's reputation as a producer who consistently turns out good, occasionally great films is second perhaps only to Clint Eastwood's. Neither Michael nor Clint might be the best actor of his generation—that would, of course, be Nicholson or De Niro—but Michael is without question the best producer/actor of his time. (Clint upsets the balance of comparison because of his career as a director, something Michael never tried.) Many of the best and most charismatic actors who are contemporaries of Michael's failed more than once to successfully produce movies with or without themselves in them.

The traditional Hollywood power structure is producer, screen-writer, star, director. In the seventies, when the studio system finally crumbled and independent movies became more viable, the director moved to the top, and the producer was put into second position. Michael, understanding his strengths and weaknesses and the times he was living in, went against the popular tide and shunned directing in favor of producing. His four-corner Oscar sweep in 1975 for *One Flew Over the Cuckoo's Nest* not only restored the producer to the top of the hierarchy of the business of mainstream filmmaking but reminded the industry that producing, not directing, was where the corporate power really was.

Through friends such as Zack and Dede (who were not specifically interviewed for this biography), and dozens of others, I was able to write this biography of Michael. And because Michael is still with us and remains a powerful force in Hollywood and New York, I feel I should refrain from naming most of the others who bravely helped. Those who wouldn't do on-the-record interviews helped to point me in the right directions. I thank them one and all.

One note that belongs in the small-world category: In the early '80s, Steve Reuther, who had the dark good looks of a movie star (tall and smart and fast and strong), was my agent at William Morris when I first moved to Hollywood and became involved with scriptwriting. I have mostly good memories of Steve. In one of the more incredulous moments of my life, I was actually shoved by a producer trying to buy the rights to one of my earlier biographies, in Steve's office. It threatened to turn into a brawl. Steve immediately got between us, settled down the producer, and by the end of the meeting, *made the deal.* This guy, I thought to myself, is going places. I can understand why Michael and Steve would want to work with each other. In theory, at least, it seemed an ideal pairing, tempered by the clash of two powerful men.

Fortunately, Kirk has written a number of memoirs that have proved extremely helpful. Even Michael's mother, Diana, wrote a highly useful family history. While those books were filled with information, some if it perhaps blurred by sentiment and failing memory, their greatest value was in leading me to primary sources. My aim whenever I write a biography is to understand the subject, and his work, and how one feeds into the other—how the man reflects the movies and the movies reflect the man. I have tried to link together the chronological, emotional, and creative in this biography of Michael Douglas.

I wish to thank the Margaret Herrick Library of the Academy of Motion Picture Arts and Sciences; I state emphatically, once again, it is the best research facility for American film in the world. I also wish to thank the Cinémathèque in Paris, the London Academy of Film, Turner Classic Films, and several private collections, which together have allowed me to see every Michael Douglas feature film, most of the documentaries, and many of his TV appearances, including several episodes of *The Streets of San Francisco*. Although I did not talk to Michael for this book, I am grateful for his continual openness—about both his work and his life—in his many illuminating interviews and recorded conversations.

I wish to thank my main researcher and fact checker, Jesse Herwitz (blame him!); my agent, Alan Nevins, at Renaissance Literary and Talent; my longtime editor, Julia Pastore, and all the good and talented people at Crown Archetype, especially Tina Constable, Mauro DiPreta, Tammy Blake, and Meredith McGinnis.

And to you, my loyal fans, I know that we will meet again, a little farther up the road.

INDEX

Note: The initials MD and KD refer to Michael Douglas and Kirk Douglas. Page numbers in *italics* refer to photographs.

ABOUT THE AUTHOR

MARC ELIOT is the *New York Times* bestselling author of more than a dozen books on popular culture, among them highly acclaimed biographies of Steve McQueen, Clint Eastwood, Cary Grant, and Jimmy Stewart; the award-winning *Walt Disney: Hollywood's Dark Prince*; *Down 42nd Street*; what many consider the best book about the sixties, his Phil Ochs biography, *Death of a Rebel*; *Take It from Me* (with Erin Brockovich); *Down Thunder Road: The Making of Bruce Springsteen*; *To the Limit: The Untold Story of the Eagles*; and *Reagan: The Hollywood Years*. He has written on the media and pop culture for numerous publications, including *Penthouse*, *L.A. Weekly*, and *California Magazine*. He divides his time among New York City, Woodstock, Los Angeles, and the Far East.

www.marceliot.net